VOICES OF THE DEATH PENALTY DEBATE:
A CITIZEN'S GUIDE TO CAPITAL PUNISHMENT

Voices of the Death Penalty Debate:
A Citizen's Guide to Capital Punishment

By

Russell G. Murphy

Professor of Law

Vandeplas Publishing

United States of America

Voices of the death penalty debate: a citizen's guide to capital punishment

Murphy, Russell G.

Published by:

Vandeplas Publishing - May 2010

801 International Parkway, 5th Floor
Lake Mary, FL. 32746
USA

www.vandeplaspublishing.com

ISBN: 978-1-60042-108-2
LCCN: 2010928139

DEDICATION

This book is dedicated to my grandchildren, Abigail, Christopher, Benjamin, and Sophia, in the hope that they will grow up to live in a more just world.

Acknowledgements

Sufficient words do not exist to express my love and gratitude for the contributions made to this book by my wife, Professor Kate Nace Day. If it succeeds, it is because of her – her critical edits, substantive input, steadfast support, soaring spirit, and, most importantly, unwavering belief in my work. My administrative assistant, Andrea Shannon Curley, was with me from start to finish. Her work was as flawless as it was invaluable. Law student Jason Chandler provided superb research and technical backup throughout the final writing of the book; a bright future in law lies ahead of him. Thanks to Suffolk University Law School Professor Bernard Ortwein for his editorial suggestions and to Reference Librarian Scott Akehurst-Moore for his sustained assistance. The insights of artist Jeremiah Day significantly strengthened the book. I am grateful to the many individuals who took the time to read and comment on drafts, particularly writer Bob Bowersox of Key West, Florida, educator Mary Schilling of Philadelphia, Pennsylvania, and legal writing specialist James Janda of the Suffolk law faculty. Work on the book was partially funded by grants from Suffolk University Law School, Boston, Massachusetts. Lastly, VOICES honors the memory of Jill Russell Cahill.

TABLE OF CONTENTS

INTRODUCTION

VOICES OF THE DEATH PENALTY DEBATE is a deliberately different book. Through the statements of witnesses who testified at historic Hearings in New York between December 2004 and February 2005, it seeks to educate a national and international citizenry about capital punishment. Its straightforward goal is to engage readers in the debate over one of the most complex, emotional, controversial, and important public policy issues of our time.

In June of 2004, the New York Court of Appeals, New York's highest court, invalidated portions of the jury instruction provisions of New York's 1995 death penalty statute. The ruling in the case of People v. La Valle[1] effectively eliminated capital punishment in the State. As a result, the Chairs of three State Assembly Committees - Codes, Judiciary and Correction[2] - made the bold decision to hold public Hearings on every aspect of death penalty practice and policy. They observed:

> Public attitudes about the death penalty have evolved. The use of capital punishment in the country and throughout the world has changed. A wave of exonerations of sentenced inmates, some through the use of newly analyzed DNA evidence, has raised new concerns about wrongful convictions. In New York, the sentence of life imprisonment without the possibility of parole has become widely applied in first degree murder cases.

A call for Hearings was issued and the response far exceeded anyone's expectations. Ultimately, two full days of scheduled live testimony were stretched into five days with 146 witnesses testifying in person and 24 persons or groups submitting written statements.[3] This book is the result of my participation in these Hearings, as a witness, and as a long-time friend of the family of Jill Russell Cahill, who, in October of 1998, was brutally murdered by her husband in up-state New York. The reversal of her killer's death sentence in 2003 started the journey that culminates with this work.[4]

VOICES organizes Hearings testimony in Chapters that present the essential facts relating to the death penalty and the major categories of debate over capital punishment worldwide. It offers the reader the collective understanding of experts as well as the thoughts and insights of ordinary citizens - victims, organizations, religious leaders, and the accused. It is the words of these witnesses that give the book its power. And, they are as impactful today as they were when first spoken.

Within this structure of major issues and arguments, VOICES adds a narrative to explain and order the quoted passages that are the core of the book. The goal of VOICES is to present a balanced analysis of the arguments for and against capital punishment. I take no position in this debate. Every effort has been made to keep the presentations simple, clear and understandable. Nonetheless, limited footnotes are provided at the back of the book in order to give technical and substantive background to the testimony where it is needed.

In the end, this project will have succeeded if citizens reach an informed and principled position on capital punishment by reading this book.

Russell G. Murphy
Professor of Law
Suffolk University Law School
Boston, MA
April, 2010

NOTE ON FORMAT AND STYLE

At the center of this book is excerpted testimony from the public record of the New York Death Penalty Hearings. VOICES presents this testimony in as unedited a form as possible. At various points in the excerpts, portions of a witness's statement may be deleted as indicated by ellipses in the text (. . .) or at the end of a sentence (. . . .). I have added letters, words, phrases or notations to testimony when needed to clarify or explain a statement or to make the statement more readable. These additions appear in parentheses ( ) in the text.

For purposes of consistency, reference is made to "Hearings testimony" or "Hearings witnesses" rather than to any one of the five separate hearings. Members of the N.Y. Assembly are identified by last name, such as "Mr. Lentol", "Assemblywoman Weinstein", or "Chairman Aubry". A list of Committee Chairs and participating Assemblyman and Assemblywomen is provided in Appendix B.

Excerpted testimony, verbal or written, has been selected on the basis of overall educational value. Not every witness statement is included. Great care has been taken to preserve the accuracy of Hearings testimony.

Testimony from the Hearings is generally presented without opening and closing quotation marks. Longer excerpts are indented. Quotes within the excerpts have been used to reflect witness references to the statements of others.

CHAPTER ONE: DEATH PENALTY FACTS AND FIGURES

In order to understand the testimony presented at the New York Death Penalty Hearings, one must examine some basic information about imposition of the death penalty in the United States and around the world. Interested readers should consult the websites for the Death Penalty Information Center (www.deathpenaltyinfo.org) and Amnesty International (www.amnesty.org) for detailed statistics. Much of the information that follows is drawn from these websites.

In the Fall of 2009, 35 states and the federal government allowed capital punishment as a sentencing option for the most serious crimes. Since 1976, the year the death penalty became constitutionally available in modern times, approximately 1196 persons have been executed in the United States. The most active year for the death penalty was 1999. In that year, 98 executions were carried out. From 2004 to 2008, executions per year steadily declined; there were 60 executions in 2004 but only 37 in 2008. (A United States Supreme Court moratorium on executions during most of 2008 resulted in this lower number)[5]. In 2009, 52 death row inmates were executed. The vast majority of these executions took place in Southern (87% in 2009) and Midwestern (13%) American states. Texas is by far the most active executioner representing over 46 % of executions in 2009 and approximately 38% of all U.S. executions.

A parallel trend has occurred relative to death sentences. The average annual number of death sentences imposed between 1990-1999 and between 2000-2007 declined by 49%. In 1999, 284 defendants were sentenced to death; that number dropped to 111 in 2008 and 106 in 2009. This was due in part to the continuing pattern of post-sentencing exonerations - "the innocence phenomenon" – which now number approximately 139. Nine death row inmates were released in 2009. At the federal level, death sentences have actually increased by almost 50% over the same periods. This may be attributable to the expansion of crimes eligible for the death penalty (60 new offenses) under the Federal Death

Penalty Act of 1994[6], heightened prosecution of drug offenses, responses to terrorism, and the streamlining of the death sentence appeals process. At the end of 2009, the total death row population in the U.S. was roughly 3279 (including 42% black, 44% white, and 12% Latino).

In terms of race and ethnicity, according to the Death Penalty Information Center, approximately 35% of all executed defendants since 1976 were African American, 56% were white and 7% were Latino. The race of the accused, and that of the victim, has a profound affect on who is executed and who is not. In modern times, there were 15 executions involving a white defendant and a black victim, while 231 executions involved black defendants who killed white victims. A California study determined that the killer of a white victim was 3 times more likely to be sentenced to death than the killer of a black victim.[7] Numerous other studies have reached similar conclusions.

In the Spring of 2009, there were 53 women on death row in the U.S. representing approximately 1.6% of the total death row population. Eleven women have been executed since 1976.

Costs and delay in carrying out death sentences are significant systemic problems in American capital punishment practice. By 2007, the average delay between sentencing and execution was 12 years.[8] Study after study shows that it is dramatically more expensive to obtain and carry out a death sentence rather than seeking life in prison without parole (LWOP). For example, in California, a special commission estimated that the state's death penalty system cost $137 million per year as compared to an estimated cost of $11.5 million a year for a life without parole system.[9] An Urban Institute study found that a death sentence in Maryland was $1.9 million more expensive than a sentence of life without parole. Over a twenty-year period, the per-execution bill in that state was $37 million.[10] Every federal death penalty trial is approximately eight times more costly than a non-death penalty murder prosecution.[11] In Tennessee, capital trials cost an average of 48% more than non-capital ones.[12] For Kansas, death penalty cases were 70% more expensive than non-capital cases.[13] A Report by the National Bureau of Economic Research estimated that the extra cost of capital trials in the U.S. between 1982 and 1997 was $1.6 billion.[14] The Palm Beach Post suggested that Florida could save $51 million per year by substituting life without parole for capital punishment. And, New York spent $175 million on capital prosecutions from 1995 to 2005 but failed to execute a single killer.

Public opinion seems relatively unaffected by these matters, at least on a straightforward "yes" or "no" question on support for capital punishment in the abstract. According to an October 2009 report by the Gallup Poll, a solid majority of Americans, 65%, favored capital punishment for a person convicted of murder. This result was a 4% drop from public attitudes in 2007 but was a slight 1% increase over 2008 attitudes. When asked in 2006 whether they supported the death penalty or life in prison without any possibility of parole, survey respondents chose life in prison by a margin of 48% to 47%. On three critical 2009 questions, Gallup found that 49% of Americans believed that the death penalty is not imposed often enough, 57% said the death penalty is fairly applied in the U.S., yet, 59% thought an innocent person had been executed in the past five years. As Americans change their opinions about the death penalty, by an approximate 3 to 2 margin, they become opponents of capital punishment.

Most countries in the world, and certainly those with democratic traditions, have abandoned the death penalty. In 2009, it was estimated that 139 countries had abolished the death penalty in law or practice. Retentionist countries numbered approximately 58. Europe is a virtually death penalty-free zone of 800 million people. In addition to the United States, large portions of central Africa, the Middle East, and Asia still practice capital punishment. But, under the influence of international law, foreign court decisions, and global sensitivity to increasing numbers of wrongful convictions, the trend is towards abolition. The December 2007 vote of the United Nations General Assembly in favor of a worldwide moratorium on capital punishment is reflective of this trend. The United States joined 53 other countries in voting against the resolution in stark contrast to the 104 votes in favor and 29 abstentions.

A similar isolation attaches to America when one considers numbers of executions worldwide. For years, the U.S. has been near the top of the list of chief executing countries. In 2007, there were 42 executions in the U.S., placing America fifth on the list of principal executing countries behind China (470), Iran (317), Saudi Arabia (143), and Pakistan (135). The U.S. (37) and Pakistan (36) changed places in 2008. The 52 executions in the United States in 2009 continued the status of America as a primary executioner worldwide. In the area of capital punishment, the United States is associated with many countries that are openly identified as our enemies and are, often, terrorist nations.

Global executions have generally been declining. There were 1252 executions in 2007, 1591 in 2006, and 2148 in 2005. These numbers probably do not to reflect the true extent of reliance on capital punishment by the Chinese Government. A dramatic increase in worldwide executions in 2008, to a reported 2390, was attributable to the 1718 executions reported by China for that year as compared to the 470 reported in 2007. The worldwide death row population is estimated to be at least 20,000 condemned men and women.

CHAPTER TWO: UNDERSTANDING THE LAW - BASIC CONSTITUTIONAL PRINCIPLES

Restrictions on modern death penalty laws originate from a series of decisions by the United States Supreme Court interpreting the United States Constitution's Eighth Amendment prohibition against "cruel and unusual punishments". Starting with the 1976 case of <u>Gregg v. Georgia</u>[15], these decisions provide the basis for references to constitutional restrictions in testimony presented by witnesses at the New York Death Penalty Hearings. This testimony is the foundation of VOICES OF THE DEATH PENALTY DEBATE.

The constitutional structure established by the United States Supreme Court for determining the legality of death penalty laws and procedures exists in the context of American federalism. As currently practiced in the United States, federalism refers to a two-tiered system of government in which the national or "federal" government (the Government of the United States) possesses limited but "supreme" powers in areas expressly granted to it by the United States Constitution, as, for example, the power of Congress to declare war[16] or the authority of the President to act as Commander-in-Chief[17], while the states hold all other powers not expressly delegated to the national government. These state powers include legislating on crime and, specifically, passing laws that impose capital punishment. Currently, 35 states impose the death penalty.

In a case of conflict between state and federal law, the "Supremacy Clause" of Article VI of the United States Constitution[18] makes valid federal law, including decisions of the United States Supreme Court, "the supreme Law of the land", while Amendment X[19] leaves all other matters to the states. In other words, where federal law or the Constitution applies, it controls, and states are not permitted to legislate inconsistently with it.

Disputes over state law and the United States Constitution are often resolved through the exercise of the power of "judicial review". The United States Supreme Court holds that power and decides, as the final decision-maker or "final arbiter" of such conflicts, what the Constitution requires and, therefore, what is the "supreme Law of the Land". Once the Court has spoken on a matter of constitutional law, the Court's decision is binding on all levels of government unless the Court reverses itself or the Constitution is amended.

The importance of this constitutional structure to an understanding of the New York Death Penalty Hearings cannot be overstated. The New York Court of Appeals decision, People v. LaValle[20], that eliminated capital punishment in the state, was based on state law. Under New York law, jury instructions in a capital case told the jurors that a failure of the jury to unanimously decide on a death sentence would result in the judge sentencing the defendant to 25 years to life in prison. The Court of Appeals held that this was potentially "coercive" because a juror might agree to a death sentence out of fear that a judge-imposed sentence would be too light or could lead to the release of a dangerous killer. The instruction therefore violated state constitutional due process requirements.

In order to reintroduce the death penalty, the New York legislature would have to remedy this state constitutional defect in the jury instruction and then pass a capital punishment statute that complied with the United States Supreme Court's general constitutional requirements for a valid state death penalty system. A reenacted New York death penalty law could not violate the U.S. Constitution's "cruel and unusual punishments" clause.[21] The Supreme Court's interpretation of this clause, which provides that "Excessive bail shall not be required, nor excessive fines imposed, nor cruel and unusual punishments inflicted", is the "supreme Law of the Land" and, under the practice of federalism, all state laws must conform to its requirements.

Because of this, readers of VOICES will be presented with extensive witness testimony on what the United States Constitution requires. The Hearings goal of some New York law-makers was to pass a new death penalty law that would withstand a challenge in state court under the state constitution and also be valid under Eighth Amendment case law. In this context, the question of what the Eighth Amendment demands in terms of state death penalty law, procedure, and practice, is a critical one.

In 1972, a majority of American states imposed the death penalty. A case before the U.S. Supreme Court that year, Furman v. Georgia,[22] was an attempt to have capital punishment declared unconstitutional in all cases or, in the alternative, to have existing state laws invalidated because of their arbitrary and capricious operation. A bare 5-4 Supreme Court majority, in nine separate opinions, accepted the arbitrariness argument and struck down existing state capital punishment laws.

In the wake of Furman, most states passed new death penalty statutes. The Court responded in 1976 by explicitly holding that state execution of a person is not automatically "cruel and usual punishment." Gregg v. Georgia[23], Proffitt v. Florida[24], and Jurek v. Texas[25] affirmed that capital punishment is constitutional in the U.S. so long as the general problems identified in Furman are avoided. Under contemporary capital punishment jurisprudence, these decisions have been construed to mean that a valid death penalty law must: eliminate the standardless jury (or judge) decision-making in death cases that Furman found led to arbitrary and capricious sentencing, and discrimination on the basis of race or poverty; advance or promote legitimate state goals in terms of justifications and theories for criminal punishment; and, be tested under contemporary societal standards for defining acceptable forms of criminal sentencing. Subsequent Supreme Court decisions building on these principles provide the currently controlling legal rules for constitutional death penalty statutes.

In applying these rules, a critical measure of the constitutionality of the death penalty is whether its application to a particular criminal or type of crime is socially acceptable according to contemporary "evolving standards of decency". The best evidence of such acceptability is state legislation in terms of the number of states following a certain death penalty practice and the trend of such legislation.

In making this evaluation, the Court in Gregg v. Georgia reserved to itself an independent authority to inquire whether execution of a particular defendant or class of criminals is consistent with the concept of "human dignity" that underlies all Eighth Amendment analysis. The Court then goes on to consider whether an execution is "excessive" in relation to two factors: the extent to which execution furthers a legitimate goal of criminal sentencing such as deterrence or retribution; and the "proportionality" of death as a sentence in relation to the crime committed or the personal traits or characteristics of the criminal. If state laws and practices show no "national consensus" supporting capital punishment in a particular case, or the Court on its own concludes that a death sentence serves no special social purpose, capital punishment is constitutionally prohibited.

Under these general principles, the Supreme Court has decided a number of cases in which a death sentence has been categorically invalidated. These include juvenile killers[26], the mentally retarded (but not the severely mentally ill)[27], non-killer accomplices to a felony-murder[28], and non-murder offenses[29]. The overarching concept in these areas is a simple but perplexing idea found in nearly all U.S. Supreme Court decisions on capital punishment: the death penalty as a sentence must be limited to cases and criminals that are clearly "the worst of the worst."

Although obvious, the "excessive punishments" provision of the Eighth Amendment also applies to the method of execution employed by a state. The acceptability of a particular method - firing squad, electrocution, hanging - is measured by societal values and standards in existence at the time the Court decides a case. In the most recent decision on this subject, the 2008 case of Baze v. Rees[30], the Court upheld the constitutionality of the "three drug cocktail"[31] lethal injection method almost universally used for capital punishment in America. The lawyers in Baze argued that this method involved excessive and prolonged suffering and was often not administered by trained medical personnel.

An important aspect of death penalty law involves the matter of race. A great deal of testimony at the New York Death Penalty Hearings focused on the disproportionate impact of capital prosecutions on African American men. That testimony was shaped by the case of McCleskey v. Kemp[32] in which the Supreme Court rejected the claim that general statistical evidence of racial discrimination in the trial and sentencing processes of capital cases constituted a violation of the Equal Protection[33] and Eighth Amendment provisions of the U.S. Constitution. To succeed on a claim of racial discrimination, the McCleskey standard requires some form of intentional or purposeful discrimination that personally affects the individual accused's death sentence. That can be extremely difficult to show.

The Supreme Court has also established constitutional guidelines for the trial of death penalty cases. At the heart of these procedures is the "bifurcated trial". Following the Gregg v. Georgia line of cases, state death penalty laws now divide capital trials into two stages, usually using a single jury: the guilt or innocence phase and a separate sentencing phase. At this second stage, jurors must be presented with, and carefully consider, "aggravating" and "mitigating" evidence relating to the crime and criminal. Only certain "qualified" jurors may sit in a death penalty case. Any juror whose views on capital punishment would "prevent or substantially impair" him or her from considering a sentence of either death or life imprisonment cannot be seated in a capital case. In other words, a juror who would never impose the death penalty, or one who would always impose that penalty, must be removed from the jury pool. The bifurcated trial system has become the accepted method for insuring that a death sentence is not imposed in an "arbitrary, capricious or freakish" manner. This weighing and balancing process is also the primary protection against impermissible forms of discrimination.

Finally, by statute and court decision, appellate review of death sentences is now regulated by complex and highly demanding procedures[34]. Detailed appellate review is mandatory. Still, there are many procedural obstacles that can make it difficult or impossible for death row inmates to obtain review of claims of trial error or, much worse, consideration of evidence showing them to be innocent. While these procedures may have "speeded up" the execution process, most death row inmates experience the "death row phenomenon" of having to wait a decade or more before final court review and, ultimately, execution. Some witnesses at the Hearings asserted that these delays alone constitute cruel and unusual punishment.

CHAPTER THREE: JUSTIFICATIONS FOR CAPITAL PUNISHMENT

The New York Death Penalty Hearings were structured around a series of specific questions, raised by the Assembly Committees responsible for the Hearings, that examined capital punishment as a state, national and international public policy choice[35]. Two of these questions focused directly on basic justifications for the death penalty as a criminal sentence:

> I. 2. Is the death penalty an appropriate societal exercise of retribution against persons who commit intentional murder?

> I. 3. What evidence is there that New York's death penalty or the death penalty in general deters intentional murder more effectively than other sentencing options?

As these questions suggest, the debate over capital punishment constantly focuses on whether the death penalty significantly advances any of the major policy justifications for criminal sentences. In the United States these justifications include retribution, deterrence, incapacitation and rehabilitation. The Hearings generated commentary on all of these sentencing goals.

Retribution is the right of society to punish a wrongdoer on behalf of the victim and society itself. Often described in murder cases as an "eye for an eye", retribution is seen by many as revenge or vengeance towards the killer. It is justified in both moral and practical terms - without a proportional response to an intentional killing, society loses moral standing as protector of its people; state execution prevents vigilantism in the form of violent retaliation by the victim's family and friends. Acts of retribution punish those who "deserve it" by inflicting painful experiences that roughly match the pain caused by the offender. As Professor Robert Blecker of New York Law School stated during the Hearings, retributivists ask "Does this person deserve to die?"

A most intensely debated justification for capital punishment continues to be deterrence. Under this theory, the suffering caused by a criminal sentence will deter the individual criminal from committing similar or other crimes in the future and will educate the society-at-large about the consequences of committing crimes. The awareness of harsh treatment of one citizen will then persuade other citizens not to commit crimes out of fear that similar punishments will be imposed on them. These two forms of deterrence theory are referred to as specific/individual deterrence and general/societal deterrence. The death penalty is, of course, the ultimate form of specific deterrence - execution conclusively prevents the murderer from killing again. It is with general deterrence that controversy continues to rage. The testimony presented in this Chapter provides extensive opinion on whether the death penalty deters others from intentionally killing.

Incapacitation justifies a sentence of imprisonment or other form of restriction on personal liberty such as probation, house arrest, or physical monitoring by ankle bracelet or similar electronic device, on the ground that isolating a criminal from the larger society protects it by preventing the prisoner from committing crimes outside of prison. Again, the death penalty is a perfect form of permanent incapacitation. The debate is over the abolitionist argument that life in prison without any chance of parole (LWOP) is an equally effective form of incapacitation.

Lastly, rehabilitation is today mostly an afterthought in criminal sentencing. Use of criminal sentences for the purpose of making the criminal a law-abiding citizen is regarded by many as an outmoded sentencing theory. Nonetheless, Hearings testimony asserted that life imprisonment without parole has "reformed" intentional killers and permitted them to make valuable social contributions, even from behind prison doors. Rehabilitation in any larger sense - education, medical treatment, drug counseling, re-socialization - is barely mentioned in the Hearings.

Retribution

· Argument over the legitimacy and benefits of retributive justifications for capital punishment were central to the New York Hearings. The very first witness, District Attorney for New York County Robert Morgenthau, set the tone for this discussion by observing "(T)he only honest justification for the death penalty is vengeance."

Professor Robert Blecker of New York Law School is one of this country's strongest advocates for aggressive use of clear and narrowly tailored death penalty laws. His testimony followed prosecutor Morgenthau's and, essentially, framed the debate over retribution as a basis for state execution.

> · We morally must have it (the death penalty). There are some people who kill so cruelly, so callously, that they deserve to die, and we have an obligation to execute them. . . . (Y)ou just ask the question of each individual. . . . Does this person deserve to die? . . . The death penalty is not only just, it is mandatory, . . . it is morally mandatory. . . . (T)he grounds, the only just grounds for the death penalty, . . . that's retribution. . . . Retribution is not revenge. . . , revenge can be limitless. Revenge can be misdirected, revenge need not be proportional. Retribution is limited, directed and proportional. It is proportional to both the acts of the defendant, the culpable mental state and the attitude of the defendant, and the harm caused.
>
> The retributivist is . . . as committed to making sure that those who don't deserve to die are not executed, as (he is) to (the notion that) those who deserve to die, do. . . . The death penalty is not violative of human dignity, not when carefully designed, not when carefully applied to the worst of the worst. . . . Yes, we know what the worst of the worst is. We do know. Mass murder, genocide, torture killing, paid assassination, and other killings that clearly demonstrate extraordinary callous and depraved indifference and a willingness to sacrifice another's life, particularly that of the very infirmed or the very vulnerable,

especially for the killers own convenience. . . This callousness, this wantonness, this cruelty, this coldness. This is what constitutes the worst of the worst.....The abolitionists...cannot distinguish between the worst of the worst and the merely horrible. . . .

Retributivists have a commitment to justice . . . even if with the death penalty there's likely to be an innocent person executed. But you don't balance the one (executing the worst) against the other (executing the innocent) retributively, you just ask the question of each individual and you do your best. Does this person deserve to die?

When asked whether the injustice of executing an innocent person would outweigh the justice provided by retributive execution, Professor Blecker observed:

I am not willing to execute an innocent person knowing that person is innocent in order to achieve the execution of other people who deserve to die. But . . . no system of justice is perfect and . . . . some error will be built in. . . . (Y)ou recognize systemically that you must . . . take a certain risk...for the sake of justice. With the death penalty there is 'actual ritual denunciation . . . .' of the convicted killer. (A) jury stands up as the representative of the community and says you are so heinous, you are so despicable, so callous, so cold, so cruel that you deserve to die . . . (and this) has value independent of whether we actually even execute.

Retribution, then, is an explicit theory of justice premised on the moral obligation of society to punish extreme criminal transgressions with the most extreme penalty. Retributive justice is often invoked in the name of the victim's family. As will be seen, these families are deeply divided over the effectiveness of capital punishment in lessening their suffering and bringing "closure".

Joan Truman Smith, whose daughter was brutally murdered in 2000 during the armed robbery of a Wendy's restaurant in Queens, New York, gave emotional expression to the survivor's need for retribution. One of the killers, John B. Taylor, was sentenced to death, but later had his sentence reduced to life in prison without parole based on the invalidation of the N.Y. death penalty jury instruction. Taylor's accomplice, Craig Godineaux, entered a guilty plea and was sentenced to life without parole; according to the prosecutor, his mental retardation was a bar to his execution. (Ms. Smith's testimony is given mostly verbatim, in her Jamaican dialect.)

In May of 2000, my daughter and five of her coworkers were murdered in the Wendy's massacre. It's just going to break my heart again to repeat what I want to say. I'm just going to say that my daughter was a 22 year old, just starting life. She went to work. It's a minimum wage (job), but what the heck in America, you have to do something to earn a living. She was my first-born daughter. She always showed her respect by trying to do something. I said, fine, you know. I come to this country -- fast food.

But I said, look, it's a living -- I have three or four kids and I have a father. She stop college to earn some type of wages (for us).

Never in my dream (could I have) learned that his could happen in Wendy's. I always try to say, come home early at night because I don't want nobody to rape her. I will do anything. I will go pick her up. At that age, I don't want -- just the fact of it, I never in my dream, to wake up one morning and on the news there's a massacre. I don't want to cry, but to come here and listen to all of this, I was against death penalty because I was born in Jamaica.....

This is for my daughter and I know that you are giving me 10 minutes --

Assemblyman Lentol: Take your time.

Ms. Smith: -- but I wake up and just to think of the pain that these people felt that night when the manager come back and tried to rob the store.... She was the only lady that night. She begged for her life. They put plastic bags over their heads. I just imagine how she pee herself up never think(ing) that this would come to her life -- she beg, she wanted to go back to school. She wanted to do everything to see life again.

And he never listened to her. He never once listened to these people that were begging, they begged for their lives and all of them were executed with bags over their heads and duct tape.

Now you tell me now, what . . . are we going . . . to give them, life in prison (?) Tell me now. This is not some innocent . . . . Tell me what can we do to stop this type of crime. Until it's at your door -- you're going to feel the same thing I'm saying . . . . Think of the crime that these people committed and if the evidence fit, I want -- kill them . . . . Until it reaches your door, you're not going to think (about these things). You sit there and see a gun in your face. You're begging for your life.

You know what, I'd rather move to Texas than. . . .

They're talking about -- they go in there (with life in prison) and they don't get no privilege? What kind of privilege should they get? What kind of privilege should that sentence get? You're going to sit for 10 years -- sit for 10 years, are you privileged? Oh my God. You getting food, you getting family. All I got is to go to the cemetery and visit my daughter. That's all I can do is visit her in the cemetery and you can see your family, and you can laugh and talk. I don't care -- tough luck. Damn it and you know you're a killer. You shouldn't have no visitor.

This is my letter, but I said I'm not going to read it. Just think of the Wendy's massacre. I'm pro for the death penalty.

I'm not changing. If my son commit a crime, kill him. I don't care.

Let's do the right thing. I don't know what to say or -- but my daughter, she die, and the guy is still living. Whatever it come down to, I'm just saying make sure justice is served for these people . . . . I listen to everybody and I said, you know, I have a child. I'm for it, kill them. Thank you.

The weight of testimony from victim's families was against retributive execution. Bill Pelke on behalf of Murder Victims Families for Human Rights, and Kate Lowenstein for Murder Victims Families for Reconciliation, gave testimony reflective of this view.

> Bill Pelke: (T)he death penalty has absolutely nothing at all to do with healing . . . in fact it just continues the cycle of violence and creates more murder victim family members. (Mr. Pelke's grandmother was stabbed to death by a group of teenage girls). Revenge is never, never, never the answer. I didn't have to see somebody else die in order to bring healing for my grandmother's death . . . . The answer is love and compassion for all humanity . . . . If there's not mercy involved then I don't think there's justice and the death penalty allows absolutely no room for justice."

> Ms. Lowenstein: Hello. Thank you for giving me the opportunity to testify today. My name is Kate Lowenstein. My father, former Congressman from New York, Al Lowenstein, was shot to death in his office here in the City. Dad agreed to meet with a mentally ill former student who took out a gun and shot him five times in the chest until Dad lay on the floor of his office, bleeding and dying. I miss him desperately.
>
> All of us who have had a family member murdered wish we could have been there to protect them. We have all been filled with a consuming anger and horror and fury at the killer. We want the murderer caught and punished. I know the rage and sense of justice that lead people to support the death penalty. I also know, from working with murder victim family members for the past four years, that what victim's families need is help to heal and (to) learn how to live with a mangled heart. They need support and counseling. We need the killer to be caught and brought to justice. We do not need an execution.
>
> After a murder, there is a shock and an obsessive need to have the murder be undone. To have it not be true. But no one can make that so. The state cannot undo a murder. Those of us

who have gone through it are forced to realize, maybe slowly, but inevitably, that nothing we do to the killer will bring back our family member from being dead. The state offers victims the death penalty as if it is some kind of scale they can use to correct the loss, but you can't, and in the process of trying, we buy into a system that we all know by now does no honor to the victims or to our society.

I know that the vast majority of victims would rather you take the $175 million New York has put into sentencing a handful of killers to death and put it into solving thousands of unsolved murders.

Murder levels us all equally with its pain. No victim is more important, but the state sends that message with the death penalty.

The death penalty does not honor our murdered family members, so, for many of us, it violates our deeply held political, social and religious beliefs. It feeds our feelings of revenge, anger and hatred and holds out to us an illusionary form of healing and what we are told will be closure. By now I hope you all know not to offer closure to victim's family members. There is no closure.

It makes a statement that it's tough on crime, but in reality, it takes resources away from the victims and police who need it and it creates more victims.

By executing a killer you have not executed their crime, but you have socialized hate and revenge and endorsed a system that is repugnant to the values we all outwardly endorse.

In our grief, the state tells us this will help you, but it is the murdered life we want back and in the end, nothing changes that and an execution leaves us silent. The murdered are still murdered, now another family is in agony and a system has gone forward that is contrary to everything we want justice to be, a system that values white life over black, rich over poor, the powerful over the vulnerable, the conviction of the innocent. All of these things my father taught me to fight against.

New York does not need the death penalty. Use this
opportunity to end it. Thank you.

Bill Babbitt testified about the execution of his brother, whom he
turned in to the police when it was made clear that his brother had
murdered their grandmother, Leah Schendel. At that time, Babbitt stated
that the police told him that his brother would "get the help he needed . . .
(and be sent to) a mental institution . . . . I was betrayed. They immediately
sought the death penalty . . . . " According to Babbitt, "I stood up to do the
right thing, and even today, now that my brother is gone, I feel that I have
my brother's blood on my hands . . . . I feel isolated from my family. Some of
my family members have not forgiven me . . . . "

On retribution and revenge, Mr. Babbitt's testimony on the execution
of his brother Manny was chilling.

> Manny was executed 37 minutes into his 50th birthday . . . .
> (W)hen I watched them execute my brother that day, I noticed
> the district attorney was there and he couldn't watch. He sat
> hunched over with his elbows on his knees . . . . But Manny did
> not want to spend the rest of his life in prison. Manny would not
> -- he said he would not open up his eyes.
>
> He made a statement before he was put on that gurney. He
> told the warden, I forgive you all. He said, I'm not going to give
> anybody any trouble. So when I watched Manny lay there and
> take what others insisted he had coming while my mother sat
> outside the gate of San Quentin prison with a big blanket over
> her head waiting for her son to die, when I beheld my brother
> laying there waiting for them to kill him, those who sought to see
> him die could not bear to see it. And I remember Manny telling
> me, do the right thing, forgive.

Representatives of religions and religious organizations presented
faith-based perspectives on capital punishment. A typical viewpoint came
from Reverend Dominick Lagonegro, Auxiliary Bishop of the Catholic
Archdiocese of New York (and also Bishop's Liaison to the Catholic Chaplain

Apostolate Committee of N.Y. and Bishop's Liaison to the American Catholic Correctional Chaplains Association).

> Vengeance is an understandable human reaction when great evil confronts us but it is not the righteous action. My experience and my faith lead me to conclude that while justice most certainly demands corrective punishment for those who have done grave harm, we as civilized people must not resort to vengeance, which is not only unhealthy to our society but ultimately unsatisfying for those who have been harmed. Victims of violence, (who) struggle to overcome the emotional loss and fear, can find some sense of peace only through reconciliation and non-violence. Vengeance through execution does not heal the wounds, control the rage, or fill the emptiness. Revenge does not bring the closure so may people hope to find. Executions merely continue the cycle of vengeance begun by the perpetrators.
>
> For victims, . . . (justice) means treatment of their physical and emotional injuries, assurance of corrective punishment for those who have done them harm, just compensation when feasible and a loving invitation to healing and forgiveness. For offenders, . . . (justice) requires penalties that offer correction as well as punishment; rehabilitation programs, healing and restoration where feasible.

Reverend Bishop Howard J. Hubbard, Catholic Bishop of Albany, N.Y., gave similar testimony and was openly applauded for it by the large audience that attended the Hearings.

> (Catholics) seek a society of peace and justice, not a society of vengeance and violence. The government of a civilized society through its laws sets an example of how we are to live. Rather than maintaining public order and protecting the health and welfare of its citizens, a government that carries out executions serves only to perpetuate the violence and destruction it seeks to end.

Reverend Hubbard continued:

Lest you think only someone who never personally experienced the horrific death of a beloved family member could oppose capital punishment, listen to the testimony of Marietta Jaeger-Lane founder of Murdered Victims' Families for Reconciliation.

Marietta's youngest daughter, Susie, was kidnapped, held for ransom and then killed. Marietta's initial response was to kill . . . (the kidnapper) for what he had done to her family. Upon closer reflection, she writes in her book JOURNEY OF HOPE, FROM VIOLENCE TO HEALING. "I came to realize that to kill this man in Susie's name would be to violate and profane the goodness and sweetness of her life. I could not honor her memory by becoming that which I deplored, someone who wants to kill. She was worthy of a more noble and more beautiful memorial than a cold-blooded, premeditated, state-sanctioned killing producing yet another victim and another grieving family. I better honored my precious daughter by insisting that all of life is sacred and worthy of protection. So I asked that the prosecutor not apply the death penalty."

. . . .

In 2000, the New York State Bishops issued a pastoral statement entitled, Restoring All to the Fullness of Life, on the concept of restorative justice. In this statement we note that the purpose of the criminal justice system is not merely punishment, but correction and redemption.

We wrote: "We must reject the traditional emphasis on retribution that manifests itself in an over-reliance on incarceration and resort to the death penalty. We must instead balance corrective punishment with efforts at healing, forgiveness, and rehabilitation."

Those who commit crime do not give up their human dignity, and those who administer justice must not deny this God-given dignity.

One short exchange between Assemblyman Kirwan and the Retired Chief Justice of the Florida Supreme Court, Gerald Kogan, captured much of the essence of the retribution argument.

Justice Kogan: I've heard people say that, well, you need to have the death penalty because it gives us closure on this particular issue, especially for the families. If somebody in my family was brutally murdered, the fact that you're putting to death the person who committed that murder doesn't give me, really, closure, because everyday for the rest of my life that will always be in my mind, that I lost a loved one, the victim of a very, very brutal crime.

Mr. Kirwan: Well, you're a nicer person than I am. Because I want to tell you, if somebody killed a member of my family, (their execution) would give me a great deal of satisfaction, (and I would know) that they weren't watching television or reading a book some place.

At times it is just not clear to victims' families what is the right thing to do. Speaking of the murderer of her sister, Debra Russell Jaeger stated "We just wanted justice served according to the law. We'd let a jury of his peers decide . . ." the fate of this killer. Debra wanted him "in a place where he could never harm his children and our family again", whether that was through death or life without parole.

Compare this feeling with the testimony of Bruce and Janice Greishaber about the killer of their daughter Jenna.

Mrs. Greishaber: Proponents of capital punishment rarely have the insight of families like ours. Our family was given an apology for the failure of our system to consider putting the killer of our daughter to death for the crime (he committed) because it didn't fit the legal definition of a capital crime.

It was at that moment that I knew without a doubt what I could never have previously been absolutely sure of, my feelings about the death penalty. It was at that moment that I realized that life without parole would be the only sentence that would even begin to ease the pain in our hearts.

I truly prefer the knowledge that he (the killer) has spent the first six years of his 25 (years) to life sentence in a special housing unit, confined and alone with his thoughts. I would prefer every murderer have a lifetime of such treatment and I consider death too easy in comparison.

I believe that a lifetime of incarceration is a judicious and ethical response to any murder. I believe that Nicholas Pryor, who murdered Jenna, is suffering daily. I do not want to see that come to an end. I hope to die before him, knowing that his entire adult life has been spent behind bars, recognizing that his own actions put him there.

While he may have been sentenced to only 25 (years) to life, I have faith in our system to keep him under the control of the prison system for the ultimate length of that sentence, eating off of a tray, unable to make a phone call when he wishes, to play a hand of poker with buddies, or order a pizza, or even take a brisk walk when he wants to stretch his legs. And this, for the rest of his life.

I'm here to tell you, as a mother of a homicide victim, that the death penalty brings as much pain as it does relief, that it creates an entirely new layer of pain, and that many survivors of homicide victims would prefer that the offender in their case spend a lifetime of unimaginably painful confinement before dying a lonely and often painful death within those walls. And then still face whatever comes next. Thank you.

Mr. Geishaber: I reflect on my feelings. That visceral sense that someone who took life should lose their life, and I can't reconcile it. I carry with me at all times the victim impact statement I made before the court at the sentencing of Jenna's murderer. Reading and re-reading it has made me realize a great deal about who she was and who I am, and it has helped me make this statement today.

We are without our daughter. I reflect on the feeling that if I wanted to take her killer's life then I would be a killer and no better than him.

I reflect on the feeling that what kind of society resorts to killing to solve problems? That any killing results in more killing. That we take revenge for someone taking a life, and then someone takes revenge for the revenge, and where does it all stop?

Bishop Jack M. McKelvey, Episcopal Diocese of Rochester, continued with these themes.

The death penalty, when carried out, increases victimization and violence . . . (and) (i)t sullies the hands of the state. (Those who carry out the execution order report) side effects of stress, anxiety, poor health, emotional upset . . . from being engaged in this death drama . . . . We hear statements which indicate that an execution will bring closure to a person's agony for a loved one who has been murdered. If that is true, then that person will have to hold on to . . . anger, pain, frustration, and heartache for an average of ten to fourteen years before those feelings are assuaged . . . by executing the killer.

Exceptional testimony was submitted by Mr. Robert McLaughlin. Mr. McLaughlin was wrongly identified as a killer by a 15-year-old witness who admitted later that the police coerced him into identifying him rather than another suspect by the same name. Had McLaughlin been sentenced to death he would have been executed as an innocent man.

Well, that's why I came here today, to oppose the death penalty. We're going to kill innocent people. It's inevitable. If we have the death penalty, it's going to happen. And it's just wrong. It's wrong.

Like I said, I was in there, I know what it's like. It's worse to keep them alive. It is. They're having a miserable time in there. It's miserable for them in there, period. It's worse to keep them alive.

When you kill them, okay, you just let them out of jail mentally, because they're out of jail and they don't think about it no more. They're dead, they're gone, it's done. So in my own opinion it's worse to keep them in there. They're suffering more.

And if that's not enough, you can put a little stipulation, you put them in segregation. If it's such a hideous crime where it's so bad, stipulate that they do not associate with the general population. Believe me, that would drive them absolutely nuts.

Jeff Frayler of the N.Y. State Association of Police Benevolent Associations insisted that the goals of retribution cannot be satisfied by life in prison. Without the death penalty a killer's "lethal actions will . . . guarantee him permanent lodging, clean clothing, food and, more importantly, his life." To many police and law enforcement organizations, that is hardly justice.

Michael Palladino, President of the Detectives' Endowment Association of N.Y., agreed.

Mr. Palladino: Good morning. Thank you for giving me the opportunity to speak before you today. No doubt the issue of the death penalty is controversial and emotionally charged as well. My appearance here today is on behalf of dedicated men and women of law enforcement and the families who love and support them . . . . Although the death penalty was declared unconstitutional by the Court of Appeals recently, I submit to you that it is alive and well right here in New York City. In the past three years, six of my detectives received death penalties . . . Detectives Patrick Rafferty, Robert Parker, James Nemorin, Rodney Andrews, Claude Richards, and Joseph Vigiano. These

are the names of the last six New York City detectives who made
the ultimate sacrifice in the line of duty. These brave heroes
were protecting the citizens of this great city when they were
issued their death sentences. They were not permitted the
luxury of public hearings, court proceedings, or appeals. All the
media coverage they received was posthumously . . . . As an
advocate for law enforcement, I tell you without hesitation that
the men and women of law enforcement place their lives at great
risk every single day to protect their fellow citizens. They are
not robocops; they are human beings, productive members of
society, and role models. They have spouses, children, goals, and
dreams, just like everyone else. Then, one day, unexpectedly,
their life is savagely taken from them. Many other lives are also
shattered in the aftermath. The spouse left behind has lost a
companion and lover and a provider for the children, with whom
an entire future was placed; gone without the chance to at least
say goodbye. Have you ever held a grieving police widow? I
have. You can feel every bone, every fiber of their being,
trembling in their body. Have you ever looked into the eyes of
one of the children left behind? I have and they all have the same
dazed, confused look on their faces, trying to make sense of this
major league curveball life has just thrown them. They are left to
cope with the death of their parent, their best friend, their little
league coach, again, with the added pain of not being able to say
goodbye. They will carry the trauma and anguish with them for
the rest of their lives . . . . And yet I read in the New York Daily
News on December 5, 2004, an editorial by a man by the name of
Mr. Jonathan Gradess (Mr. Gradess testified at these Hearings),
who is the Executive Director of the New York State Defenders
Association and an opponent of the death penalty. It states that
the execution of a police officer in the line of duty is, "part of the
delicate fabric of human life." What a chilling statement. What is
this guy talking about? Put simply, Mr. Gradess opposes the
death penalty for convicted murderers, but will tolerate and can
accept the killing of sworn law enforcement officers. I would
love to see this gentleman explain his position to the widows and

children of my slain detectives .... Law officers in this State put their lives on the line each and every day, on duty, as well as off duty. They are entitled to some legislative advantage. As citizens, as union officials, as lawmakers, we have an obligation to enact laws that give our protectors better odds of returning home to their loved ones at the end of a dangerous tour of duty. You, the members of the Assembly, can give these law officers the legislative protection they deserve by amending the language (of the capital jury instruction) and reinstating the death penalty .... (Y)ou (must) take into consideration the expense to house, feed, clothe, medicate, educate, rehabilitate, entertain and protect a killer for the rest of his or her natural life - which could be for 30, 40, 50 years or more .... Another popular position of the opponents to capital punishment is that it is selectively enforced based upon race or ethnicity. I don't believe that for one minute. Capital punishment is an issue of old-fashioned good versus evil. It's about the just punishment for heinous and egregious acts of murder ....

Mr. Palladino gave this example.

(W)hen I asked him (a killer in custody) why he went to such great lengths to murder this innocent lady, he said to me that he was in and out of the building quite often because he had friends that lived there. For the most part he was a vagabond. So he felt that he could gain entry into the apartment just by speaking to her because he had seen her and she had seen him in the past. And he did, he got in. The purpose was to rob her of her money and her valuables. And when I asked him why he decided to kill her he said to me that he had nothing to lose and everything to gain. I said, 'How so?' He said, "well, if she was dead she could never come to testify against me." I said even though she's dead, you're under arrest. And he said, "Yes. What's the worst that can happen? After all, I'm not going to lose my life; (there is) no death penalty here in this State." What's the good part? He said, "The worse that could happen to me, I spend the rest of my life in jail. It's a better life than I have now. I get fed. I can exercise. I can do whatever I want . . . ." So, put simply, this man traded the life of Lucille Klein for what he considered a better life style, going to jail.

Marguerite Marsh's daughter Catherine was "strangled by a 6'4", 320 pound monster, who (chopped her up and) hid her body in various places in his house." In total, the killer, Kendall Francois, murdered eight women. When it came time to prosecute him, most of the victims' families pressed the District Attorney to seek the death penalty. Mrs. Marsh did not. Later, after a guilty plea was entered and Francois was sentenced to life without parole, Mrs. Marsh described her feelings as "satisfied with this sentence."

> Justice had been served. This brought an ending for me. The nightmare was over. But certainly there was no closure. There are many who believe closure comes only with a death penalty . . . . How ridiculous.
>
> I am grateful that I will not have to bear the pain of going through appeal after appeal, and Cathy's two little daughters will not have to grow up subjected to accounts of their mother's murder over and over again in newspapers and on TV. . . . Capital punishment serves no purpose. As a civilized society, how can we sanction the taking of life as punishment. That is not justice but revenge. It is legalized killing. If it is wrong for man to kill, how can we say it is right for the state to kill . . . . Does murder give the state permission or a license to also kill? Are we a people who kill people? I do not believe that we can cure murder by murder . . . .

Professor John Blume, Director of the Cornell University Death Penalty Project, added:

> It is easy to forget that all death row inmates have mothers, fathers and grandparents. Many have wives. Many have children. Most of these people did nothing wrong, but when the death sentence is carried out, a new set of victims is created. In

other words, in many instances, the death penalty only perpetuates a cycle of violence.

Returning to the religious and spiritual dimensions of retribution, testimony on behalf of the New York Religious Society of Friends, the Quakers, by Ms. Linda Chidsey echoed the views of Catholic, Baptist, Congregationalist, and Jewish witnesses that revenge is an unacceptable reason to practice capital punishment.

As early as 1699, Friend John Bellers wrote: "Society has done enough for its own protection when it has rendered a murderer harmless by putting him in prison. If it does more, it is acting in a spirit of revenge . . . ." And in 1868, Friend John Bright wrote: "The real security for human life is to be found in a reverence for it. A deep reverence for human life is worth more than a thousand executions in the prevention of murder, and is, in fact, the great security for human life. The law of capital punishment, while pretending to support this reverence, does in fact tend to destroy it . . . ." We have seen how capital punishment creates new victims, the families and loved ones of those who have committed murder. We have seen how it undermines the opportunity for murder victims' families and loved ones to move through the necessary states of grief in a way that opens the door to forgiveness, healing and reconciliation. We have seen how execution diminishes and degrades the humanity of all involved, how it leads to a gradual execution of the soul . . . . In 1956 when a bill was before the British Parliament for the abolition of the death penalty, London Yearly Meeting wrote: "The sanctioning by the state of the taking of human life has a debasing effect on the community, and it tends to produce the very brutality which it seeks to prevent. We realize that many are sincerely afraid of the consequences if the death penalty is abolished, but we are convinced that their fears are unjustified . . . ." I (Ms. Chidsey) see us at a crossroads, a time when we are being given an opportunity to do away with an antiquated and barbaric notion of justice. Just as we did away with slavery, child labor and limited voting rights, so now may we do away with the death penalty, and I urge us to seize this opportunity.

Not all religion-based testimony condemned the death penalty. Tim Taylor, speaking for The Brethren, "a Christian fellowship of believers in our Lord Jesus Christ", stated, "In relation to the evil of murder, the scripture (Genesis 9:6) says, Whoso shedeth man's blood, by man shall his blood be shed.... This scripture still stands. The lord never changed it and we hold that it applies only to murder."

Bud Welch, the father of Julie Welch, who was killed by Timothy McVeigh, Tim Nicholas, and others in the April 1995 bombing of the federal building in Oklahoma City (prior to 9/11, the greatest act of domestic terrorism in American history; 168 people were killed), eventually rejected this form of retribution.

> All my life I opposed the death penalty. It had never been a big issue for me, never been caught on either side of it. But I had been told by friends sometimes that if it ever happened to me I'd change my mind. And when Julie was killed I became so full of rage, so full of vengeance, that the first month after Tim McVeigh and Terry Nichols were arrested and charged, I didn't even want trials for either one of them. It took me a month to accept the fact that we needed to have the trials to hopefully learn the truth.

After visiting with Bill McVeigh, Tim McVeigh's father, Mr. Welch concluded:

> I finally came to the conclusion that the day that we would take Tim McVeigh or Terry Nichols from their cage to kill them, (that day) would simply not be part of my healing process. That. .. was an act of revenge and hate. And revenge and hate was the very reason that Julie and 167 others were dead in that great city .... It was revenge and hate that McVeigh and Nichols had against the U.S. government for some of the things that happened to them in Desert Storm, they both served there; and what

happened at Ruby Ridge, Idaho; and what happened at Waco, Texas, with the Branch Davidians. Waco, Texas was April the 19th, 1993; the Murrah building bombing was the second anniversary of Waco.

> (E)very morning Bill McVeigh wakes up with that noose around his neck that his son was convicted of killing Julie Welch and 167 others. And I think it's most difficult for him . . . . (When McVeigh was executed) (w)e had what I called a huge staged political event happen in this country. It was a Monday morning, seven a.m., in Terre Haute, Indiana, June 11, 2001. We took Tim McVeigh from his cage and we killed him, and like Michael Ross in Connecticut, Tim McVeigh was a volunteer. He had asked for his appeals to be stopped . . . . I'm on the board of directors of the Oklahoma City National Memorial and I know most of the family members. And I know that about half of those family members were looking for some type of relief that Monday morning. They simply did not find it . . . . Since that time I've had any number that had come to me, and most commonly they say, "It just didn't do for me what I thought it would."

The execution of Ethyl and Julius Rosenberg for treason against the United States is one of the most famous incidents of capital punishment in our Nation's history. As the following lengthy quotation from the testimony of the Rosenberg's son, Robert Meeropol, points out, exacting retribution through the death penalty has "collateral" consequences for the families of the executed.

> My name is Robert Meeropol. I'm a resident of Massachusetts, but I was born and raised in New York City and Hastings-on-Hudson, New York.
> I am an attorney, although I'm not in private practice. I am here today as a private citizen and in my capacities as the executive director of the Rosenberg Fund for Children, and as a founding board member of a new organization, Murder Victim's

Families for Human Rights, of which Bud (Welch) is the president.

I have a personal relationship with the death penalty. I'm Robert Meeropol now, but I was born Robert Rosenberg. My parents, Ethyl and Julius Rosenberg, were executed in Sing Sing Prison on June 19, 1953, when I was six.

My name was changed when Abel and Anne Meeropol adopted my brother Michael and me after the executions. I believe my brother and I are unique in American history. We are the only people to have had both their parents executed by the government. Although my parents were convicted in federal court of conspiracy to commit espionage they were executed at Sing Sing, a New York State prison, because the federal government had no execution chamber at that time.

But in many ways my parents' case was, and remains, a New York case. They lived on the lower east side of Manhattan and were tried at Foley Square Courthouse just a mile from where they lived. They were killed under federal auspices, but in a New York State prison by a New York State executioner.

You might wonder why I'm addressing you on behalf of Murder Victim's Families for Human Rights. In Murder Victim's Families for Human Rights we believe state-sponsored executions, that is, the killing of helpless human beings by the state, are murders. I address you as a murder victim's family member.

We in Murder Victim's Families for Human Rights also believe that all extrajudicial killings and judicial killings violate Article 3 of the Universal Declaration of Human Rights[36] and thus constitute human rights abuses.

Now, I'm not going to address you on the politics of my parents' case, although I will say that the overwhelming body of evidence was that they were wrongfully executed, regardless of whether one or the other of them may have done something illegal. I'm not going to talk about why, for almost 30 years after my parents' deaths, I supported the death penalty, particularly for those who engineered my parents' murder. I'm also not going to discuss the many reasons why I oppose capital punishment today. Instead, I want to focus on one aspect of capital punishment that others may not have addressed.

As a child who survived his parents' execution, and as an adult who works with many children whose parents are in prison, or in one case, on death row, I have an unusual perspective to share with you.

I was three when my parents were arrested and six when they were executed. I believe you've heard little or no testimony about capital punishment from the perspective of a child who has had one or both parents executed. How does a child who has just turned six understand such a mess? How does something like that affect a six-year-old? How much do I remember?

Actually, I remember a lot. I don't remember by parents' arrests. In fact, my earliest distinctive memories of my parents are of visiting them on death row. But I have clear memories of the last week of my parents' lives.

On Monday, June 15, 1953, when the (U.S.) Supreme Court adjourned for the summer, my parents were scheduled to die that Thursday. On Tuesday a special petition was presented to (Supreme Court) Justice Douglas as he left for vacation. On Wednesday, Douglas stayed the execution and went on vacation. But on Thursday the Supreme Court was recalled into special session. On Friday morning Douglas' stay was overturned by a six-three vote.

My parents were executed that evening, Friday, June 19, one minute before sundown, so as not to desecrate the Jewish Sabbath. Although I couldn't read the newspapers I saw this on T.V. and heard about it on radio. My six-year-old's interpretation of these events was that the Supreme Court's justices asked my parents' lawyer to give them 10 reasons why my parents should not be killed, and he did, so the Supreme Court stayed the execution. But then they recalled the Court and asked the lawyer for the 11th reason and he was unable to provide it, so my parents were killed. I think I confused repeated radio references to 11th-hour appeals with giving an 11th reason. I pretended not to understand so adults would not fuss over me. In some ways I did not understand, but I got the essence.

What kind of an impact did this have on me? Clearly, I didn't completely understand what was going on, but I had a sense that "they" were out there and "they" were very powerful and "they" were attacking "us".

Of course, I didn't know exactly who "they" and "we" were and what these groups represented, so I had a generalized sense of anxiety, an incomprehensible sword of Damocles hanging over me. I was frightened, angry, and grew up with a suppressed need to attack those who attacked my family.

I survived because a supportive community surrounded me. But what about other children who do not have such a support system? This raises a very disturbing question. If New York State passes any death penalty statute, what will the impact be on children whose immediate family members are executed or placed on death row?

No one can deny that it is qualitatively worse to have a family member on death row or executed than to have a family member in prison, but that's not much of an answer. You must have a better answer to this question, because as legislators you have a solemn obligation before passing a law to understand its impact. That obligation becomes even more serious when you are dealing with matters of life and death, as you are here.

Before enacting capital punishment legislation shouldn't you consider its impact on children with family members on death row? Nationally, there is an apparent disregard for children who have a family member on death row, or who have had a family member executed. We don't even know how many children have an immediate family member on death row in the United States today.

Worse, we don't know the effects that having a parent executed will have upon their impressionable lives, and the cost society may pay for that impact. As far as I can tell, no one has bothered to study this, even though these children are all innocent victims of the state's efforts to kill their loved ones.

If you must consider bringing back state-sanctioned ritualized killings, shouldn't you at least study this issue first? It is past time to realize such collateral damage is yet another powerful reason to keep the death penalty out of New York.[37]

In response to a question about the often-stated justification for retributive execution - "an eye for an eye" - Mr. Meeropol commented

Mr. Meeropol: Well, you know, first there's Gandhi's response . . . . if we have no eyes left, we will not see at all.

But I think that - - I'm going to speak from my own experience of how I reacted. And speak a little bit about what I didn't talk - - said I wasn't going to talk about, because you raised this issue.

I was in favor of the death penalty as a child and as a teenager and as a young adult, because I believed that my parents had been murdered. And I thought it would be a great idea if the people who had conspired to have them executed were brought to justice and executed as well . . . . I continued to harbor this anger and hostility in me, and it wasn't until in the middle of the night when I was miserably in private practice years later, and woke up and realized what I really wanted to do.

That I wanted to start what became the Rosenberg Fund for Children, which is a public foundation that provides for the educational and emotional needs of what I call the children of targeted activists in the United States . . . . (W)hen I figured out a way to do that, I lost all of my desire for revenge because that was the sweetest revenge of all, to make something good, to help children today who are experiencing the kind of thing that I experienced, to turn the destruction of my family into something constructive for the benefit of other families.

And that's how I would respond . . . . We need in this world, in this country, we need constructive responses, we need positive responses, we need good to come out of bad. We don't need more bad to come out of bad. There's enough bad in the world already. That's what I would say to them.

Some of the most critical testimony relating to theoretical justifications for capital punishment in the United States was presented by Gary Abramson of the Legal Aid Society of Orange County (Los Angeles) California.

Mr. Abramson: I'm going to limit my testimony to . . . one of the questions on your list of proposed topics. Mine is: "Is the death penalty an appropriate societal exercise of retribution against persons who commit intentional murder?"

The question itself demonstrates a fundamental problem of capital punishment. Using a word "societal" abstracts the killing, when in stark fact, the killers are the officials of the government, its courts and prisons, acting as our representatives. Using general terms falls short in saying fallible individuals determine guilt, impose the death sentence, and administer it.

Beyond a reasonable doubt, the standard applied before a person may be found guilty, is less than certainty. So, no matter how selective the process is in determining which murderer's life the state takes, an innocent person is eventually the government's homicide victim.

People involved with dangerous government projects, bridge construction, for example, sometimes die. But the death penalty is unique in that it is a government activity with death as its purpose, rather than a sorry consequence. Regrets and compensation may soften the impact of a builder's death, on the survivors. But what does society, or the individuals who work in a legislature, say to the loved ones of an executed person later found to be innocent? That the death was part of a societal retribution project that (went) awry at this time?

Shouldn't there be a criminal penalty for a society that intentionally kills an individual, mistaking the person for someone else, as there is for any citizen who does? A misdeed is no better for being committed in our behalf rather than in mine.

Even assuming the possibility of guilt's certainty, the question remains whether society, which is the sum of us imperfect persons, has both the authority and the wisdom to make a decision of a sacred nature. In a democracy, as opposed to a theocracy, the intelligence of our leaders is regarded as human and limited, not divine. The key moral difference between a murderer and the rest of us is the murderer's evil presumption of the authority to end a life. With capital punishment that distinction erodes or vanishes, and authority is abused.

The issue is not whether defendants deserve to die for committing intentional murder, but whether we should act on our instinct that they do. An execution may provide emotional gratification to the victim's family and outraged citizens, but since the enlightenment, public officials have been expected to base their decisions on reason, not rage. A government, in theory, is superior to a mob.

In a secular, liberal, that is, free society, restraint in the exercise of power demonstrates worthiness of it. Our reason tells us that because we are people, not angels, that awesome choice of who should die is beyond our authority and our intelligence.

When we put a person in prison for life we are protecting ourselves from someone whose criminal conduct requires a permanent suspension of liberty. We have the right to make such a decision because it's provisional, not ultimate. Allowing for the possibility of error is a logical and deeply moral act, while wanting revenge is only an emotion, one that diminishes a society that acts violently on the urge.

Societal retribution cannot be called inappropriate, to use the language in your question. That's a term more applicable to manners. The word is "wrong."

A different perspective on retribution was presented by Marsha Weissman of the Center for Community Alternatives. A death sentence is premised on a jury's determination that "mitigating circumstances" relating to the crime and defendant were insufficient to avoid the death penalty. Ms.

Weissman questioned whether consideration of mitigators could ever lead
to a just and accurate death sentence..

> I am Marsha Weissman and I am the executive director of the
> Center for Community Alternatives. We provide a number of
> programs and services, including sentencing advocacies,
> sentencing mitigation, and through that work we have become
> engaged in death penalty mitigation.
>
> Since 1995 when New York reinstated the death penalty,
> C.C.A. has been involved in more than 50 cases providing death
> penalty mitigation services. And our opposition to the
> reinstatement of the death penalty grows out of this work.
>
> Mitigation work involves the telling of life stories of people
> who are facing the death penalty. And most of the stories that
> we have chronicled are those of tragedy and cruelty that began
> when our clients were children.
>
> The circumstances of the lives of many people facing the
> death penalty in New York, and across this country, do not
> excuse murder, but they do help to explain the circumstances
> that cause one to commit a capital crime.
>
> Best intentions notwithstanding, New York's efforts to craft a
> just death penalty will never come to pass with absolute
> certainty. We can never be sure of the accuracy of the imposition
> of the death penalty across the board .... Our work as mitigators
> takes us to families and places that are secrets in America. It is
> not to disrespect or discount the loss suffered by victims of
> murder, but the death penalty, our death penalty work as
> mitigators, unveils the pain and suffering of families on both
> sides, and I think the witnesses in the earlier panel, Bud Welch
> and Robert Meeropol, certainly spoke to that in ways that I
> cannot.
>
> Our mitigation work has brought us into the secrets of
> American life: the families with histories of unspeakable trauma,
> untreated mental illness, physical and sexual abuse, abject
> poverty and desperation. Conditions that were neglected or
> ignored until murder forced us to pay attention.

Capital punishment is in many ways addressing a problem that should have been attended to decades earlier. Our work as mitigators indicates that capital punishment perpetuates what Craig Haney, who is a law professor . . . and a psychiatrist, has called a myth of demonic agency. It allows us to deny the humanity of people who commit heinous crimes. Capital defendants become nonpeople, without context, life connections, social relationships, wants, or hardships, yet our work as mitigators belies this effort. Capital defendants are indeed people, and tragically they are people that our community and society have helped to shape in their often horrific, but all-too-human behavior.

There are enough pragmatic concerns that we have heard today to argue against the reinstatement of the death penalty in New York; the cost, the disparity, and the eventuality that New York too will make a mistake and condemn an innocent person to death.

Yet we believe that the moral issues should be (considered) as well. New York State should not be engaged in the immoral act of taking a life. We should not be complicit in perpetuating the myth of demonic agency.

Professor William Bowers of the Capital Jury Project at Boston's Northeastern University joined Gary Abramson in adding a political dimension to the retribution rationale.

Mr. Abramson: I think that . . . this is a very angry country. And the rage of the public for the defendants, I think, has a lot to do with -- it's in some ways displaced. I think you see a frustration with their own lives. I mean, the urge for revenge is fundamental to the human. We all feel satisfied when we feel like we've gotten back in some way.

So, when you translate that into the criminal justice system, and the defendant becomes this sort of straw figure for a lot of public animosity and fantasies about rage, and the need for revenge, and then you translate that into a system where politicians are acutely sensitive to the emotions of their constituents, that in this society the death penalty -- I mean, the fact that you're having these hearings and that there is even an impetus (to restore the death penalty), after the Court of Appeals has said the statute is messed up, and so now the government wants to fix it.

It shows that there is still this tremendous need in society to kill intentional murderers. And I think it's explained -- you know, I'm not a psychologist, but I think that it's a mass cultural phenomenon around vengeance fantasies that get played out with my clients and our clients. . . .

Professor Bowers: (In) America, criminal law is not national, it's a state issue, and that's very different . . . . Here the politics is state and it's local. And I just finished working on (the) question of what happens when judges have the override of a jury's sentence. That's true in Alabama and Florida.

When you look at the campaign(s) -- oh, our judges -- you know, judges here are elected. Well, you may not be surprised when I say it, but when you think about it, it's surprising. The overrides, life to death overrides, you can't go the other way . . . . You know, it's twenty-to-one death override (by the judge) of a life sentence from a jury.

That's happening more commonly . . . . It's more likely to happen in the run-up to elections, the judicial elections. But you can see that the newspapers provide these judicial candidates a place to be hard on crime and to accuse their opponents of being soft on crime . . . . One thing more, working here in 1991, I helped design a survey, and using the standard polling question, do you favor or oppose the death penalty, 73 percent of the people of New York said they favor the death penalty. Well, we decided, because I had seen from an earlier poll conducted in Florida, actually, by people that were working with Amnesty International. If you asked about -- if this state could impose a sentence of life without parole, would you prefer that to the death penalty, and the majority said yes.

(W)e went on to ask other questions - what if the defendant would have to work in prison for money that would go to the families of victims, (based on that question) support for the death penalty shrank down to 17 percent from 73.

I mean, it's a mile wide and not very deep, this death penalty support, but it is a knee-jerk and a very potent reaction, in the absence of something that feels like an effective alternative, which I think life without parole is. In other words, retribution can be easily trumped by practical concerns.

Very late in the hearing held on February 8, 2005, a panel of religious leaders returned to the question of whether support for retribution as a justification for the death penalty can be found in scripture or religious doctrine. Barbara Zaron, representing the Steering Committee of the Reform Jewish Voice of New York State, phrased the moral question as follows:

I will (ask). . . . the same question asked by Rabbi Marc Gruber who testified at the New York City hearing on behalf of the Reform Jewish Voice: "How will we respond when our children ask, 'why do we kill people who kill people to show that killing people is wrong'?"

A good answer to that question is difficult to find in religious doctrine. Reverend Geoffrey Black, President of the New York State Council of Churches, pointed out that the "teachings of Jesus Christ . . . clearly renounce retribution . . . as it's applied to capital punishment."

In the Gospel of John, Chapter Eight, Jesus challenges those who would execute a woman caught in adultery. While the Mosaic law would have supported her being stoned to death for her offense, Jesus admonishes the crowd to let the one who is without sin throw the first stone. No stones were thrown that day, because no one present was himself sinless, or thereby perfect, and thus in an appropriate position to execute such an absolute punishment.

It is ironic, or perhaps timely, that we hold these hearings on the eve of Ash Wednesday, the beginning of the Lenten season, which in itself culminates with Good Friday, the day of Jesus' own execution by crucifixion. We are reminded that it is at his execution that Jesus, from the cross, again challenges the practice of retribution, in that he asks forgiveness for those who are taking his life. There he prays aloud, "Father, forgive them for they know not what they do."

As Lloyd Steffan, professor of religious studies at Lehigh University explains in his 1998 book, EXECUTING JUSTICE, Jesus is certainly not taking the occasion of his own crucifixion to lend support to the idea that the state has a legitimate right to do what it is doing. Rather, by his words, Jesus condemns this execution act, and his condemnation is clear from the fact that he asks God to forgive his executioners.

More generally, our faith tradition holds to the centrality of Jesus' essential teachings in the Sermon on the Mount. There Jesus challenges the practice of retribution with this teaching: "You have heard it said an eye for an eye and a tooth for a tooth. But I say to you, do not resist an evildoer. But if anyone strikes you on the right cheek, turn the other also."

Now, I want to pause here to say that often this is seen as a kind of a very passive, ultra-passive way to go about dealing with conflict, when, in fact, it is an act of defiance to turn one's other cheek to the evildoer.

The sum of the - - to sum the matter up, Jesus teaches us not to return evil for evil. Of course, this is not always the way of the world in which we live, but as Christians we are challenged not to conform to the ways of the world, and the requirement of retribution is one of those ways.

Beyond the position prompted by the theological and biblical and spiritual aspects of our faith, our position is shaped by our belief that any system devised and administered by human beings is subject to error and corruption, as our criminal justice system has proven itself to be time and time again. And I need only refer to many of the previous testimonies this afternoon.

Such a system cannot be allowed to render an absolute and final judgment, as it would in the death penalty, for which there is no possibility of redress or correction when mistakes are made. In our view, a mistake of this order is itself the ultimate injustice.

The Reform Jewish position was described as paralleling that of the U.S. Conference of Bishops. Barbara Zaron observed (quoting Rabbi David Saperstein).

Though the Bible calls for execution for dozens of offenses, some of them being murder, adultery, idol worship, disrespecting parents, and desecrating the Sabbath, over 2000 years . . . of rabbinic wisdom teach us to reject an ultimate punishment that removes even in the possibility of redemption and rehabilitation. Our opposition is even stronger in the case of juveniles, who do not have the full capacity to distinguish between right and wrong.

Continuing on the same theme, Dominic Candido expressed the position of the Religious Society of Friends.

We hold that the death penalty is, first and foremost, an act of weakness, be it for retribution or for deterrence. It is an impotent act that gives an illusion of control, just as the murderer's act imbued him with a false sense of power.

You ask whether the state has a right to take life in retribution. Please think more deeply. Retribution means to pay back. What has been paid back when a life is taken?

I once read that Roman soldiers gave money, called ransom, to the citizens of Rome prior to setting off to war. The payment was meant to recognize that the act of killing which they were about to undertake in the name of the state was wrong. Do we similarly absolve ourselves today, paying six times the cost of life without parole just to put someone to death?

In this post-9/11 age of retribution, it is easy to fall prey to the notion that we have made ourselves more secure by punching back. Instead, we Friends believe that all communities should rise above fear and work toward restoration, affirming that while self-defense is appropriate, vengeance is not. It is a lustful moment that does not sustain.

Given our respect for the integrity of human life, why should we be complicit in the death or suicide of another? Many of those sentenced to death look forward to the self-perceived moment of transcendence. Even if retribution is the goal, the mark is missed as the state ends up rewarding the killer by being the very instrument of the individual's wish to die.

The difficulty in this line of argument lies in a contradiction. From the religious point of view, according to Wanda Goldstein of the Unitarian Universalist Church, "(t)o take those completely captive persons and deliberately kill them in an empty, stark, sanitized manner seems far beyond any concept of humanity" recognized by spiritual teachings. Yet, retribution is premised on the inhumanity of the killer's actions. Americans who are not strongly religious may not be able to accept the imbalance that exists when the murderer's inhumanity is ignored but the killer is permitted to live for humane reasons.

Bianca Jagger, former wife of rock star Mick Jagger, appeared as Goodwill Ambassador on behalf of the Council of Europe and Amnesty International. Her testimony presented the harsh reality of retribution in its pure form - the witnessed execution of death row inmate Gary Graham. In her words,

> Ms. Jagger: I would like to commend this Assembly for exercising this great democratic process and for allowing me (to speak). Thank you very much for allowing me to be here. I am the . . . Goodwill Ambassador and a member of the Executive Director's Leadership Counsel of Amnesty International USA.
>
> I am here to speak against the death penalty because I have been working on issues pertaining to human rights for more than

20 years and for almost 10 years I have been working with men and women . . . (on) death row and what I want to ask, before I tell you the story of a man that I witnessed his execution, Gary Graham, (is whether) society (is) operating at it's highest moral level when it's only solution to prevent violent crime is to kill? And I am here to urge you that the only thing that deserves to be killed is the death penalty.

In 1998, I received a phone call from a Steven Halking, the Executive Director of the Coalition to Abolish the Death Penalty, and he urged me at the time to join him and . . . to participate in a press conference to try to stop the execution of a man he believed to be innocent. Later on, I worked as well with Amnesty International on his case. Gary Graham was 17 when he was convicted and sentenced to death for the murder of a white man, Bobby Lamber(t), shot in a grocery store parking lot in Houston on May 13, 1981.

From the moment of his arrest until the last moment of his life, Gary Graham proclaimed his innocence. However, his lawyer at trial did very little to help him and conducted no investigation. As a result, evidence (that) would have prevented him from being mistakenly convicted, sentenced to death and executed was never presented at his trial and was never . . . seen or heard by the jurors.

Gary Graham, who later wanted to be known as Shakin Cincoffa, to re-vindicate his African origins, was convicted on the basis of a single eyewitness testimony. She picked him out of a line up following an extremely suggestive identification procedure. In fact, she saw him from 40 meters away behind a windshield in a car. There (were) 7 other witnesses who said that Gary Graham was not the killer. In addition, there was absolutely nothing that linked him to that murder.

Gary had released a statement (when I went in 1998 to Texas) where he said when I was a 17 year old juvenile, I became the victim of poor legal representation and a racial bias prosecution system that is more often criminal than just. I was wrongfully convicted of capital murder and sentenced to death by (a) nearly all white jury despite overwhelming and compelling evidence to my innocence. My trial was a travesty of justice and a strong people's movement is the only hope to prevent my legal lynching and to stop my execution.

By 2000, Gary had lost all his appeals and was scheduled to be executed on June 11, 2000. I knew the wheels of the machinery of death were at work when I watched on ABC Nightline (it) being proclaimed by the prosecutor that Gary Graham was the killer and that all the witnesses had pointed to him, which was not true.

(I) woke up at 4:30 to do CNN early news right after I drove to the airport to meet with Reverend Jessie Jackson. He was flying to Texas to lend his support to Gary Graham and to call on Governor Bush and Chairman Garras to grant him a pardon, a commutation, or 120 day reprieve. Gary Graham could have been saved if that had been applied but unfortunately it did not take place.

(I) had met with him twice before he (was) executed and in his, in my first meeting with him, I said to him that if he needed me to be a witness to his execution that I was prepared to do it. Little did I know that that was going to happen and I learned on a television program that he had asked for me to be present at his execution. Of course, I was filled with horror by the reality that I was going to watch the death of a man I believed to be innocent.

In my capacity as a representative of Amnesty International I witnessed the shocking and controversial execution by lethal injection of Gary Graham at Huntsville, Texas, for the murder of Bobby Lamber(t) outside an American supermarket in 1981. Gary Graham was on death row for 19 years and proclaimed his innocence until the end.

It is difficult to describe my horror at witnessing his death. We entered into a little room: gazing through a plexiglass window I could see Gary Graham was tied to a hospital trolley and about to be killed. It reminded me of a modern day cross and I was there to witness the execution of a man I believed to be innocent. I was in a state of disarray and I was revolted and terrified at the thought of witnessing another human being killed.

His whole forehead was held in restraint by a leather strap and he had to strain his head to look at us. He told me in fact that he had been beaten that day because he always said that he was going to oppose his execution. He was black and blue, and that's the reason why he was covered from the neck down on his body.

His look was intense, suddenly he began to speak with a strong, clear voice. He knew they would be his last words he .... He turned to the family of the man he had been accused of murdering and said "I would like to say that I did not kill Bobby (Lambert). I am an innocent black man that has been murdered. It is lynching, what is happening in America tonight."

It was at that point that I broke down. He had so much he wanted to say, but so little time to say it. We told him that we loved him. I put my hands and face on the glass. We were just 4 feet away.

It was ironic. I was in Texas in the United States of America, a country that proclaims itself to be the world's most progressive force in humans rights, but we were about to witness the execution of a man about who's alleged crime, there (were) so many disturbing doubts.

As I watched his execution, I could not come to terms with the failure of American Justice. With his last breath, Gary Graham implored us to let the world know of the injustice that had been done to him, and he urged us to carry on the fight to clear his name after his death.

We thought that they would begin the execution procedure when (he) stopped making his last statement, but we were wrong. They had begun to kill him as he was talking to us. In the process of his death, he made a powerful, eloquent speech, he said that it meant a great deal to him that we had asked to be at his execution and he called us by name. I could not believe the State of Texas was executing Gary Graham based solely on the eyewitness identification of one person. I was witnessing the State machinery of death at work. As he put it himself, they are going to keep lynching us for the next hundred years if you don't carry on the tradition of resistance.

Two men came in and checked for his vital signs and looked at his eyes. I didn't realize he was dead. I had hoped that perhaps he would be able to resist death. On the Tuesday before he had said to me that if the sacrifice of his life would expose the sham of the justice system in Texas, then he didn't mind dying, but we were going, we were hoping the Board of Parole would grant him a reprieve, a pardon . . . .

I am here because what I witnessed with Gary Graham is not an exception. I believe that if there have been more than 116 people . . . exonerated, the possibility that a person is executed when they are innocent, it is much too real. We, as a society that proclaim to be a democracy, a leader in democracy in the world, we cannot allow . . . the possibility of executing another innocent man. I'm here to urge you to not allow the death penalty to be reinstated. Thank you very much.

Ms. Jagger's sense of what "humanity" requires may not be shared by large segments of American society. As explained by former New York City Public Advocate (and, presently, President of the New Democracy Project) Mark Green:

Mr. Green: Good morning panel, Mr. Chairman, Assembly members . . . . The raw power of the death penalty dawned on me personally and emotionally when some 25 years ago I was engaged on a TV panel before a live audience in New Jersey and someone who was in favor of the death penalty said among the reasons for it is retribution, an eye for an eye and a tooth for a tooth. And so by giving in to the Socratic method I said, are you saying sir that if an accused has tortured a victim to death that the state should then torture . . . that defendant? And the audience spontaneously cheered "yes, yes, yes". I was surprised, I was dismayed, I was educated, but my mind certainly wasn't changed.

In April 1989, a 29-year-old jogger in New York's Central Park was brutally raped and beaten. Five boys between the ages of 14 and 16 were quickly convicted. Twelve years later the real rapist, Matias Reyes, confessed to the crime. His story was confirmed by D.N.A. testing of hair and semen specimens still in police custody. The boys were released from jail. Some of the most dramatic testimony at the New York Hearings came from one of the exonerated, Yusef Salaam.

Much of Mr. Salaam's statement dealt with the subject of Chapter Six of this book, innocence. He was convicted of rape because the victim in the jogger case, who was in a coma for 12 days, did not die. Had she done so, the case would have been a capital one. With violent crime soaring in New York City in 1989 – 1990, and fear everywhere, the cries for retribution were loud and intense. The retributive attitudes then in play help us understand the dangers associated with revenge-based sentencing. Mr. Salaam's testimony was a direct challenge to the legitimacy of retribution as a basis for capital punishment.

> Mr. Salaam: To the distinguished panel and members of the Assembly of the State of New York, I am Yusef Salaam. I was one of the 5 innocent youths convicted of brutally attacking and raping the Central Park Jogger, Ms. Patricia Meili.
>
> In addressing you today, I am reminded of the recent resolution just weeks ago enacted by the Congress of the United States. In that resolution, the Congress officially proclaimed an apology to its African American citizens in an attempt to address its prolonged failure to act during the early turbulent periods of our history, where thousands of African American children, women and men, were lynched and otherwise murdered by vigilante mobs without benefit of any fair and non prejudiced judicial law processes.
>
> Sadly to say, while that resolution, as helpful as it may have been with regard to true reconciliation and healing processes concerning mob justice, it doesn't at all cover the

authorized injustices and legal lynchings still prevalent in society today.

It is only by sheer happenstance that I appear before you today, in flesh and spirit and a free man rather than as one more statistic, unjustly mob or state murdered or incarcerated, and therefore (a) lost human being.

During the trial against my co-defendants and me, Donald Trump spent $85,000 to place full-page ads in all of New York's major newspapers, The New York Times, Newsday, the Daily News and the New York Post, calling for the reinstatement of the death penalty and how we should be hated and how we were murderers.

I respectfully submit that the ad reads:

"Bring back the death penalty, bring back our police. What has happened is the complete breakdown of life as we knew it. Many families, many New York families, (have) had to give up the pleasure of a leisure stroll in the park at dusk, the Saturday visit to the playground with their families, the bike ride at dawn, or just sitting on their stoops. Give them up as hostages to a world ruled by the law of the streets as roving bands of wild criminals roam our neighborhoods dispensing their own brand of twisted hatred on whomever they encounter. At what point did we cross the line from the fine and noble pursuit of genuine civil liberties, to the reckless and dangerous permissive atmosphere which allows criminals of every age to beat and rape a helpless woman and then laugh at this family's anguish?

And why do they laugh? They laugh because they know that very soon they will be returning to the streets to rape and maim and kill once again. And face, and yet, face no greater personal risk to themselves. Mayor Koch has stated that hate has run its course and should be removed from our hearts. I think, I do not think so.

I want to hate these muggers and murderers. They should be forced to suffer. And when they kill, they should be executed for their crimes. Yes Mayor Koch, I want to hate these murderers and I always will. I am looking to punish them. I no longer want to understand their anger. I want them to understand our anger. I want them to be afraid. Let our politicians give back our police departments power to keep us safe. Un-shackle them from constant charges of police brutality which every petty criminal hurls immediately at an officer who has just risked his life to save another. We must cease our continuous pandering to the criminal population. Send a message loud and clear to those that would murder our citizens and terrorize New York. Bring back the death penalty and bring back our police."

All this was in the papers before the trial even started.

The would-be President of the United States, Patrick Buchanan, suggested that it would be helpful to public order if the oldest rape defendant who was my co-defendant Karey Wise, who was a 16-year-old boy, were tried and convicted and hung in Central Park. My co-defendants and me faired no better during television coverage of the case. In one notable instance, on the nationally aired Donahue television show, lawyers for two of my co-defendants were confronted by the show's audience where one woman cried "Castrate them" to great applause. And if this woman (the victim) dies, then they too should be put to death. A vicious, almost machine- like cycle began to fester.

(T)he media, who influence public opinion, and without benefit of trial, aided in filling the people with hate against us. Get politicians and elected officials to act accordingly . . . .

This death machine . . . is in essence no different . . . from the escaped slave hand bills and lynching rally calls of past gone eras. (T)his death machine is an exact re-enactment of the same forces that were at play which now the U.S. Congress seems compelled to apologize for.

Members of the panel, I respectfully submit to you that you collectively and individually can and indeed have an obligation to stop this cycle of death and sanctioned murder. It's only by happenstance that I appear before you today. I was 15 years old, just a boy, when these events changed my life forever.

Because I was the tallest and presumably the darkest skin of my co-defendants, people pointed at me saying things like what we need to do is hang him; for what they did they don't deserve a trial; he needs to be made an example of; he needs to be under the jail; death threats and much more of the like.

We were labeled as scourge of the earth, wolf pack, wilding. So vicious was the media-inspired atmosphere that even few people of color sought justice for us. Not even the judge in the case sought justice. Until exoneration by the courts, I had spent and lost nearly 14 years of my life under the weighty, spiked heels of the Criminal Justice System. That period represents my life between the ages of 15 through 28.

In normal life, what would have happened to me by the time I turned 16? In a normal life, what would have happened for me by the time I would have turned 18? In a normal life, what would have happened for me by the time I turned 21? And likewise, what would have happened in a normal life by the time I turned 25?

In a state with the death penalty, what would have happened had Ms. Patricia Meili unfortunately died as a result of the attack? In all likelihood, instead of being here with you now I would have either been executed or instead of being here with you now, I'd be waiting execution. Honorable members of the panel, again, it's only by happenstance that I sit before here, sit before you today.

In 2002, thirteen years after our false confessions, convictions rather, the real rapist of the Central Park Jogger, Matias Reyes, voluntarily came forward and confessed to the crime and he confessed that he was the only one involved. Our convictions were reversed but fourteen years of our lives had been erased. At the time of his confession, Reyes was already in prison for the rape and murder of other women. Ironically, by the time of his confession, the statute of limitations had run out on the crimes that he committed in the Central Park Jogger case. Some still say, however, that justice was served because we served his time. Had this been a capital crime, we also would have served his death penalty.

Honorable members of the panel, the wrongful convictions of the Central Park Jogger case speak volumes concerning serious and disastrous flaws in advocating for an implementation of the death penalty. This is so regarding the likelihood of innocents being executed by the state and it also speaks volumes concerning the processes involved in a state making the choice to sanction the death penalty. With the foregoing notwithstanding this case speaks volumes concerning the desperate number of people of color in prison and languishing on death row.

Some politicians and other advocates for the death penalty have been known to glibly remark that justice can't be perfect. In effect . . . admitting that some innocent people have to die for what Patrick Buchanan calls help to public order. What a despicable and backward and inhuman position for a person to take. What a despicable and backward and inhuman position for the state to take. Members of the panel, I respectfully submit that you (must) end the State sanctioned death machine. This from a man who appears to you today only by happenstance.

This section on retribution ends with the voice of a key citizen in the Hearings debate, Assemblyman Joseph R. Lentol of North Brooklyn, Chair of the Assembly Committee on Codes. Mr. Lentol raised the issue of vigilantism and whether retributory execution contributes to the preservation of public order by restraining individuals from participating in mob violence or private executions.

Speaker Lentol: Thank you. Thank you Mr. Rogers (President of the Association of Legal Aid Attorneys). (O)ne of the things that I've been thinking about throughout these hearings and even before is the awesome responsibility that we in government have, not only regarding this issue, but just in general in maintaining public safety, protecting the public, maintaining order if you will.

And I want to give you a chance to respond to what I think is probably the argument that has not yet been made, at least before these hearings, by proponents of the death penalty. They've come close but they haven't made this argument, and that is this, that if it is indeed our responsibility to maintain order, is it not a legitimate purpose of the death penalty (to prevent vigilantism) because we have individuals who require . . . revenge or retribution, so that (with capital punishment) society is well served and order is maintained among society and we don't have a mob out there . . . . ?

James Rogers, President of the Association of Legal Aid Attorneys, responded.

Mr. Rogers: I'm, I am personally morally opposed to the death penalty in any event, but I'm not so dogmatic that I wouldn't consider and listen as you have to . . . what are the merits? Does it work? Is it a deterrent and if it's not a deterrent, is community vindication, is societal vindication and retribution a legitimate goal? Even if one were to conceive that (retribution) is a legitimate goal, I think society can do a whole lot better in identifying values than that.

But even if one were to conceive that (retribution) is a legitimate goal, the risks are so profound of what happens to an innocent person caught up in that system, and (the risks) particularly to poor people and people of color, the risks are so profound that even if people agree that (retribution) is a goal and society should strive for (it), they wouldn't . . . accept the risk of an innocent person knowingly being put to death.

But since the overwhelming evidence sir is that the risks are that great, and that the chances of executing innocent persons are significant, . . . I don't think anybody in their right mind would say . . . that . . . (even with) retribution I'm willing to take that risk. And that is why I don't think you have seen a stream of people sit in this chair and say to you retribution is the value above all values.

Deterrence

 The primary alternative to retribution as a justification for capital punishment is deterrence. The argument that the death penalty is needed to deter potential killers from committing murder is extremely controversial.[38] In 2006, a Gallop poll reported that only 34% of persons surveyed thought capital punishment deterred crime. Proponents contend that the threat of capital punishment prevents homicides. They assert that executions educate citizens about the consequences of committing murder and persuade potential killers not to kill. Death penalty opponents strongly argue that existing scientific and anecdotal evidence does not support these propositions. Cases of provable deterrence are extremely difficult to find. This clash of opinion appeared frequently during the New York Death Penalty Hearings.

Professor Robert Blecker argued the case for deterrence as strongly as he justified retribution as a basis for capital punishment. He did so by appealing to what many would regard as instinct, common sense, a "gut reaction". Professor Blecker:

 The question is not does the death penalty deter, of course the death penalty deters, but that wouldn't make it sufficient because life in prison also deters. Neither of them deter perfectly. Neither of them deter adequately. As the Commission (that explored capital punishment in N.Y.) said in 1953 about deterrence and the death penalty, we can number its failure(s), look at every murder, but we can't number its successes. We can't tell how many people would have been killed but for the death penalty. But the question is not does the death penalty deter, all punishment to some degree deters . . . and the death penalty deters to a great degree, but so does life imprisonment. The question, the only rightful question in terms of deterrence is, does the death penalty deter more effectively than its principle alternative, life, or life without parole. And here the evidence is not exactly as has been presented, although we don't tend to read about it much in the abolitionist media . . . . The last six studies, rather sophisticated, have indicated a significantly greater . . . deterrent effect of the death penalty over the principle alternative, life without parole.

Now there are critics of those studies and there are criticisms starting to be published about the methodology and I'm not here to enter into it. I'm not qualified to enter into it. But do be aware that recent studies have shown consistently and marginally greater deterrent affect(s). It's not only statistics that are on the side of deterrence, it's also psychology and logic. Of course the death penalty should operate as the greatest marginal deterrent. It makes sense. Death is the ultimate threat, (and this) threat is the ultimate punishment. There are things that we would not do out of fear of dying that we might otherwise do out of fear of loss of liberty.

And especially for those who themselves have become used to prison, who know that they can handle it. And I base this by the way on 2,000 hours over 12 years inside Worton . . . Prison with convicted killers, exploring with the trust of the inmates and full cooperation with the administration . . . their lives . . . their minds . . . (and) their attitudes.

And it's very common to hear them say, I can handle prison. I know what that's about. Death is something else. You don't handle death the same way you handle loss of liberty.

So it makes sense that the death penalty would be a marginally greater effective deterrent, and advertently it also makes sense. I've heard instances that people, who have killed . . . in Washington, DC, . . . did not murder under the same set of circumstances in Virginia and Maryland, two neighboring jurisdictions, and when I asked them why, the anecdotes that I got were, for example, the memories as a child of looking up at the - when DC had the death penalty - looking up at the DC jail and the electric chair, you could see it from the parking lot. Or one who spent time in Virginia and used to clean halls around the electric chair, where the bodies were executed, and the answer was, the reason . . . I did kill in DC and I didn't kill in Maryland and Virginia . . . (was) because I couldn't handle what they had waiting for me there, I couldn't handle the death penalty.

It is said . . . that deterrence is one of these questions, in terms of the death penalty, that is so fundamental and so obvious that it's more obvious than any argument that we can construct against it. So logically, psychologically, anecdotally and statistically, the odds are overwhelming that the death penalty is a more effective marginal deterrent than its principle alternative, life or life without parole. But let me make it perfectly clear, for me that's irrelevant. If the death penalty were a more effective deterrent and it were immoral, if it violated human dignity, we should reject it and soundly reject it, notwithstanding the fact that it deterred. And if it failed as a more effective deterrent but was itself morally commanded, then we should embrace it, notwithstanding the fact that it failed as a deterrent . . . .

By the way, you've also heard that deterrence requires that punishment be swift and certain. That is the classical view. That's no longer embraced. Punishment need not be swift and certain, for those who are this adverse about dying, it may be highly contingent and improbable and nevertheless will advert certain behavior threatened with death that we cannot tolerate. So it need not be swift nor certain in order to be a more effective deterrent. ·

Two academics, Jeffrey Fagan of Columbia University and John Blume of Cornell University, stated the case against deterrence.

Professor Blume, Director of the Cornell Death Penalty Project, observed:

> Now, is the death penalty a deterrent: Well the overwhelming weight of the scholarly research indicates that the death penalty does not deter persons from committing murder. I will not discuss these studies in detail. There will be a new study which will soon be published in the Journal of Empirical Legal Studies at our law school which essentially indicates (this) again and reaffirms that it is not.[39]
>
> But I do want to say several things I guess more anecdotally. First, our research reveals that the states that have abolished capital punishment by and large have lower murder rates than states that retain capital punishment.
>
> By way of contrast, all of the former slave states have the death penalty, and most routinely sentence persons to death. Yet, on average, southern states have higher murder rates than other regions of the country.
>
> Second, I have spent some time studying serial killers, which I think we would all agree, to borrow a phrase which has previously been used in these hearings, would constitute "the worst of the worst."
>
> For the most part, these individuals are more intelligent than the average murderer, and also again as a general rule, do not suffer from a psychotic thought disorder. Thus, these persons would seem to be the most susceptible to the deterrent effect of capital punishment because they have the ability to make the necessary cost-benefit analysis.
>
> But the most notorious serial killers in recent times -- Ted Bundy, John Wayne Gacey, Donald Pee Wee Gaskins, Aileen Wornos[40] -- to name a few, all committed their crimes in states with active death penalties. They were also ultimately apprehended, convicted and sentenced to death. The threat of capital punishment, in short, was no deterrent to them.
>
> Third and finally on the issue of deterrence, my study of death row volunteers (inmates who waive all appeals and ask to

be executed) uncovered cases where some individuals in fact committed murder for the purpose of being apprehended and sentenced to death. Thus, there are cases where retaining capital punishment may lead an individual, admittedly a mentally ill one, to actually commit a crime as a form of suicide.

Some very concrete information on deterrence came from Professor Fagan who, at the time of his testimony, was a member of the National Research Council's Committee on Law and Justice. His lengthy testimony follows, including criticisms of studies showing a deterrence effect from capital punishment.

Mr. Fagan: I want to thank the members of the Committee for allowing me to address you today. Normally I would not make a statement of my qualifications, but I think in this case, because of the subject matter that I want to talk about, a few qualifications might be in order.

I'm a Professor of Law and Public Health at Columbia. I got my PhD from SUNY Buffalo in 1975 where I was trained in econometrics, statistics, and engineering, all things which qualify me deeply to be a law professor. I am a Fellow of the American Society of Criminology, and a member of the National Research Council's Committee on Law and Justice, where we have taken up issues of the death penalty and of its deterrent effects. And I have served on a number of federal scientific review boards and federal agencies. I was editor of . . . peer-reviewed journals for six years, and I serve currently on the editorial boards of a number of peer-reviewed journals in criminology, law and public policy. And I say that because I come to you today to talk about the technical question of deterrence and the death penalty.

Since 1995, more than a dozen studies have been published claiming that the death penalty has a very strong deterrent effect. And, in fact, (that) each execution can prevent anywhere from three to 18 homicides. These are astonishing effects, pretty much unsurpassed in other realms of social policy. I believe that

Professor Blecker cited some of this work in speaking to this panel at the last hearing here in New York.

Several of these studies claim that pardons, commutations and exonerations, all together, lumped together without distinction, cause murders to increase. Others say that even murders of passion, among the most irrational lethal acts, can be deterred by . . . execution. Some say that deterrent effects of execution are so powerful that executions will not only reduce murders but also will reduce robberies and a whole wide range of non-violent crimes.

So, for these folks, the deterrent effects of execution and capital punishment apparently are limitless and some proponents suggest that execution might, in fact, be a cure-all for every day crime. These are published in peer review journals, by the way.

The bar is very high, however, when science makes these kinds of claims, whether it's in medicine, whether it's in engineering, or whether it's in social policy. The standards are neither technical nor are they particularly mysterious. They just simply reflect a lot of common sense that you and I would apply when we were asking somebody to back up some strong claims that they were making. These include, for example, the ability of somebody to replicate the original research under different conditions by an independent researcher . . . . These standards include the use of measures and methods that avoid biases from inaccurate yardsticks and faulty gauges. And most important, I think, is the ability to tell a simple and persuasive casual (causal?) story that tests and then rules out any other competing explanation.

Well, a close reading of the new deterrence studies shows quite clearly that they actually fail to touch this scientific bar, let alone cross it. Let me cite just a few examples of some of the limitations in this body of work.

All but one of the studies lump together all forms of murder claiming that they're all deeply deterrable. But logic tells us that some types of murders are probably poor candidates for deterrence such as crimes of passion or jealousy. Yet the one study that looked at this particular category of domestic homicides found that these were the only category that were actually deterrable. This is a claim that flied in (the face of) a century of research on homicide and a century of research on deterrence. And it also ignores the empirical fact that domestic homicides have been declining steadily since the early 1970's during a time when there was no execution in the United States and long before its re-imposition (in the mid-1970s) .... Can we trust a science that so deeply contradicts what are the known facts?

Second, the studies tend to produce erratic and very contradictory results and some find, in fact, that there is no deterrence at all. One state (study) shows that executions are ... likely to produce an increase in homicides ... following execution, in a handful of states ... what we call a brutalization effect; homicides will increase in some states, and in some states homicides will decrease. Moreover, some of these studies show that a particular state will change direction somewhere in the middle of a course of 25 or 30 years. A state that was a brutalizing state (homicides increase with executions) in one period of time will all of a sudden become a deterrent state (murders decrease). Can we trust a policy and a science whose effects change direction on any given decade without any reasonable explanation?

Third, these studies generally all fail to control for the performance of the criminal justice system overall. Specifically, clearance rates for violent crimes. And there's something important about clearance rates. Some of the studies do control for imprisonment, and that's helpful, but very few control for the ability of local law enforcement to identify, detect, and arrest homicide offenders or high rate offenders generally. This is what we call the clearance rate.

And ... decades of deterrence research tell us that it's the risk of detection and apprehension, not the severity of the punishment, that actually deters individuals.

So it's very hard to evaluate these claims of scientific evidence about execution without first understanding whether or not we have taken into account the clearance rates for homicides. But, in fact, none of the studies do take into account the clearance rates for homicides. Again, we have an incomplete picture of the effects of deterrence.

Fourth, there's been a recent paper, an analysis of executions and murders going back to the 1970's, by Professor Richard Berk. And basically he shows that all of the deterrent effects that are being claimed in this body of research are confined to one state - Texas. And even in Texas only for a handful of years, and that was a handful of years when there were five or more executions in a given year.

No state has reached that threshold of execution in a single year, no other state, and it's highly unlikely that any will do so in the future. And, in fact, what Berk shows is that if you knock Texas out of the study and out of the data set, any hint of deterrence vanishes and so there's no longer a relationship between execution and homicide.

Statistically, when you have a tyranny of these small number of observations that drive a very deep and complex, and large, and elaborate database, it leads you to a false conclusion and it's a false conclusion born out of what we call these out layers (outliers?). I would think that lawmakers would be reluctant to generalize from the Texas data . . . to any other state and any other set of conditions, particularly in the State of New York.

Fifth, and perhaps one of the most important, is that the most frequent sentence that exists today is life without parole (LWOP) for a capital murder. LWOP is the most frequent sentence of murder convictions today, far more frequent than death sentences, even in some of the high murder rate states. For example, in Pennsylvania in 1999 and 2000 there were 137 LWOP sentences in Pennsylvania compared to 15 death sentences in '99. In 2000, there were 121 life LWOP sentences compared to 12 death sentences in Pennsylvania. In California there are 3,163 inmates serving life without parole as of February 2004, but there are only 635 on death row.

None of the studies of deterrence take LWOP into account. It is not a variable in any of them. We cannot rule out LWOP as a cause of the decline in homicide rates that we have seen all over the country, both in New York and elsewhere. The omission of LWOP from these data sets and from these analyses rules out that alternate and complete competing explanation that good science demands and leaves us a little bit puzzled, scratching our heads really to understand the decline of murder rates in California and elsewhere. This omission is not just misleading, but it's actually irresponsible. Were this a tort situation I suppose they would be in line for some kind of malpractice suit. But we don't do that in academics.

In fact, if you actually examine the homicide rates in California, Texas, and New York, since each state's peak homicide rate, we go back to the early 1990's on this, one can see the strong incapacitat(ing) effects of such sentences (LWOP) on murder rates. For example, in New York, a state with no death penalty until April 1995 and no execution, homicide rates declined by 65.5 percent since the peak rate in 1990, a decline that began in 1992 long before the death penalty was reinstated, and accelerated throughout the decade.

In comparison, homicide rates in Texas declined by 61.4 percent (a lower rate than N.Y.) since its peak rate in 1991. Texas has no life without parole statue. So, which state saves lives? Which state saves more lives? And which one does so without the expense and other complications of execution?

Finally, the studies fail to consider other alterative causes of fluctuations in the murder rate. Murder is a complicated story. For example, nearly all of the increase and decline in U.S. homicides since 1985, and they (homicides) peaked nationally in 1991 and then declined again thereafter, nearly all of the increase and decline was in the category of gun homicides, yet none of the studies take into account the fact that . . . non-gun homicides have been declining steadily since way before the re-imposition of capital punishment, since roughly 1972. Why would there be a deterrent effect on non-gun homicides?

Second, none of the studies account for gun availability. It's not that easy to account for gun availability but it can be done. But none do. And none have controlled for the ravaging effects of the crack epidemic in the nation's cities in the late 80's and early 90's and its complex interactions with gun violence. So we don't know if these factors, in fact, influence the homicide rates because the deterrence researchers never considered them and never put them into their studies. So, in fact, we have an illusion of deterrence and this illusion disappears quite quickly when subjected to a careful, and critical and scientifically rigorous analysis.

There are serious flaws and omissions in this body of work that render it unreliable, and certainly not sound enough . . . to base life and death decisions such as whether or not to reinstate the death penalty. The omissions and errors are so egregious that the work falls well within the unfortunate category of junk science or, as we say in . . . scientific review, these studies fail both the smell test and the legal test.

So, let me conclude. Murder is a complex and multiply-determined phenomenon. It's a very complicated business. It has gone up and down in cyclical patterns for the last 40 years. It goes up. It goes down. There are distinct periods of increase and decline. And, in fact, if you look at it it's not unlike the patterns that you would see in a number of contagious or epidemic diseases. There is no reliable or scientifically sound evidence that execution can in fact exert an effect that either acts separately or sufficiently powerfully to overwhelm these consistent and reoccurring epidemic patterns. Execution is a very small effect. It's a very rare event. But things like prisons, guns and drugs are very big, sustaining, reoccurring factors that in fact do a far better job of leveraging the murder rate up and then down than does a very small thing like execution.

The infrequency of execution and of capital punishment is spread geographically across the country with relatively very little publicity. All of these fail to provide a reliable test, much less a dispositive test, of the effects of deterrence on homicide. And so to accept it uncritically invites errors that have the most severe human costs.

Thank you.

To law enforcement officials like Michael Palladino, President of the New York Detectives' Endowment Association, these alleged flaws in the technical studies of deterrence and capital punishment are not really relevant. Palladino relied on his 26 years of service in the N.Y.P.D. to support this passionate testimony.

Opponents of capital punishment would like you to believe that it does not act as a deterrent in preventing murder. This statement, coming from those involved in the criminal justice system, is so pathetic that it would be laughable were it not such a serious matter. The spirit and intent of the Penal Law, the whole concept of a Penal Law, is to deter the commission of crimes by using the threat of punishment. Surely it is the priority of the law to prevent people from committing crimes rather than punishing the culprits after the fact . . . .

Make no mistake; it is the sanction that deter(s).

From my experience, I believe that capital punishment is most definitely a deterrent. The problem is the difficulty in tracking or accurately measuring the statistic. However, what can be tracked is the crime and murder statistics when the death penalty is in favor. When capital punishment is law, the murder rate is lower.

In the 1960's, the death penalty was law and the crime rate held steady and low and the quality of life was better. When the death penalty was repealed in the 1970's, the crime and murder rates rose steadily, right through the 80's and into the 90's. One day we woke up and the New York City murder rate was out of control, topping more than 2,000 murders a year in the five boroughs alone.

(I)n 1994, Governor Pataki was elected and in some regard (he) could be considered a savior. He resurrected the death penalty and the crime and murder rates began to quickly and steadily decline to rates not seen since the good old days of the 60's. The common denominator linking those two lowest crime periods is capital punishment as a deterrent. I, for one, do not want to return to the bad old days of the 70's, 80's and early 90's . . . .

Capital punishment is an issue of old-fashioned good versus evil. It's about the just punishment for heinous and egregious acts of murder. It's about deterring . . . reprehensible deeds. Although we cannot definitely measure the statistic, if capital punishment prevents or deters just one horrible deed, if it saves just one innocent life, then it has performed its duty.

As an advocate for law enforcement on a local and national level, I regard capital punishment as a necessary tool in the arsenal for traditional crime fighting. Moreover, in this post 9-11 era, law enforcement, especially in the State of New York, has stepped up to meet the challenge by taking on the added dangers of counter-terrorism duties. Along with those added responsibilities comes greater risks. At a time when life, liberty, and the pursuit of happiness are under attack, government should be giving the law enforcement community additional weapons in the fight against violent crime, not diminishing them.

I do not believe that every convicted murderer (should) be sentence(d) to death. However, absent the death penalty, how do you properly punish cop killers? What sanctions do you give to those who exercise an extreme disregard for society and murder sworn law enforcement officers? How do you bring to justice serial killers or heinous acts of terrorism given the magnitude of the World Trade Center tragedy? Do these people deserve life with no parole on the taxpayer dollar? I think that is adding insult to injury.

(O)pponents of the death penalty contend that they would rather pursue a less barbaric form of punishment, like life without parole. To those individuals I say their hypocrisy knows no bounds. Is it not far crueler to lock someone in a steel cage, ten feet by ten feet, for 40 years or longer? Given the choice of incarceration for the rest of my natural life or death by lethal injection, I'd have to give death serious consideration.

In closing, I ask you, the lawmakers, to reject the subjective arguments from the opponents of capital punishment. During the last four police funerals I attended, many politicians paid their respects and asked me and the grieving families if there was anything they could do to help. My response to you is yes. Today I am asking you to take a proactive approach. Let's not wait for the bad old days to return. Capital punishment works as a deterrent; the statistics prove that. I urge you to amend the problems in the language (of the jury instruction law) and reinstate the death penalty. Don't dismiss it, fix it . . . .

It is imperative that lawmakers send the message that government will not tolerate cops being slaughtered. If a criminal can take a police officer's life and escape with his or her own, where does that leave an innocent, defenseless citizen? It leaves them in fear.

The first witness to testify at the Hearings, Robert Morgenthau, District Attorney for New York County, presented historical information on the death penalty to support his conclusion that "the death penalty serves no useful purpose and has no place in a sensible and civilized justice system".

More than 150 years ago, in 1846, Robert Rantoul, Jr., a member of the Massachusetts legislature, conducted an unusually sophisticated study of the death penalty in Europe . . . . In a series of papers to the governor and the legislature, he called for the abolition of capital punishment. Rantoul, who also served as United States Attorney in Massachusetts and as a U.S. Senator and Representative in Congress, said, "After every instance in which the law violates the sanctity of human life, that life is held less than sacred by the community among whom the outrage is perpetrated."

Rantoul . . . found in his research that nations with a low proportion of executions to convictions had declining homicide rates, and that periods with unusually high numbers of executions were followed by increased incidents of homicide, the opposite of what deterrence theory would predict.

The case against the death penalty has also been made over the years in New York.

In 1841, a report of the New York State Assembly recommended abolition of "Punishment of death by law." Among other things, that Assembly committee report said that, "The uncertainty of conviction by juries for capital offenses has grown almost into a proverb, in the clearest cases it is constantly seen that they will not convict."

That was in 1841, and more than a century later, in 1965, the Temporary Commission on the Revision of the Penal Law and the Criminal Code, chaired by Assemblyman Richard J. Bartlett, Republican of Glens Falls, concluded that the death penalty was a "barbarism," which had a "seriously baneful effect on the administration of criminal justice."

(This) Commission observed that erroneous convictions and executions were inevitable and would "destroy the moral force of the entire penal law". (It stated that) the death penalty could not be administered in the United States with even "rough equality," and that the number of cruel and repulsive murders, "never will be greatly influenced by abolition of the death penalty." Numerous studies since the Bartlett Commission have reached similar results . . . .

In 1994, Congress enacted a new Violent Crime Control and Law Enforcement Act[41], which increased the number from two to 60 federal offenses for which someone could be sentenced to death and created more than 60 new federal crimes for conduct already harshly punished under state law.

Legislators who think these measures will reduce violent crimes fool themselves and the public. Such proposals may be good politics, but they are not good law enforcement. They divert our attention from present needs. I know of no law enforcement professional who believes that the (federal) death penalty provisions and all the new crimes covered by that 1994 Act have affected public safety in the slightest. The criminal laws we needed were already on the books. What was missing was the commitment to enforce them.

Even proponents have been forced to concede that 150 years of experience since the Rantoul report has not produced credible evidence that executions deter crime. There is no correlation between executions and low homicide rates. For instance, Texas, which has the highest number of executions in the nation, with 336 executions since 1976, also has one of the highest murder rates. FBI statistics show the homicide rate(s) in states that have the death penalty are 44% higher than in non-death penalty states.

Here in the northeast, and in nearby Philadelphia, the district attorney has been an avid proponent of the death penalty.

There are 124 inmates on death row in Philadelphia County, the third highest total for any county in the nation. Nevertheless, and this is important, in 2003, Philadelphia, which has a population equal to Manhattan, had nearly four times as many murders as Manhattan did, 348 versus 93.

To serve as an effective deterrent, punishment must be prompt and certain. The death penalty is neither. According to a Columbia University study[42], the review process in capital cases takes an average of nine years to complete, and as the Florida case(s) show, that process can take a great deal longer. As a result of the seemingly endless litigation, there are now 3,490 inmates awaiting execution in the United States. In addition, the imposition of the death penalty varies so greatly depending on geography, race, gender and other factors, that receiving it is somewhat akin to being struck by lightening. The arbitrary manner in which the death penalty is applied can only deepen cynicism and disrespect for the law among those who are disposed to commit violent criminal acts.

Some crimes are so depraved that execution might seem a just penalty. But even in the virtually impossible event that a statute could be crafted and applied so wisely that it would reach only those cases, the price would be too high. When the state kills, it sends the wrong message. The death penalty is an endorsement for violent solutions, and violence begets violence. In the words of George Bernard Shaw, "It is the deed that teaches, not the name we give it."

There are far better methods of reducing murders and other violent crimes than imposition of the death penalty. When I became district attorney in 1975, Manhattan led the City with 648 murders, 39% of the total (for the City). In 2003, by contrast, there were 93 murders, the lowest number in any of the four major boroughs and only 16% of the City total.

Those numbers went from 39% to 16%. That is an 86% reduction in the number of murders. Today, only Staten Island has fewer murders than Manhattan.

If the trend continues through the end of the year, Manhattan will have had, in each of the last three years, fewer murders than in any year since 1937, the first year for which we have reliable statistics. In fact, we have less than half has many murders in Manhattan as in 1937, and the death penalty was in full force in 1937.

This was accomplished in large part by rigorously enforcing the law, assigning experienced and well-trained prosecutors to homicides and other serious cases early on in the process, and concentrating resources on drug gangs and violent recidivists. Of course there are many other aspects to crime reduction, including specialized bureaus for sex crimes, domestic violence and other areas that require particular expertise.

Capital punishment merely allows proponents to convince themselves that they have done something to fight crime. It is a mirage that distracts society from more fruitful, less facile answers. . . .

Assemblyman Jeffrion Aubry, Chair of the Committee on Correction, asked a question.

Assemblyman Aubry: Mr. Morgenthau, in the last part of your statement, you talked about the reduction of murders in New York County, and kind of intuitively, you say that the imposition of, or the ability of having, the death penalty as one of those penalties, would work against the reduction of murders, and yet, how do you view that? How do you rationalize - -

Mr. Morgenthau: I don't think the possibility of the death penalty had any affect whatsoever on the reduction of crime in Manhattan. I think it was the concentration on drug gangs, on the younger, highly active criminals, our insistence that punishment be prompt and certain. I think that's what led to that reduction. I think the death penalty was totally irrelevant to what happened.

For example, you have Philadelphia, which has got basically the same population as Manhattan, Philadelphia County, and they have three times as many murders as Manhattan did, with a record number of people on death row.

Assemblyman Aubry: So in your estimation then, the safety of our population is not enhanced by this provision . . . (the proposed death penalty restoration statute)?

Mr. Morgenthau: No, it's not.

As a practical argument, deterrence as a justification for capital punishment works only if the criminal makes some kind of conscious cost/benefit analysis of the possible consequences, for him or her, of committing a death-eligible crime such as murder, terrorism or, in this modern age, extreme corruption. Assemblyman Daniel O'Donnell, a former public defender, zeroed in on this matter during Professor Blecker's testimony.

Assemblyman O'Donnell: (F)or seven years I was a public defender in Kings County, and one of the things that I find most interesting about your presentation about deterrence, was that the vast majority, if not all of my clients, did not have the forethought to think about deterrence. That when committing the act, from the most simple shoplifting (of) a piece of gum, to the most heinous act of committing murder or rape or whatever you define as the most heinous, they were not thinking about either getting caught or the punishment involved. And yet, you said in your presentation, that of course, it (capital punishment) deters crime, which requires that the people committing the crime are, at the time of their commission, thinking they're going to get caught and thinking about what their punishment will be once they go through the system.

So, I have to just tell you that from that perspective, I was intrigued by you're thought that in your discussions about people on death row, that you believe that, of course it deters . . . .

Assemblyman O'Donnell: (O)ne of the things that you talked about . . . was something called red collar killers. Could you please explain to me what you meant or mean by that? . . . .

Mr. Blecker: New York has as one of its aggravating circumstances in the death penalty statute that (it applies to) a person killed with the expectation to receive something of a pecuniary value or benefit. In short, it's the notion that those who kill for money, especially the hired assassin, but also those who hire the assassin (are death penalty eligible).

(T)hose who kill for money are thereby aggravated in murder . . . . That's a value that we hold deeply in this culture and that I embrace. However, we don't apply it in the way that we claim to apply it. Because what we do is, on the one hand, we assume that it (the death penalty) should . . . extend to robbers, that . . . robbers rob from a pecuniary motive
. . . . But (we do not extend it to) the red collar killers, to specifically answer your question . . . (this is) a group to whom we not only don't extend the death penalty, but we generally don't penalize at all and often don't even indict. Those are our corporation executives, who maintain deadly workplaces, not caring whether their employees, often third world and under-class, will in fact suffer horrible deaths. And they kill by the tens, and sometimes by the hundreds, but we don't recognize them in

this society for who they are, because we think they're killing from the best of all motives, the profit motive.

So we don't, we implement the death penalty with a class bias. We go after the under-class. We go after the street criminal, we go after the robber. What we don't go after is the corporate executive . . . for example, the Ford Motor Company executives, who, knowing that Pinto was put on the road with an exploding gas tank from rear end collisions, calculated the number of deaths on the highway, the cost of modifying the Pinto, the cost of defending the lawsuits, and came out with the conclusion that it was cheaper to keep the Pintos on the road, with overwhelming high priced legal counsel, so that they would settle for cents on the dollar, and let people die and be immolated on the highways. Those are the red collar killers.

Assemblyman O'Donnell: In that example, who are you suggesting, from, in the Pinto example, from the Ford Company, should be somebody who should be executed for doing that?

Mr. Blecker: At least should be death eligible - -

Assemblyman O'Donnell: That's good enough for me. Who should be death eligible from the Ford Company because of the Pinto experience? Because I'm curious to know how far down the food chain we intend to go before we cut it off. So tell me who from the Ford Company, under your theory, should be death eligible.

Mr. Blecker: Those who with the projections in front of them, as to how many people would die on the highways, as to how much it costs to modify it, as to how long they could delay the lawsuits, and as to the cents on the dollar -- it came out to be something like $11.00 a car. Those who made the decision to leave that car on that highway, understanding, assuming and embracing, that hundreds of people would die in fires as a result, and that they could settle for cents on the dollar.

Those actively involved in the managerial capacity should be death eligible, and what's most remarkable about that, for those of you who are fans of deterrence, just one, just one capital trial of one corporate executive in the United States of America, and you will see reformed corporate behavior like you've never seen before, because if you're looking to deter a class, look for corporate executives whose lives might be at stake. And you will see a class whose behavior . . . will change overnight. You want deterrence, there's your maximum bang for the buck. Not against the street robber.

Thomas Sullivan is a lawyer from Chicago with 50 years of experience. He served as U.S. Attorney for the Northern District of Illinois, worked on pro bono death penalty cases before the U.S. Supreme Court, and was a member of the Illinois Governor's Commission that recommended a moratorium on capital punishment in the state. On the deterrence issue, his comments were blunt and succinct.

(I) am opposed to the death penalty because I think it's a terribly dumb idea . . . . It doesn't work right . . . . But, it is not popular to be regarded as not being tough on crime . . . . (T)he truth of the matter is that if you favor the death penalty you are not being tough on crime. It has nothing to do with . . . the effect on crime (or achieving deterrence). Zero. Zip. It's just irrelevant.

Attorney Russell Neufeld, a 9-year veteran of the N.Y. Capital (Death Penalty) Defender's Office, continued.

(T)he issue of deterrence is, I think, a very important issue. There's nothing that's more important for government than to be able to protect all of us, to protect all the people.

So looking at the issue of deterrence is really important. And like my former colleague, (Assemblyman) Dan O'Donnell, I've talked to hundreds and hundreds and hundreds of people who either did kill people, or almost killed people, or tried to kill people, or did things where somebody could have gotten killed.

And at this point, dozens of dozens of (these) people have been charged with murder and capital murder. The death penalty does not function as a deterrent. It absolutely is not something that people think about when they've decided not to shoot somebody or to shoot somebody. Time and time again, it's been robberies where they thought they would go into a bodega and because they had a gun, they'd just (take) the money and the shopkeeper decided to resist to some extent and shots were fired. Or they were so angry at their lover, their wife, the person who rejected them, that they killed them or tried to kill them. The people in the criminal justice system, people overwhelmingly who we represent, those people decided to kill people, or tried to kill people, and (these) people . . . are not functioning on a rational level. It's just not what's going on. It's not the reality of the people that I've represented for the last 25 years.

(On deterrence), (o)ne of the questions that was asked was have there been comparisons done between jurisdictions that had the death penalty now and didn't have it beforehand to see if there's been a change. And one of the studies that was done was of Oklahoma.[43] And the Oklahoma study found that there in fact had been a brutalization effect by bringing the death penalty to Oklahoma. That is, that before they had capital punishment in Oklahoma, they had a lower murder rate than after they brought the death penalty back.

The investigation said that there's actually a brutalization effect. That is, when government sends out the message that if you think somebody did something really wrong, when you think somebody is really the worst of the worst, it's okay to kill them, then people tend to internalize that and act off that themselves.

This "brutalization effect" is the opposite of what death penalty supporters seek to achieve through deterrence. If we accept the theory, it operates on two very different groups. One consists of citizens in communities in which executions occur who are incited, energized, to commit acts of violence that they would not otherwise commit. The second is made up of families and friends of executed death row inmates, who may seek revenge for an execution. Testimony on their experiences was presented in the retribution section of this Chapter.

Patricia Perry, a citizen and New York voter, made a related common sense point about the brutal consequences of execution.

I'm opposed to the death penalty for all the reasons you have heard. But I'm also opposed to it for a reason that hasn't been mentioned, at least not directly. I'm opposed to it because it teaches our children that some murder is okay. State murder is okay. I submit that there is no more calculated, cold-blooded murder than that which a state imposes on a prisoner. And you and I are parties to this execution. We're not there. We pay somebody else to do the dirty work. The officials of the prison have a member of the clergy who comes in to bless the whole thing, not necessarily to bless, but to give counsel to this poor soul and make us feel better.

We have this -- ironically we offer this little gift to the prisoner. He or she gets to designate his last supper. That is so sick. And then we walk this person -- but we don't, you don't, I don't -- we make the correctional officers who have interacted with this person for months, maybe years, who know a lot more about this person than you or I will ever know, be a party to his or her death. And then we expect these persons to go home to their families and just forget about it. Just another day at the job. We send men and women to war and we know that they come back with something called post-traumatic stress syndrome. What do you think happens to men and women who take care of killing in peacetime? What does that teach our children?

You can call it retribution. You can call it revenge. You can call it justice. But it is murder and we have a little audience. You see, even those who want the death penalty and the states that have the death penalty must understand that this is a very dirty business, so most executions are held about 12 a.m., midnight, in the dark.

Only a few people are allowed to come see this little charade, the families of the victim, the families of the accused, maybe some clergy again. And then -- by the way, there's also a hearse waiting, because we know what we're doing, we've got to get the body out of there. Have a service and get rid of it. And then the newspapers and the letters to the editors and the sensational journalists all over the country print that justice was done to this person. How do you think the children of the family of that accused person that's been killed feel when they face their classmates? Oh, yes, their uncle, their dad, their grandfather, their mother, was an evil person and did some bad things.

They won't want revenge, will they? You wouldn't want revenge if the state killed your father, would you? Or are we just perpetuating our need for revenge? I'm here because my son, Police Officer John William Perry, was one of thousands of men and women who assisted in a rescue (at the World Trade Center after the terrorist attacks on September 11, 2001). He didn't make it. Unlike some other victims, I have no one person, I have no one person I can put in prison for life. But I certainly would prefer that anyone accused of a crime of that nature would have to live with what that person has done, rather than get a nice, quick exit from the world.

Shuajaa Graham was tried four times for the killing of a prison guard at the Deuel Vocational Institute in Stockton, California. The second trial sent him to death row at San Quentin prison in 1976. That conviction was overturned because of the prosecutor's systematic exclusion of African American jurors. After four years on death row, and another trial ending with a hung jury, Mr. Graham was finally acquitted and released. His is the "insider's view" of the deterrent power of the death penalty.

(D)eath row is nothing that you can even really explain. I lived with the condemned. I lived with the worst of them. And in all my years of living on death row, I never heard a prisoner say that "if I knew that I was going to face the death penalty, I would never have committed this particular crime." (From) those who say that they are guilty, I never heard in all my life of being on death row, (them) say to themselves that if I would have (known) that I was going to face death itself, that I wouldn't have done this particular crime. (These inmates) were basically black and brown and people of color....

Attorney Jennifer Cunningham appeared on behalf of 1199 Service Employees Union and echoed Mr. Graham's testimony, from a slightly different perspective.

> (T)he fact is that capital crimes are perpetrated primarily by family members or professional killers and in neither case is the death penalty going to serve as a meaningful deterrent.... If the death penalty has not served a deterrent purpose it means only to exact revenge ... (and) this is purely and simply barbarism.

A different view came from Reverend James Fitzgerald of the Riverside Church in New York City

> The death penalty has to do more with those in power manipulating the public's anger into a desire for blood than with the penalty being an effective deterrent or an appropriate punishment for crime. Even a cursory examination of the data shows that states without the death penalty have lower serious crime rates than those with the death penalty. A generation ago rehabilitation was taken seriously in prison, resources were made available for social betterment programs and the recidivism rates were significantly lower ... It is easier to fan public anger into support for the death penalty than it is to allocate resources for social betterment, which (allocations) have proven to make serious crimes by repeat offenders less likely to happen.

Deterrence can be looked at from several levels: deterring citizens from acting violently; deterring convicted violent criminals from committing more lethal types of crimes; and preventing further killing by the executed murderer. Detective Palladino of the Detective's Endowment Association addressed this latter form of deterrence. He described a 1989 case in the Bronx, N.Y., in which Harold Bow (real name, Harold Verley) killed an elderly woman, Lucille Klein, in order to steal her money and valuables. At that time, there was no death penalty in N.Y. Verley had committed a prior murder leading to a short time in jail. Mr. Palladino pointed out that during interrogation, Verley explained that he had nothing to lose by killing Ms. Klein because Klein couldn't testify against him and even if he was convicted he would still not die, and would have a decent life in prison.

In response, Assemblyman Ortloff observed.

> I'm just going to ask you to address deterrence in a slightly different perspective than most of us commonly do. Some of us on the panel were elected after '95 and some of us were there when the vote was taken in '95. Personally, I voted for the death penalty ten times before it was finally not vetoed but signed into law. Each and every time I did, first of all let me say I did it prayerfully with fresh consideration each time. My final conclusion of the reason that I supported it had to do with what I called the three individuals involved; the first victim of a repeat murderer, the murderer, and the murderer's next victim. And it came to me, and I would like you to comment on this as well, if Harold Verley had been executed for his first murder, it stands to reason that Lucille Klein would not have been killed, at least certainly not by him. And in that sense, her murder would have been deterred had the death penalty been invoked on Mr. Verley for his first crime. Does that add. . . to the . . . deterrence that someone might feel, that (if they kill) they might get caught and . . . (executed)?
>
> Mr. Palladino: I'm sure, of course it does.

The law enforcement point of view changed when testimony was given by representatives of non-white organizations. Ron Stalling, Judge Advocate of the National Black Police Association (and a 32 year veteran of the Secret Service), and Anthony Miranda, Executive Chairman of the National Latino Officer's Association, asserted that the deterrence justification for the death penalty was invalid.

Mr. Stalling: The fear of death itself does not appear to prevent individuals from committing capital crimes or any other crimes. My experience as a police officer involved in many arrests of assailants suggest(s) that these suspects, upon apprehension, gave no thought to the consequences of getting apprehended or, possibly, what the penalty might be.

The death penalty as a method of protecting society from crime has not been shown to have a special deterrent effect on crime in a society that faces the need to combat violent crime, including acts of terrorism. The National Black Police Association is not aware of any convincing evidence that the use of the death penalty deters crime. Comparisons in crime rates in different states and countries that have retained or abolished the death penalty do not indicate that the threat of execution has been effective in preventing capital crimes.

Mr. Miranda: The . . . deterrent to crime is good police work . . . . It is the fear of getting caught . . . (that) deters crime, as evidenced in the current drop in crime statistics throughout the United States, including New York. It's not the death penalty; it's the increased ability of law enforcement to actually catch and apprehend individuals. That is the deterrent. . . . The threat of the death penalty does not stop somebody because nine times out of ten if you probably ask them, it was not a consideration in the acts that they were engaged in . . . . If you have that individual case (a potential killer who does not commit murder out of fear of the death penalty), which was what was mentioned, it is the extreme case. It is not the normal . . . standard of the cases of the people who are on death row currently. So in fact, we don't agree with the death penalty.

I, too, believe that incarceration is the greater deterrent. I (would) rather have somebody tortured for 40 years or doing three life terms in a ten by ten cell and having to walk back and forth, than having to say well, he took it (execution), it's over, he's finished with. I think more families and more people will find more justice in the fact that if they're going to be in jail . . . .

At least they're going to remember the victim's life every day that they're in there. Every day that they're in jail for the next 40 (years) - if they live to 100 - they'll still remember the family and the victim because they're forced to be living in that type of situation where they've given up their freedoms.

The President of the New York State Corrections and Law Enforcement Guidance Association, Marsha Lee Watson, who testified with Mr. Stalling and Mr. Miranda, stated succinctly, "People fear more going to jail than they do . . . dying"!

Randy Jurgenson, retired New York homicide detective, spoke for himself based on experience going back nearly 40 years. He described a 1971 case (the first capital case in New York since 1963) in which two well-publicized police killers were on trial, "looking at the electric chair", and, despite all the publicity, while the trial proceeded, five more New York police officers were murdered. "This case was no deterrent" to these killings.

Mr. Jurgenson's testimony elicited the following comments:

Assemblyman Kirwan: So now you (Mr. Jurgenson) deduced it's not a deterrent to those five people. But you'll never know who it deterred because they didn't commit the crime. Like when they used to execute pick pockets in London, while they were executing pick pockets there were (other) people picking pockets. But, again, you'll never know who was deterred because they didn't commit the crime.

Mr. Jurgenson: May I answer that?

Assemblyman Kirwan: Sure.

Mr. Jurgenson: We'll never know that, but we do know five were killed. That's a fact.

Assemblyman Kirwan: Clearly those people (killers) weren't deterred. But you'll never know who was deterred because they didn't commit the crime. That's my point. So you can't just say it deters everybody, but it deters some people. . . .

> Mr. Miranda: (Criminals) don't think about getting sentenced to 25 to life or (being) executed. You know what? Life without parole is a deterrent. When you know you commit these crimes and that's the ultimate sentence that you're going to get and there's no chance in coming out, that is an effective enough deterrent because if you grab the wrong person or an innocent person you can give their life back. (If you make a mistake and execute the wrong person) then you're just as guilty as ... the individuals who take another life wrongfully. ...

> Ms. Watson: (T)o a person that does not value life, taking it is nothing. But making them stay in it (life), stay in something that they don't even value and like, is a punishment. So that's why I think ... (such a person is being effectively) punished (by life without parole).

As one reads this testimony on deterrence, the relationship between numbers of executions, costs of executions, and level of deterrence achieved becomes more clear. Many executing states have no more than 1 or 2 executions per year and they are extremely expensive to obtain and carry out. These few, exceptional, isolated, cases accomplish marginal deterrence. As Hearings testimony indicates, greater overall deterrence might be achieved by spending this money on law enforcement, crime detection, speedy prosecutions, and prompt and severe punishment short of death. Chapter Four of this book presents detailed testimony on the issue of costs, but the testimony of Ursula Bentele, Professor of Law and Director of the Capital Defender and Federal Habeas Clinic of Brooklyn Law School, made the basic point.

> Under this approach (a new death penalty law for New York) what you can predict after about 20 years of applying a new death sentence (statute) ... (is) one or two executions per year statewide. ... The expected cost for the state over that 20-year period will be something like $500 million or about $200 million ... beyond what it would cost to rely solely on life without parole

.... (I)f the State thinks of itself as having this sort of discretionary $500 million pot of money, that it's going to apply to law enforcement over the next 20 years, is it the best ... (use) of that $500 million to buy two or three executions. Or, on the other hand, would the State of New York gain more in the way of law enforcement, deterrence, saving lives, by taking that same money and using it, for example, to fund additional police detectives, prosecutors, judges and corrections officers so that we could arrest, convict and incarcerate the many murderers, rapists, and robbers in this State, who currently escape any penalty at all because they never get arrested because we don't have any sufficient law enforcement resources in place to find them, convict them, and incarcerate them.

The testimony of Hal Weiner, Convener, St. Savior Chapter, Episcopal Place Fellowship, took the deterrence issue head on. "We know the argument of deterrence is a red herring". Mr. Weiner cited a survey of U.S. leading academic criminological societies showing an 84% rejection of any deterrent effect of the death penalty and an F.B.I. 2003 Uniform Crime Report indicating that southern states account for 80% of executions and (yet) have the highest murder rates while the northeastern U.S. has 1% of executions and the lowest murder rate.

Professor Evan Mandery of the John Jay College of Criminal Justice offered a less adversarial view of the state of the evidence on deterrence.

I think that each side in this debate overstates its position to some extent. I think, for example, it is unfair for abolitionists to contend that there is no evidence of deterrence. I think Professor Fagan makes a very important critique of the methodology of some of the recent studies that have found evidence of deterrence. But they're not crackpot studies, and I think it's a mistake for us to characterize the state of evidence as being entirely one sided. I think a social scientist examining this data would say that it's ambiguous, leaning towards more evidence for the lack of deterrence than no deterrence.

Discussion of deterrence often occurs without context. A more careful analysis of the issue reveals distinctions based on the type of murder involved and, more importantly, the type of killer. Onondaga County prosecutor William J. Fitzpatrick made this point by comparing the "cold-blooded" killer James Cahill to the typical domestic violence murderer. James "Jeff" Cahill murdered his wife, Jill Russell Cahill, pursuant to a sophisticated six-month plan he developed after initially injuring her by hitting her in the head with an aluminum baseball bat during a domestic dispute. Jill's death, and my involvement in the Cahill case, brought about this book.

> Mr. Fitzpatrick: You know, in terms of deterrence, if that's the thrust of your question, is the death penalty a deterrent. My response is, of course it is. How could it not be? Is it a deterrent that a person who is in a bar fight is going to consider, absolutely not.
>
> James Cahill didn't think he was going to get caught. I mean, that's why he wore a disguise (when he entered his wife's hospital room in order to poison her with potassium cyanide). And that's why when police came to question him, he pretended he had been sleeping, and that's why his mother tried, on his behalf, tried to find the potassium cyanide remaining in his house and tried to destroy it. His intent was to get away with this crime.
>
> If there was a greater understanding on his part that he was going to be caught, then it may have deterred him from doing what he did.
>
> Ms. Weinstein: To follow-up on this question of deterrence and the suggestion by my colleague of adding domestic violence as an aggravating factor (for capital murder). The major reason proffered for the death penalty is its deterrence effect.
>
> Do you think that in these 20 percent of homicides that are based on domestic violence, that if DV (domestic violence) was an aggravating factor, those individuals would stop before they

kill their spouse because of the threat of the death penalty? Or does it more follow what you talked about, the bar fight where the emotional level is so high that no one's thinking of the consequence?

Mr. Fitzpatrick: I think that a good percentage of them would not be deterred. But if a number of them were deterred then it would be, in my judgment, worth the cost. The vast majority of the domestic violence homicides that we see do not fall into the Cahill category (deliberate, planned executions). They fall into a long, simmering pattern that explodes one night, usually as a result of alcohol or drugs.

But if there is a (single) person to be deterred, then I say that it would be worth an effort to save an innocent woman's life.

Mr. Fitzpatrick's argument was that when there is actual reflection and calculation, as there was in the Cahill case, and the potential killer is aware of a reasonable likelihood of apprehension and conviction on a capital charge, deterrence is possible. To prosecutor Fitzpatrick, the threat of the death penalty literally saved lives in New York.

Mr. (Assemblyman) Kirwan: Just one quick question Mr. Fitzpatrick. We've had a few questions today about . . . (deterrence). Obviously we don't know . . . who's deterred . . . because they didn't commit the crime. So we'll never know who is deterred by something . . . . I'm with you, that we'll never know how many are deterred, but clearly it deters some. And that to me makes it worthwhile.

Mr. Fitzpatrick: Well I don't think there's any question. And you know, of the things I say about my job or any one of my sixty (prosecutor) colleagues around the state is, there are people who are both alive and enjoying the comforts of life and the happiness of their homes, and the safety of their bodies, because of the job that we do. We just can't tell you who they are.

A retired Justice of the New York Court of Appeals, Stewart Hancock, dismissed deterrence as a justification. Justice Hancock:

Deterrence basically doesn't work when you've got somebody who is committing a crime of passion. (T)hey're doing it when they're angry. Or . . . they're under the influence of drugs, or under the influence of alcohol. Now that leaves the other group (of cold, calculating, premeditated killers), which by and large makes up again a small percentage of the overall homicides that are committed.

Those people you don't deter for the very simple reason, they don't think they're going to get caught. So if they don't think they're going to get caught, deterrence has absolutely nothing to do with whether or not you're going to prevent . . . (the killing) from happening.

In a different vein, I testified at the Hearings very briefly on deterrence (but more extensively on statutory modifications for a proposed statute reinstituting the death penalty in New York). I noted "You will get more deterrence, of course, from . . . (Professor Blecker's) proposals (from the Ford Pinto case) then you do in traditional crimes of passion and violence. I often tell my students that if you want deterrence, you impose the death penalty on tax fraud cases".

Mr. Richard Bartlett stated his credentials before providing a rich historical framework for considering the deterrence rational:

Mr. Bartlett: I come before you today as a former member of this House, having served from 1959 through 1966, as a former member of the Temporary Commission on Revision of the Penal Law and Criminal Code, which I had the honor to chair from its inception in 1961 until our work was completed in 1969, as a former Supreme Court Justice and Chief Administrative Judge, as a former Dean of Albany Law School, and as a lawyer who was practiced in the state and federal courts of New York for 56 years. That's a lot of formers, I know.

It was my service on the Penal Law Commission, and the Report we issued nearly 40 years ago on Capital Punishment, which was followed by the virtual abolition of the death penalty in New York, which the Legislature and Governor Rockefeller accomplished in 1965 . . . (that) motivate(s) my participation in this proceeding . . . . (I)n the process of our studies, our public hearings, and the earnest discussions among us on this most important issue, I concluded, with the majority of the Commission, that the death penalty could not be rationally supported, that its retention would be bad public policy. Forty years later, I am of the same mind.

If it could be established that the death penalty is a uniquely effective deterrent, as opposed to another strong deterrent . . . to the commission of murder, my position might be different. But the simple truth is that such a conclusion cannot be reached by rational analysis.

I must note that the majority statement (for the Report's recommendations) was drafted by Professor Herbert Wechsler, one of the great legal minds of our time and an invaluable member of our Commission.

I will not summarize all the reasons stated in support of abolition set forth in our Report. You can read them for yourselves. But I do want to focus on our final reason, and briefly summarize it.

"There may indeed have been cases in which the threat of the death penalty was a uniquely effective deterrent to murder, but we are confident that this factor has no major quantitative significance. There will be cruel and repulsive murders in New York whether capital punishment is retained or abolished, but their number will never be greatly influenced by abolition. We may be confident, therefore, that in proposing action that is right upon so many grounds, we shall not jeopardize the safety of the people of New York."

As you know, Assemblyman Lentol, your father was one of the sponsors of the bill which abolished capital punishment. Ed was in the Senate at that time, and Assemblyman Joe Corso had the bill in the Assembly.

And in its final form, as it was finally adopted, it had two narrow exceptions to abolition: murder of a policeman acting in the course of his duty, and murder committed by an inmate already serving a life sentence.

It's hard to believe this when you think of what more recent experience has been in the Legislature on the issue of capital punishment. But that bill passed the Senate on May 12, by a vote of 47-9, 47-9.

And as you might expect in the more contentious upper house, larger house I like to say, it passed the Assembly by a vote of 78-67. It was signed into law by Governor Rockefeller on June 1, 1965. It can be said that the death penalty in New York was virtually abolished that day.

You will . . . of course we all recall - - how the death penalty then became a major political issue, and how Governor Pataki, after his election in 1994, claimed a mandate from the people to reinstate capital punishment in New York.

This he accomplished that year with the passage of the Governor's Program Bill Senate 2850, and capital punishment for conviction of various categories of murder has been on our books ever since . . . . I urge you to look carefully at the Memorandum in support of the Governor's 1995 Program Bill #1 to restore capital punishment.

Under the heading "Justification" the Memorandum very clearly identifies retribution as a major justification for restoring capital punishment. And frankly, members of your Committees, for retribution, read vengeance, because in this context the meaning is the same.

Then the Memorandum recites statistics to demonstrate that since virtual abolition in 1965, the murder rate steadily climbed, suggesting that the deterrent effect of the death penalty . . . called for (a new capital law).

If statistics were relevant then, current statistics should be relevant now. The fact is that the murder rate has steadily declined since 1995, in spite of there having been no execution in New York since 1963.

The real truth is that these statistics were not relevant in 1995 and they are not now. There is no established correlation between the murder rate and the presence or absence of the death penalty . . . .

There is no overwhelming public demand that the death penalty be restored in New York. There is no compelling reason for the Legislature to act in haste. There is every reason to proceed cautiously and deliberately in making this very important determination.

I, for one, urge you to do nothing, for by doing nothing you restore New York to the status it briefly claimed and should claim again, as a state in which capital punishment is virtually abolished. Thank you.

The thesis of this book is that ordinary citizens, when motivated, can sort out the arguments for and against the death penalty, understand these arguments, and reason from them to an informed judgment on whether to support or oppose capital punishment. A good example of that process is presented in the testimony of Ms. Diane-Marie Frappier:

Ms. Frappier: Good afternoon. My name is Diane-Marie Frappier. I live in a small town in Afton in Chenango County. Thank you for giving me the opportunity to speak.

I'm a layperson, a wife, a mother, a grandmother, I'm a Catholic, I am a professed Secular Franciscan. In no way am I a political person or expert, and I have never spoken before a group of people in this manner, and I do find this quite intimidating to me.

I have done a little research on my own into the death penalty in our state and other states and countries in the world, and I do not see where in states and countries that have the death penalty that the murder rate has been decreased. In fact, it seems that the states that have a death penalty have a higher murder rate.

One of the things I can point out, I did make copies of this FBI report that is in all those packets. According to the FBI Uniform

Crime Statistics of 2003, which was published in October 2004, the nationwide murder rate for 2003 is 5.7 persons per 100,000. In the latest National Crime Victimization Survey, the Bureau of Justice Statistics reports that the US murder rate for 2003 was 5.6 per 100,000 people.

Both reports state that by region, the south, which has the highest number of states with the death penalty and executions, has a murder rate of 6.9. While the northeast, with the lowest number of states with the death penalty and executions, has the lowest murder rate of 4.2.

According to the FBI report on the individual states, the average murder rate among death penalty states is 5.3. (T)he average murder rate among the non-death penalty states is 2.9, almost half. New York is right in the middle of rankings .... New York State has an average of 4.9.

Louisiana, which has a death penalty, comes in on the top of the list with 13 homicides per 100,000 people. And Maine, which does not have a death penalty, is on the bottom of the list with 1.2 homicides per 100,000 people.

When we look at the executions, we find that almost 80 percent of the executions in the country occur in the south. The report noted that the Texas crime rate rose 4 percent (that year), nearly five times the national average, and the state posted a 7.6 increase in homicides. At the same time the total number of executions in Texas is more than three times that of any other state in the nation. The northeast, the region with the lowest murder rate, has had no executions since 2001.

When Canada in 1979 stopped the death penalty, there was speculation that Canada would see an increase in the homicide rate. That has not happened.

Statistics report that the number of homicides in Canada in 2002 was 554, and it's 23 percent lower than the number of homicides in 1975.

The United States has a homicide rate of 5.7 or 5.6, depending upon what report you're going to look at. Canada has a rate of only 1.8. Canada currently sentences those convicted of murder to life sentences with parole eligibility.

I believe that in considering these facts, we can come to the conclusion that the presence of the death penalty does not deter homicides.

Let's look for a moment at the effects of the death penalty on law enforcement personnel. According to statistics from the latest FBI Uniform Crime Report, regions of the country that use the death penalty the least are the safest for police officers. Police are most in danger in the south, which accounts for 80 percent of all executions.

From 1989 to 1998, 292 law enforcement officers were feloniously killed in the south, 125 in the west, 121 in the Midwest, and 80 in the northeast. The three leading states where law enforcement officers were feloniously killed in 1998 were California, the state with the highest death row population, Texas, the state with the most executions since 1976, and Florida, the state that is the third highest in both executions and death row population.

Midway through the Hearings, Professor Samuel Donnelly from Syracuse University College of Law presented a focused summary of abolitionist views on deterrence:

> Mr. Donnelly: Pope John Paul II summed . . . (it) up when he described capital punishment in modern times as cruel and unnecessary. A reason for this is that since the 19th Century we have had major metropolitan police forces, strong district attorney's offices, an elaborate network of prisons, a large and effective system of law enforcement, which together provide the greatest deterrent effect for crime.
>
> Capital punishment is a distraction from the measures that can most effectively control murder and other crimes. In New York State, despite the absence of executions, the murder rate has fallen remarkably, particularly in major cities such as New York, Rochester and Syracuse.

In Syracuse, two summers ago and continuing, a remarkable drop in the murder rate followed the prosecution . . . of the Boot Camp gang, which in effect cleared the streets (of) the most serious threats to public security. The prosecution was brought and the murder rate dropped like that.

In Rochester, a 39 percent drop in the murder rate has been credited to the joint task force of Rochester police, state troopers, and sheriff's deputies, supported, I believe, by Operation Impact.

The most remarkable developments have been in New York City since the policing and crime control measures introduced by Mayor Giuliani in the 1990's. I think, if you observe, the death . . . (rate) was dropping around the country at the time, and in most of the major cities, and suddenly it dropped (in NYC) much more rapidly, which creates a hypothesis that if it's already dropping and you introduce these policing measures, which are more complex than normally understood, then you're going to get a more rapid drop.

Our attention should be focused on studying these very effective measures, and capital punishment, the attention that you are appropriately paying today to capital punishment, is a distraction from the necessary focus on more effective means for crime control.

In contrast to these careful analyses, the extreme extension of the deterrence justification was expressed in a statement attributed to a pro-death penalty advocate, Pastor James Melton of the Bible Baptist Church in Sharon, Tennessee:

A common argument is that statistics do not show that the death penalty deters crime when we compare death penalty states with non-death penalty states. Of course it doesn't . . . . The states that have the death penalty do not use it enough to show anything.

Less than fifty executions out of 18,000 murders isn't going to accomplish much. I bet 18,000 executions would deter some crime. I bet the murder rate would fall quicker than the 1929 stock market.

The non-deterrence argument was presented in a different light by Sean Byrne, Executive Director of the New York Prosecutors Institute, and a death penalty proponent. Abolitionists contend that life in prison without parole achieves the same deterrence as capital punishment. Attorney Byrne pointed out a weakness in this position.

> As the law now stands, if Osama Bin Laden were captured, New York could not prosecute him to the fullest extent allowed by our state and federal constitutions (by executing him). Bin Laden, like prior World Trade Center bombers, would be free to plot additional terrorist attacks from his prison, while living under better conditions than are afforded by an Afghanistan mountain cave.

Attorney Byrne continued in his written testimony.[44]

> The debate over whether the death penalty deters other homicides (or other crimes in general) is diversionary and over emphasized. Nonetheless, there are statistical and analytical monographs that prove that capital punishment has a deterrent effect. *See,* Zimmerman, Paul R., *State Executions, Deterrence, and the Incidence of Murder,* Journal of Economics Literature Classification Number: K42, H00(2003); Vangrack, Adam L., *Serious Error With Serious Error: Repairing a Broken System of Capital Punishment,* 79 Wash. U.L.Q. 973 (Fall 2001); Dezhbaksh, Haslem et al., *Does Capital Punishment Have a Deterrent Effect? New Evidence From Post-Moratorium Panel Data,* January 2001, Department of Economics, Emory University, available at http://userwww.service.emory.edu; Vangrack, Adam L., *Elevating Form Over Substance: A Reply To Professors James Liebman, Jeffrey Fagen and Valerie West,* 80 Wash. L.Q. 427 (Spring 2002).

Despite these scholarly studies that stand for the proposition that the death penalty deters as many as 14 homicides for each person executed (*State Executions, Deterrence, and the Incidence of Murder*, Zimmerman Paul R., page 2), there are also academic studies inapposite. The deterrence inquiry invites respondents to produce would-be murderers who did not kill because of the death penalty. Such testimonials are understandably very difficult to produce . . . .

(H)omicides in New York have dropped from 1,980 murders in 1994 to 923 in 2003, resulting in homicides rates not seen in this State since the 1960's, before Governor Rockefeller imposed a moratorium on the death penalty and New York homicide rates started to climb steadily. New York City is <u>not</u> on the Justice Department's list of 150 most violent cities in America. To turn the prove-a-negative deterrence argument around, death penalty opponents cannot prove that the re-enactment of the death penalty did not contribute to the rapid decline in murders in New York.

Raymond A. Kelly, then President-Elect of the New York State Association of Criminal Defense Lawyers, addressed the deterrence question from the perspective of 30 years of defense work in over 200 trials, 60 murder cases, and 8 death penalty prosecutions.

Now, just briefly, the experience that I've had during the course of 30-plus years is that the death penalty itself is not a deterrent to the people who commit the murders. If you go to the great majority of the homicides that take place in this state, and indeed this country, even all over the world, the great majority of them come from people who have -- who are enmeshed in a highly charged emotional situation, generally fueled by the ingestion of alcohol and drugs, and it never crosses their mind during the course of these highly charged emotional states that there's a death penalty on the books . . . . (You must) look at the people who are involved in the turf wars, the drug wars, the kids, generally speaking - and it is kids who are on the street. These are individuals who live death 24/7 in battles over drug turf. They're not worried about the death penalty that the state of New York has. They're worrying about the real death penalty that exists on the street, and the death penalty is no deterrent whatsoever to them. They're trying -- the great majority of the people who it has been my privilege to represent - are people who are trying to get out of poverty. They're not the Cali (drug) cartel. They're people who are trying to break away, and working at McDonald's at seven bucks an hour you're not going to break away. The kids want to try and get out. And the cost of getting out, to them, is very simple; it's worth the risk and they do it.

So, to think that the death penalty is going to deter them is simply a fiction. The sociopath, the person who is the killer for hire, is somebody who thinks that they're not going to get caught. They think there's no chance in the world they're ever going to get caught, and because they have the mentality of never being caught, the death penalty doesn't bother them.

(T)he killer for hire is a person who is so lacking in self-esteem that the one thing that they do not -- that they do not fear is the death penalty. The one thing that they do fear is being warehoused for the rest of their life. If you were to give the sociopath the choice, the sociopath would say to you, "Give me the death penalty. That's the easy way out. I'm not going to spend the rest of my life caged."

Chairman Charles Billups of the Grand Council of Guardians, a fraternal organization of African American law enforcement officers, opposed capital punishment, even for killers of police on the street or corrections officers. He observed "It actually makes them (the killers) bigger than what they are."

Catherine Abate, former State Senator, past Commissioner of Correction and Probation, and former Chair, N.Y.S. Crime Victims Board, observed that in New York the "crime rate started to drop in 1992 and further dropped in '93, '94, '95. Huge drops . . . well before . . . the reinstatement of the death penalty" in 1995. It just had no effect."

Strong opinions on deterrence and the practical problems of applying capital punishment came from Attorney Mark Green, former New York City Public Advocate, President of the New Democracy Project in N.Y.C., and co-author of the book CHANGE FOR AMERICA: A PROGRESSIVE BLUEPRINT FOR THE 44TH PRESIDENT (January 2009).

> There is no serious evidence that the death penalty deters or is in any way related to the reduction in crime in New York State . . . . (When the present Governor argues that the death penalty is responsible for reducing crime he) is illogical and unempirical. He has taken a position for which there's no supporting data. Of course crime is down in New York, thank God, in the last decade.
>
> Of course it's down throughout the country, of course it's down even more in New York State. The smartest people cannot tell you exactly why. I asked Bill Bratton this when he was Police Commissioner, he's a very thoughtful man (and), he said we have some reason to guess the younger brothers and sisters of kids who indulged in crack during the cocaine outbreaks of the '80's saw what happened and now are using that dangerous product far less. More police on the street may have a role. There are a lot of cultural and law enforcement reasons . . . . I think Governor Pataki would be laughed out of a debating society if he tried to argue for the point that the existence on paper of the death penalty starting in 1995 had anything to do, much less a lot to do, with the reduction in the (crime rate). It's emotional. It's political. And that's cruel and unusual . . . .
>
> (O)f course the state has a moral right to execute people in a war and so if you're in combat and Osama Bin Laden is standing there, I don't know . . . (of) any people in this room (that) wouldn't want to kill him, cause he killed 3,000 of our neighbors based on his open admission. But once someone's captured (like), Saddam Hussein, of course you have to have a trial.

You know, I understand the blood lust of leaders saying we've got to kill these people, but now that we have Saddam Hussein, President Bush . . . talked a lot about American Justice (but) by that he meant frontier justice. It's not complicated. He wouldn't urge summarily killing Saddam Hussein. So, of course -
-

Whenever you get into a debate like this, someone can say the words Hitler and Osama Bin Laden and . . . (there) I win the argument. The problem is that you should kill these people in combat, and that's according to the protocols of war, but for every time you kill somebody (in the civilian context) who you think is a horrific murdering person, you are opening the door to executing innocent people who are not as notorious. That's the fact.

The last word on deterrence, as a topic for Hearings testimony, went to Leonara Wengraf of the organization Campaign to End the Death Penalty.

(S)tudies were presented at the last round of hearings in Manhattan as to why deterrence doesn't work. But the real, but the real research . . . actually shows though, and this I don't think has been presented as much, that investment in job training, investment in social programs, investment in education, in other words getting tough on the causes of crime, putting societal resources into where all these mountains of research have proven that they are effective, (these actions reduce crime, and) that has not been . . . as fully considered as it needs to be.

Crime, including murder, is driven by the disinvestment of resources from poor and working class communities and . . . it is very difficult for us to talk about the death penalty as a solution to crime when we, when according to the (N.Y.C.) Amsterdam News for example, 50% of black men in the City of New York are unemployed. How can we waste money on an execution machine for society's victims who have barely seen a fraction of these resources invested in them before they commit a crime?

Incapacitation and Rehabilitation

′ The death penalty is the ultimate form of incapacitation: capital execution of a murderer guarantees that he will not kill again. The focus of debate at the N.Y. Hearings was over the viability of the alternative sentence of life in prison without possibility of parole or "LWOP". Question I. 5. of the call to Hearings asked "Is the currently available sentence of life imprisonment without the possibility of parole an effective alternative to the death penalty in New York. Or is it imperative that this current sentencing option be supplemented with the death penalty?"

The primary responses to these questions came from those arguing against the viability of LWOP. First, on a moral or philosophical level, LWOP leaves the killer alive, functioning, and capable of enjoying life, and that offends principles of retribution. Second, LWOP prisoners are extremely dangerous in prison and are not incapacitated from killing guards or other inmates. Finally, a LWOP sentence does not always mean life in prison - laws may be changed and parole may be made available to a killer at some later time.

Professor Robert Blecker testified to these points by focusing on his concept of justice. For him, certain killers are given the death penalty "rightfully, justly." To the most vicious murderers, LWOP is not worse than death and, even if it was, "the question at the penalty phase (of a capital trial) is, did . . . (the accused) deserve it (the death penalty) . . . . It is a moral question, not just a factual question." "If you are a retributivist, independently of the future (and whether a murderer can be rehabilitated during LWOP), you understand . . . that the past counts." "(W)e as a society have an obligation not to reach the point where we ever find out whether . . . (rehabilitation is) to take place." We must "be committed to connecting the crime with the punishment . . . . so that the sentence will correlate with the seriousness of the criminal . . . ." When dealing with "the worst of the worst", Professor Blecker questioned whether LWOP could ever be the moral or functional equivalent of the death penalty. ,

As noted in the prior testimony on deterrence, experts differ on whether LWOP is perceived by some killers as worse than death. Professor Blecker's views on this, based on his personal experience with death row inmates, were crystal clear.

> Take the time to investigate what is the quality of life among those who serve life. I've taken that time. As I've mentioned, I spent 2,000 hours over 12 years.
>
> I'm continuing to travel to death rows and other prisons. I'm continuing to look at the quality of life, because make no mistake about it, punishment is not only about the duration, it is not only a number, it is not only the number of years spent confined, it is about the quality of life while confined. . . .
>
> What you discover about the quality of life of those who serve life is (that) life takes on new meaning. It takes on new joys, new satisfactions. They watch movies, they exercise, they have tournaments, baseball tournaments, volleyball tournaments, basketball tournaments. They read. They watch television. A new society forms. New pleasures.
>
> (I)t's . . . a terrible injustice when I go to death row in Florida and I see Danny Wolling, the Ninja Killer, the Gainsboro Killer, who used to stalk females, break into their apartments, rape them and mutilate them and pose them nude and put their heads on the mantelpiece and take their nipples in a baggy, and I see Danny Wolling from 15 feet away lying in bed, reading a book, with his reading glasses propped on his nose on Florida's death row, fully into life, 12 years later, and something deep inside me says why aren't you dead.

There are legal and pragmatic reasons for providing "livable" conditions for death row inmates. The "cruel and unusual punishments" clause of the Eighth Amendment prohibits extremely harsh treatment such as lack of heat, food or medicine; total isolation; or torture. Prison officials make death row living tolerable in order to "keep the peace." Professor Blecker:

Understandably, (prison officials are) trying to keep the people safe, (and) the department of corrections see(s) privileges as a management tool. Thus, they are in the forefront of saying make the quality of life spent while serving life without parole, make it pleasant, relatively pleasant, in that you provide all sorts of amenities, canteen amenities and, as I say, tournaments, baseball tournaments -- I was shocked to find what goes on in both Oklahoma and in Florida on death row and among lifers.

You provide it, not necessarily because you think they deserve to enjoy life that way, but because the threat of removing these privileges allows you to maintain order and safety in the prison and because if prisoners are focused on them, they won't be focused on hurting each other and hurting staff.

So, it's not just the human capacity to adjust to horrible circumstances, it's the built in disavow on the part of the public officials in the various aspects of the criminal justice system, that it isn't anybody's job to punish. In the words of R.D. Lang, punishment becomes everywhere elsewhere.

Sparing the worst and most vicious killers from capital punishment also leads, inevitably, to further murders in prison.

Of course, there's also likely to be innocent people killed by prisoners while in prison who would have gotten the death penalty and but for (that) would have been incapacitated, and instead (they are) turned back into the dangerous monsters that they were out here. And so in effect, by sparing their lives, you're allowing them to take other innocent lives. That's happened too. How do you feel? Sick.

Professor Blecker's concluding comments on this topic added an international dimension to the debate over the finality of LWOP. When public opinion polls show greater support for LWOP than the death penalty, it is because the public (d)oesn't think about the possibility of commutation by the governor . . . . (T)he abolitionist press in this City has not reported it, including the leading media outlets, or reported it in one article only briefly. Do you know that Europe has abolished life without parole? My guess is that none of you here know that. Life without parole has been abolished in Europe. So, once we abolish the death penalty, what do you think is the next target of the abolitionists, life without parole. They will attack life without parole. And if they are successful in attacking the death penalty, they are likely to also be successful in attacking life without parole and it would be done on the same basis. It would be done on a humanity basis . . . (and asserted that) to put (a person) in prison, put (him) in a cage, when he may or she may evolve as a human being, and may become a rich, vital non-threatening person, (is unconstitutional and at that point you must) let them go (based on the Eighth Amendment).

Reevaluate periodically. So if that then becomes – then this assurance of life without parole is no longer an ironclad assurance. If we follow in the steps of the governments of Europe, in their abolition of the death penalty, we're likely to follow with life without parole. So my response to you is, if you state the question fairly, you will find a much higher level of rejection for life without parole and you will find a much greater embrace for the death penalty . . . . (which) is nevertheless still principally based upon retributive values.

Yet, surprisingly, even Professor Blecker was willing to acknowledge that rehabilitation of even the worst murderers is possible. That would not stop him from executing such a killer on other, retributivist, grounds. But his concession requires careful consideration by those trying to form an opinion on the death penalty.

Do I believe in rehabilitation? Yes, having spent all those hundreds and hundreds of hours in the prison, I came across someone, David Brooks, someone I got to know intimately.

Someone, by the time I met him, who was a humane, dignified, vital, rich person, who was a positive influence for the kids.

Someone whom at 19 had shot 57 people. Someone who, when I didn't know him, was a vicious killer and had deserved to die. By the time I met him, he was a dignified, humane human being. So how is it that I could possibly have said that he deserved to die if he could grow into that? If you are a retributivist, independently of the future, you understand because you feel certain that the past counts. That rehabilitation, while rare, is real. It cannot be forced and it can easily be faked, but it is real. But sometimes, we as a society have an obligation not to reach the point where we ever find out whether it's to take place. And if you think that's somehow inhumane, then search your own souls, you advocates of life without parole, because you are committing yourself to the very same proposition, that no matter how a person develops, no matter how a person is rehabilitated, you're committing yourself, now and forever, that you will never rethink it and will never release him.

Monroe County District Attorney Michael Green gave a concrete example of a case in which a LWOP sentence was lifted because of a subsequent change in the law.

We tell juries that life without parole means just that, that a defendant will remain incarcerated for life, and will never come before the parole board. But our experience with the James Moore case in Monroe County tells us otherwise.

Moore raped and murdered a young girl in the early 1960's and entered into a plea bargain where he was spared the death penalty in exchange for his plea and sentence of life without parole.

Thereafter, the New York State legislature eliminated life without parole sentences and commuted all those sentences to sentences of 20 years to life. Since 1982 Moore has appeared before the parole board every two years seeking his release.

Every two years the victim's family and the entire community
have their wounds reopened.

This past year, 42 years after this brutal crime, 8,000 people
responded to a petition drive, and notified the Department of
Parole that they were opposed to Moore's release to parole.

Kathryn Kase, a New York lawyer working at the time for the Texas
Defender Service (an organization providing post-conviction legal counsel to
capital defendants), attempted to counter this testimony by challenging the
assumption that some convicted first degree murderers are predictably so
dangerous that only execution will keep society safe. She offered a study by
her organization, "Deadly Speculation: Misleading Texas Capital Juries with
False Predictions of Future Dangerousness (2004)", that showed that such
predictions are significantly imprecise. If that is true, execution forecloses
any chance for the redemption or rehabilitation that even some hard-core
death penalty advocates admit exists.

The testimony of Professor Emeritus Bell Chevigny of Purchase
Collage, SUNY, provided some final examples of rehabilitation.

Ms. Chevigny: Good afternoon. My name is Bell Chevigny.
I'm very grateful that you are holding these hearings and that I
have the opportunity to address you about this important issue.
I am a writer and a retired professor of literature from SUNY, but
I'm here as Chair of the Pen Prison Writing Program. Pen is the
International Writers Association.

Since 1973, the Pen American Center here in New York City
has offered an annual literary competition to incarcerated men
and women nationwide. More than 1,000 (prisoners) from 49
states send us manuscripts. In 1999, we published an anthology
of winners doing time, 45 years of prison writing, which I offer to
the Assembly.[45] In the 60's and 70's, testimony from prison
writers was often best selling, I'm thinking of the autobiography
of Malcolm X, George Jackson's work, Eldridge Cleaver, Angela
Davis.

Since then, our prison population has grown 6 or 7 times larger. Yet in the same years, the publication of prison writing has plummeted. What does this mean? That as prisons grow, we know less and less about the lives of those inside. And we elect representatives to build more prisons and keep us ignorant of what happens in them.

Many writers who win our contests have lived on death rows. Writings by 7 of them . . . , I've marked that in the contents, who they are. Since its publication we have awarded prizes to 3 other condemned writers. My testimony draws on my privileged acquaintance through writing and correspondence with these men.

I will address the second question you want to discuss. Is the death penalty an appropriate societal exercise of retribution against persons who commit intentional murder? I am convinced that it is not. You have heard excellent testimony about how the death penalty is unfair. . . . How it is impossible to eliminate the possibility of error and how more than 100 condemned people have been exonerated. Most condemned writers I know experienced great violence as children, most were poor, most were assigned disastrously incompetent lawyers. But I'm not here to debate their guilt or innocence. I come before you to argue for the guilty as well as the innocent.

I oppose the death penalty even for the guilty. No one put the case more simply and eloquently than Patrick Nolan, a prisoner in Sacramento, California, and I have a piece about him for you if you'd like to see it. He realized that he could never undo his crime, but he could honor the victim by rededicating his life. "In taking a life, I owe a life. My own."

Patrick Nolan wanted to pay for his killing, pay with his own life. Not by offering it to the executioner, but by dedicating it to serve his fellow man. How did he come to this belief? By reading when he was in solitary confinement the works of Thoreau and Martin Luther King and The Concentration Camp Memoir by Victor Frankl, Man's Search for Meaning. Even in the worst conditions Frankl observed life has meaning because we always have choices.

Determined to live a meaningful life, Nolan studied poetry and found that poetry enabled him to face the pain he dealt and the pain he'd received. Nolan encouraged other men to write. Then, sickened by a race riot in Folsom (prison), he took another step. With the prison Chaplin, he initiated meetings where black, white and brown men could share feelings and thoughts and develop the trust they needed to explore and reshape their lives. These remarkable meetings challenged and reversed the destructive culture of the prison yard.

Nolan learned to feel remorse and to begin to heal and develop a productive life. He died in 2000 of Hepatitis C, the furtive executioner now ravaging our prisons. In Nolan's honor, the organization Inside Circle continues and expands his work to hundreds of men in California prisons.

When Nolan killed a man he was not sentenced to death. In dedicating his life because he had taken another man's life, he revised the concept of retribution as it is often understood. He reinterpreted it as restorative justice. Permitting Patrick Nolan to live and to discover how to make his life meaningful and the lives of men around him meaningful was a profound act of recompense, and an appropriate societal response if ever there was one.

My dictionary gives recompense as the primary definition of retribution, though it's usually understood as revenge. Recompense, it's a neutral term. To be sure Patrick Nolan was an exceptional man, but his transformation is not unique.

Let me tell you briefly about 4 men convicted of murder who have in similar ways redefined retribution as giving their lives to society through their work. Jessie Wise was convicted of 2 murders (and sentenced to death). Growing up in a St. Louis ghetto and a boy's home, Wise longed to become a writer and a musician. In prison he wrote, I quote, "I gathered all the books I could, made drumsticks out of pencils and fret boards and keyboards out of cardboard and went to work." He began, he taught himself to compose and was put in charge of the music room in his Missouri prison.

Weiss went on to, I'm sorry, his name is Wise, Wise went on to teach music fundamentals and instrumentation and to lead prison bands. Here's a picture of a band with Jessie Wise in a foreground of condemned men in Missouri, the band called itself Final Appeal. When one of the men, marked here, "Tony executed", was executed Jessie wrote, Jessie Wise wrote, "his creativity and musicianship were stripped from the world, people do change while incarcerated. But no one takes notice of this fact."

Wise himself took notice and composed a piece called Lement for Tony M. Jessie Wise also became an accomplished writer. He was executed in May of 1999.

Consider Steven Wayne Anderson. While robbing a darkened house, Anderson shot and killed a woman. Instead of fleeing he turned on all the lights and waited for the police to arrive. In 20 years on San Quentin's condemned row, Anderson educated himself and wrote poems about the more than 500 men waiting with him. He wrote me "we carry eminent destruction with us constantly. We eat, sleep and breathe death." California's then Governor Davis insisted on honoring the wishes of murder victim's relatives, but in Anderson's case, these relatives said they did not want their mother remembered in this way (by execution).

In my opinion, Anderson's capacity for feeling made him freer than those who sent him to his death in January 2002, and he wrote "As I walk to that greater darkness I will go wearing their chains, not mine."

Two others, and I'm about to finish, currently on San Quentin's death row were convicted as teenagers and sent to prison together. One, Steve Champion, writes "The day that I was sentenced to death I made a commitment to better myself. I placed myself under the microscope and in honestly looking at myself gave, it gave me the strength to remove the negativity in my life that hinders my growth. I started writing to unleash my emotions, to place them in front of me like a mirror so I can see and understand them."

Champion and his co-defendant (Anthony Ross) taught themselves to read and write. Often they were permitted to write only with stubs of pencils or the flexible cores of bic pens. When I visited Ross he described prison as "part monastery, part university and part cemetery because I left my old self there."

Now 45 he's an old man. When he gets into conversation with a newcomer to prison, he asks the young man to name 5 principles that he lives by. They don't have any, except odd hope values, Ross told me. Then I say no, no, let's just make that 3, 3 principles you live by. This is the beginning he told me of their moral awareness.

I'm not arguing that the lives of such men should be spared because they have literary talent, but because they have regained their lives and now struggle to make some reparation, some contribution to society. To deprive people convicted of crimes of a chance to grow, to recover the values they held before turning to crime, compounds the original evil done to society. Allowing them time to experience remorse and make something of their lives, even in prison, is more in keeping with the humanitarian values of a democracy that values justice and equality.

Thank you again. In the future, people will look back at this period in our history and wonder how it lasted so long. The ending of capital punishment in the US is the drama of this new century. You have an opportunity to let New York lead the way.

CHAPTER FOUR: COSTS AND THE PROSECUTORIAL PROCESS

There's a county (in Texas) called Waller County, it's a rural county, it's right next door to Houston. They have never in the entire history of the county prosecuted anyone for capital murder, and it's not because they don't have murders there. It's because they can't afford it.

County commissioners in rural counties in Texas say, we can get a road grader for that kind of money. And you know what? They're right. And they prefer to have a road grader. Kathryn Kase Esq, Texas Defender Service

This Chapter draws together one of the most powerful issues in the death penalty debate – the extraordinary costs incurred to obtain a capital conviction and execute a capital defendant – with diverse matters affecting the prosecution of death penalty cases such as prosecutorial discretion, geographic disparities in seeking capital punishment, competencies of defense counsel, and the functioning of capital juries.

Several Hearings questions invited testimony on these matters, as follows:

I. 4. Are the results which New York has achieved over the past nine years in administering the death penalty worth the significant public resources which have been expended? Could those resources have been used more effectively for other crime control or public purposes.

I. 1. Is it possible to design a death penalty law that is fairly administered and consistently applied, free from impermissible racial, ethnic, or geographic bias . . .?

II. 5. New York's law provided a system of capital defense through a Capital Defender Office and contracts with other institutional defenders and private attorneys. Has this system worked effectively? How might it be improved?

II. 6. Under New York's death penalty law, prosecutors were given unfettered discretion to seek or not seek the death penalty in any first degree murder case. Is such unlimited discretion appropriate? Did this system of prosecutional discretion work effectively and fairly?

II. 7. Three death sentences imposed under the 1995 law came from Suffolk County with one each coming from Kings, Queens, Onondaga and Monroe counties. The chances that a defendant would be subject to a death penalty prosecution in New York over the past nine years varied widely, depending upon the county in which a defendant's crime occurred. Is this a permissible result in a death penalty system? Should the imposition of the death penalty vary, depending upon the county in which a defendant is prosecuted?

II. 15. The 1995 law contained provisions for disqualifying jurors from death penalty guilt and penalty phase proceedings who harbored opinions for or against the death penalty which would preclude them from rendering an impartial verdict or exercising their discretion to determine an appropriate sentence. Has the provision, as it has been interpreted by New York's courts, been applied fairly and appropriately? Should this provision be modified in the event the death penalty is reinstated?

To the "public resources" questions, many witnesses answered that it is vastly more expensive to impose the death penalty rather than life in prison without parole (LWOP). The specific dollar amounts assigned to this added cost varied, but Hearings witnesses generally asserted that, in difficult economic times, this money could be far better spent on effective policing, crime prevention, and prosecution of crimes associated with murder (gangs, drugs, domestic violence, aggravated robbery). It was also strongly argued that LWOP achieves the same deterrence, and provides the same social protection, as capital punishment.

The following testimony by Richard Dieter of the Death Penalty Information Center addressed the issues of cost in exceptional detail.[46]

> My name is Richard Dieter. I'm the Executive Director of the Death Penalty Information Center, a position I've had for the past thirteen years. I'm an attorney and also an adjunct professor at Catholic University Law School, and a native of New York.
>
> To me, the issue of the cost of the death penalty is not a secondary one, but actually one which is central to the discussions you're having here today. I believe it's central for two reasons.
>
> First of all, the death penalty is about justice and about making the community safer. There are many ways in which a committee or a legislature can decide to do that. Most of those kinds of changes in the law have costs associated with it. The death penalty also has a cost associated with it.
>
> I have reviewed every cost study that I am aware of that measures these costs versus life without parole. Every cost study has concluded that there's at least a net cost to the death penalty. So when considering this issue, you have to consider that of course there's no bottomless pit – no bottomless pot, rather – of money that you have to pull from.
>
> And having the death penalty, therefore, means perhaps sacrificing other things such as compensation for victims' families, better lighting in crime areas, more police on the streets, even more prison cells. A lot of things can make communities safer, can bring justice to the community. The death penalty has a cost associated with it, and so that kind of calculus has to be taken into account.
>
> I can tell you that around the country, states that are (facing) fiscal challenges are closing libraries, some are setting inmates free early, as cost-saving measures. And these are states with the death penalty, with this burden of expense.

The second reason why I think costs are an essential issue and not a secondary one is that cost will determine what kind of death penalty a state would have, if it should choose to have it. It's intricately related to issues such as innocence . . . to issues on representation. You can have, of course, a death penalty on the cheap.

Illinois, we . . . have heard . . . its experience where more innocent people were freed over their period of the death penalty than were executed, and they stopped the whole thing. Why did they do that? They studied it, and the commission came up with 85 recommendations to try and improve or change the death penalty.

Almost all of those recommendations have costs associated with them. So when you're considering the death penalty, and you're considering whether it's going to meet challenges of accuracy and fairness, you're also considering cost issues. So I think it is essential to look at how much the death penalty costs.

Well, there are obviously costs associated with every aspect of the death penalty. There's also costs associated with life without parole. Imprisonment is a very expensive process.

What would be the worst system would be one which had all the expenses of the death penalty, the jury selection, the multiple lawyers, multiple prosecutors, the experts, the two-part trial, the appeals, all of that, and then add on to that life without parole.

But that is essentially what New York has had. That is essentially what a lot of states have had. The experience around the country is that the death penalty is bogging down. Actually last year, the time between sentencing and execution of the inmates who were executed was 12 years, and that was longer than in prior years. The system is not speeding up.

There are only a handful of states that have executed more than one person a year in the 30 years that the death penalty has been in existence . . . . So, . . . over the 30 years that we've had the death penalty, only 12 percent of the people sentenced to death have been executed.

(W)hat we're having is this very expensive system. Kind of the Cadillac of all (systems), where you have the death penalty and add on the expenses of life without parole, and that's what makes it so expensive.

If there's any doubt about all of this, I would also refer to Professor James Liebman who may have testified before this Committee about his review of the death penalty. He again, studying the death penalty nationally, looked at all the cases from 1973 on. He found that 63 percent of the cases were overturned. That is, either the conviction or the sentence was thrown out and it had to be done over again. So for one thing, that's of course adding to the expenses.

When those cases were then retried with a fairer trial, over 80 percent did not result in the death penalty. That's the system that we have, and that's making this system very expensive.

Now you can look at the individual steps in the penalty process. I noticed that District Attorney Fitzpatrick, for example, testified earlier today about a case (<u>People v. Cahill</u>). He said, well the trial took two weeks, but the jury selection took five months. You know, that's long, but it's not unheard of.

The federal system has had cases like that. Other states where – especially where the death penalty is controversial, you know, that's just the start of the process. Every death penalty trial takes longer than a non-death penalty trial. Every jury selection in a death penalty case is more expensive than its comparable non-death penalty case.

And that's true for every aspect of the death penalty. You know, it just takes longer, and time is money.

The only place in the system where there might be a savings is when there's an execution. Because after an execution, obviously the state does not have to incarcerate the person, care for the person. But as I was pointing out earlier, that's the rarity. And it's not just New York.

Only two states outside of the south last year had an execution. Most of the country has this symbolic death penalty which is causing the expense, if anything, to rise rather than decrease.

A quick look at some of these cost studies. One thing to notice I think is that death penalty costs are experienced up front; whereas, life without parole costs are spread out over something like 40 years.

(I)f you take the state having to pay $1 million, a lot of that for the death penalty comes up front with the representation, pre-trial, and all of that. $1 million over a year or two is a lot more of a burden on the state then (the) $1 million which you can pay out over 40 years. So that's one thing to be considering in all of these studies.

If people, judges, and the judges' staffs, and the courtrooms and prosecutors ... are spending more time on the death penalty, that is a net cost, and that's what's taken into account in these studies.

And just a few examples. I won't go into all the details .... North Carolina I think is the best study. Federally funded, two-year study, looked at the costs, concluded that it was costing about $2.16 million per execution, extra. That's not a flat cost, but that's the extra cost attributable to the death penalty.

Of course when you say per execution, those costs are very dependent ... on how many executions you have. But the study said even if North Carolina executed 100 percent of the people who were sentenced to death, the net cost would still be $200,000 per case.

(I)t's going to be expensive if you have a system like Texas where say a third of the people are executed, as opposed to nationally where it's more like 12 percent, it's a little more efficient, but still very expensive.

The studies in Florida bear this out. There was an early study, I think Justice Kogan referred to it, of the costs in Florida that said about $3.2 million per execution. And then Florida got bogged down. They had, you know, legal controversies, as happens in many states. They had a controversy over their electric chair. Things slowed down to one or two executions a year.

Now, just recently, they re-evaluated the costs in Florida, and found that the costs were about $54 million a year, and since the executions had slowed down, actually slowed down to sort of a normal pace, the costs were now $24 million per execution. So you can start to see how this gets to be serious money.

The amount in California . . . (for) a state (that might be) comparable to New York, although I don't know that you'd ever have as many people on death row, but they've been at it for 30 years there in California. The costs estimate there are close – well $90 million per year extra attributable to the death penalty. Huge death row, lawyers, appeals, the whole process.

Now they have about one execution every two years. You know, it's rare. So the cost per that execution is approaching $100 million per execution. So that's when these kinds of numbers I think should make a difference. We're not just talking about a little money. We're talking about large amounts of money concentrated on a very few . . . people, as opposed to programs that might affect a much larger group of people, prevent crime . . . .

There's also some federal numbers about the costs of the death penalty. They're not federal in the sense that they're applied in every state, they apply to the federal (U.S. Government) death penalty, and they're very much in line with what the states are finding. It's about four times more expensive if you have a death penalty case than a similar non-death penalty case.

They also said that the prosecution costs were about 67 percent higher than the defense costs. So there's a lot of costs that may not appear in line items of budgets here. A lot of these costs in a state are going to be experienced on a county level, where sometimes they can be least afforded, and that of course can help decide whether the prosecution seeks the death penalty or not, you know, in a county that doesn't have as much resources versus one that does . . . .

Many of these costs are actually getting larger. The Supreme Court last year decided a case that said mitigation experts have to be provided to the defense or we're going to overturn the convictions.[47] The time between sentencing and execution is getting longer. States are having to have good lawyers, both at trial and appeal, good prosecutors. The whole thing is actually getting more expensive . . . .

And so, you know, they are slowing down. Executions are down 40 percent in the country. Death sentencing over the past five years is down 50 percent. Public support for the death penalty has dropped, although still a majority . . . . Support for life without parole has increased considerably.

(W)ithout even going into the intangible costs, such as the risk of executing (the) innocent, the perception of racial divisiveness, the death penalty is putting an enormous amount of money, millions of dollars, into a few cases without a lot for the state to show for it.

I certainly can say with a high degree of confidence that if New York re-instates the death penalty, you will not have an execution for ten to fifteen years, if then. And that's assuming that the whole statute doesn't get thrown out again.

And that will occur at a cost of probably hundreds of millions of dollars, and will not necessarily make the state any safer. So I think the state has to chose where to put its resources. It's not just a question about which costs more, but which brings more justice and more safety. Thank you.

Thomas Sullivan, who practiced law in Chicago for over 50 years, served as U.S. Attorney for the Northern District of Illinois, and was a member of the Ryan Commission that studied the death penalty in Illinois, put it simply: "the death penalty is damn expensive".

Mr. Sullivan: This is my analysis of costs, state by state, to the extent that I am able to do it, and showing a view of states, about 20 of them, that it costs anywhere from a third to twice as much to three times as much a death case as a non-death case.

And in many instances, I mean, I can go through this with you, but you can read it, Kansas, Indiana, Connecticut, double the costs in Connecticut, 35% more in Indiana, and about a third more in Kansas. North Carolina. 10 years ago they found that it costs a quarter of a million dollars more per death case.

The Hearings report outlined some of Attorney Sullivan's reasons for asserting that capital prosecutions are more costly than non-capital LWOP cases.

- Investigations are longer and more costly;
- Representation costs are higher;
- Every procedural phase is longer, involving more experts;
- Many jurisdictions require a separate sentencing phase;
- Appeals are generally automatic;
- There are usually extensive post-conviction proceedings in state and federal court; and
- Death row cells are more expensive and death row inmates require greater security.

Professor Robert Blecker of New York Law School was, once again, a strong advocate of the view that death penalty costs are not excessive.

We've heard about costs. It costs four times more, $2 million more (to obtain a death sentence instead of LWOP). Recent studies show 30 to 60% more to execute than to imprison for life. A Kansas study was mentioned, a 2003 Kansas study. Well in that kind of study, for example, what was not mentioned, but it was only in a footnote in the study, was (that) there's one benefit and one subtraction from the costs that's never taken into account ... and that is the hundreds of thousands of dollars saved for everybody who pleads guilty, thus waiving trials and investigations in order to avoid the death penalty. Now, that (plea) can't be coerced, the Court of Appeals has upheld and the

Supreme Court has upheld, it can't be coerced, but it can be negotiated.

When those savings are added in, it can well be argued that the death penalty is in fact cheaper . . . . As we become more and more discriminating, not discriminatory, but discriminating, about whether or when we execute and who we declare to be the worst of the worst, then the . . . costs of running a death penalty regime remain fixed and they get spread less over each individual, so the fewer we execute, the more expensive it seems to be in order to execute . . . .

(W)hen one does a cost benefit analysis (costs become clearer). That is, in the resources expended, you must subtract the hundreds of thousands of dollars saved for each guilty plea in a murder case, which has come about because a guilty defendant prefers to plead guilty to the crime committed rather than face the possibility . . . (of a death sentence).

Although not mentioned directly, Professor Blecker's analysis implicates another factor relating to cost. Keeping a person on death row under a LWOP sentence may, in many cases over many years, result in an expenditure that equals the cost of executing that inmate.

The New York experience with prosecution of death penalty cases is representative of state cost issues and illustrates may of the stresses put on state systems by capital trials. Schenectady County District Attorney Robert Carney testified against restoring the death penalty in New York and offered expense as one of his reasons.

"We (must) . . . consider the commitment of resources necessary to prosecute a death penalty case for an office as small as mine, with 15 full-time lawyers, and the impact that such an allocation of resources would have on the prosecution of other crimes.

(T)he most compelling argument against this continued experimentation with the death penalty is, in my opinion, the misdirection of resources necessary to maintain capital punishment. At $13 million per year to fund the (N.Y.) Capital Defender Office, together with all the money spent for capital qualified assigned counsel, and prosecutors costs, the death penalty has cost us as much as $200 million. Can it truthfully be said that putting seven people temporarily on death row was worth the expenditure of those monies? For this cost, a handful of defendants have temporarily confronted the remote prospect of execution, the families and loved ones of their victims have believed that retributive justice would be theirs only to be cruelly disappointed, like Deborah Jaeger, the sister of Jill Cahill, and many lawyers have prospered.

There are so many criminal justice initiatives that are effective in reducing crime that could be enhanced for a fraction of this money. The Pataki administration just last year launched two. Both are operating in my county. Project Impact gives grants to the 15 upstate counties with urban crime problems to devise strategies and collaborations emulative of New York City's Compstat program.

Under this program, for example, the city of Rochester has already experienced a 66 percent decrease in homicides among the target population of young African-American males. This has been done, in part, through systematic engagement of street gangs, by police, parole, probation, and prosecutors, working under (Project) Impact, warning them that they will be held collectively responsible for gang violence. The total cost to the state of Impact is only $4.3 million, but its positive effect on our communities is priceless.

A second initiative, Road to Recovery, gives prosecutors resources that screen defendants ineligible for drug court because of prior convictions who commit nonviolent crimes because of substance abuse. Modeled after the drug treatment alternative to prison program started by District Attorney Hynes in Brooklyn, this program allows the small upstate counties to divert qualifying defendants out of prison and into treatment. If this recidivist population reforms their criminal behavior, the crime rate will be reduced and the state will save money.

Continuing to spend millions of dollars to take a murder defendant who has already been caught and subject him to death rather than life without parole will not prevent the next murder. Redirecting money to more vigorously apprehend and prosecute armed robbers, rapists, burglars, and those who commit gun crimes, will prevent murders and save lives. Expanding funding for Impact, Road to Recovery, and other equally compelling crime reduction strategies is, in my opinion, a much wiser way to spend scarce public resources.

Similar testimony was presented from the defense attorney point of view by Mr. James Rogers representing 800 members of the Association of Legal Aid Attorneys (ALAA).

In one case out of Queens County, a death case, 4 to 5 lawyers tried that case on each side. On the prosecution side and on the defense side for over a year, each side spent well over $100,000 on jury consultants, and when it was time for that case to be appealed it took an appellate lawyer over a year to do that appeal. We have spent 5 to 10 million dollars per case, as you all know, for the 8 (7) death sentences that have been secured in New York State.

So I can't say that all the money that goes to the death penalty could fix the criminal justice system. But it is a start, a good start at that. At Legal Aid right now, we have caseload grievances in every single division that handles criminal cases. In our criminal trial offices, and in the Juvenile Rights divisions that handle delinquency cases, some . . . attorneys have over 130 cases.

Attorneys handling delinquency matters and juvenile . . . (cases) . . . (have) around 90 cases and if you know how family court works, which I know you do, that is an astronomical number. No one can stand up and say that that is consistent with our vision of justice and no one can say that anything over 80 cases, just to pick a random number , but I won't swear by it, is somehow okay in any arena. Particularly (the) criminal arena.

So we have the millions and millions and millions of dollars to go to prosecute a death penalty (case) without any evidence that (it) is a deterrent, with evidence quite to the contrary, and evidence only that it can be unfairly applied, and the risk that innocent people will be executed is severe, and we can take those tens of millions of dollars and even out the playing field a little bit in the rest of the criminal justice system . . . .

I want the criminal justice system to work in a way that we envisioned. And not to dump hundreds of millions of dollars down the drain on the death penalty when we could be evening out the playing field, guarding against innocent people going to jail.

The theme of counterproductive diversion of funds by death penalty prosecutions – past, present and future – was continued by Jonathan Gradess of the New York State Defenders Association, Professor Bennett Gershman of Pace University Law School, and Columbia University Law Professor James Liebman.

Professor Gershman stated that a recent 8 month capital case, People v. Alvarez, cost $4 million, resulted in a sentence of LWOP, and took place at a time when cuts in the County budget hampered prosecution of probation violations and other non-capital serious crimes. "On day one" the defendant offered to plead guilty to LWOP. The prosecutor refused and this costly trial resulted.

Public defender Gradess pointed out in written testimony that conservative estimates set expenditures in New York at $170 million for death penalty prosecution and defense for the 10 year period 1995-2005. Approximately $24 million was spent for each death sentence. None was carried out. In a time of rising health care costs, Mr. Gradess argued that it made little sense to divert critical state funds to try to execute "one nineteen-year old, impoverished youth" at the expense of placing "thousands of elderly New Yorkers at medical risk." Mr. Gradess:

Let me just share with you five conclusions. Capital punishment is more expensive than life imprisonment; capital cases cost more than noncapital cases; criminal justice systems with death penalties face higher design and maintenance costs than criminal justice systems without capital punishment; the major costs of the death penalty arise from the trial and penalty phases of capital proceedings; and as I think you've begun to hear, and Bud Welch pointed out, the death penalty drains resources from other critical areas of the criminal justice system and the state.

In the weeks ahead as the children of the foster care system march before you in budget discussions, as you find it impossible to open more domestic violence shelters, as you debate over the cost of drug treatment beds, I want you to remember the high cost of capital punishment.

When the victims of AIDS plead with you for needed money to save their lives, and legal services lawyers ask for restoration of money to prevent evictions, and firefighters seek pension reform, remember the high cost of capital punishment.

And when I come before you, this is particularly important, and I seek simply to restore NYSDA's (the Defenders Association) research unit, which has been unfunded since 9/11, or when the food pantries seek a new initiative so that the poor might eat, or the police plead for bulletproof vests, recall the waste, the tragic foolishness, remember the high cost of the death penalty.

You don't have to hold a degree in economics to know that New York today represents the worst place to reinstate capital punishment. As you struggle to meet the school funding mandate, as highways crumble and the demand to fix Medicaid reaches a crisis, the question of how New York will pay for the needs of its people should precede the current death penalty discussion.

Death penalty proponents like to condemn the cost argument as the ravings of Chicken Little. But the sky is falling in New York, and it has nothing to do with those of us who are describing the process, a process of short-sightedness; a process that buys guns and discards butter; that trades the needs of the homeless to purchase judicial time to hear death penalty cases; that barters away crime victims' compensation to pay for hours of appellate review; that yields to an image of execution in exchange for the reality of highways, homes and healthcare. . . .

(T)his figure of $170 million puzzled me when I first heard it, and so I traced it a little bit. You should know where it comes from and why it is low.

It is an extrapolation from a (N.Y.) Times Union investigation conducted in 2003. That's 18 months ago. So, even if its figures were correct 18 months ago, just a straight mathematical calculation would already place the cost of the death penalty at $185 million.

But looking more closely at that study, the Times Union by its own report underestimated prosecution costs. They stated simply (that) the exact cost of prosecuting capital murder is difficult to determine.

Yet assuming, as I think we could, because the president of the D.A.s' Association in 2003 purported to suggest at least this ratio, assuming a one-to-one ratio, we now know that $200 million, as Bob Carney said this morning, would already have been spent just on the costs of prosecution and defense alone.

We also know, and I can provide an awful lot of information on this to you, we also know that prosecution and defense expenses have never been in parity in this state, let alone one-to-one. When (the) capital losses (report) was written, disparity ran at a rate, in some places, of eight-to-one or ten-to-one, prosecution to defense, and we know that in the last capital case under the old law . . . the prosecution outspent defense by a ratio of ten-to-one . . . .

Thus, using even a still conservative figure of one and a half to one, prosecution to defense, the costs could easily be closer to $250 million, that would exceed current estimates by $80 million, and that would all precede adding in the costs of enhanced police investigation, (and) attorney general involvement under executive law, and we all can think back to just nine years ago when we had an Attorney General who felt very committed to the prosecution of the death penalty and its attendant expenditure.

The cost of courts were reported by the T.U. as 20 – more than $2900 per day. State corrections has reported spending $200,000 a year just to guard death row. And no one of these estimates has looked at enhanced local jail security during lengthy pretrial incarceration. This issue has not been studied, but when it is, it will reveal a figure substantially higher than $170 million.

Columbia Professor Liebman gave another perspective.

In most states it is, in fact, the case that people on death row are more likely to die of old age or of being injured by some other inmate than they are to be executed. Now whether or not a person is eventually executed, every defendant who is tried capitally and sentenced to die costs, on average, about to two to $4 million . . . more than . . . (the) cost if that person was convicted and sentenced to life without parole. But that's not the way to look at it. When you realize that most of those people who get sentenced to death are going to have their verdicts overturned and they're going to get re-sentenced to something else, you want to ask the per-execution cost. What are you paying for each execution? Because it's the execution that gives you the retribution, it's the execution that gives you the deterrence. The best study of that is in Florida, and it found that between – each execution cost that state between $25 and $50 million per execution more than it would have cost if the state only used life without parole for all people convicted of murder. Things, of course, cost more in New York. Between 1995-2004, New York spent about $170 million on its death penalty with no executions and, at the time, no executions were at least within ten years of occurring.

In our . . . study what we tried to do was identify the factors, what causes, what leads to capital error. And what we found was that those states that tried to cut the high costs of capital cases actually experienced a very counter-productive result. Because it is states with cheap, mass production, capital processes that have the highest reversal rates. Specifically, we found that high capital error rates are related to high capital sentencing rates, ineffective law enforcement practices, low per capita spending on the courts, and sub par state court review procedures. And the last two of those figures are quite relevant in New York which, unfortunately, has one of the slowest, least efficient, and least reliable state post-conviction systems in the country, on a par, as I say, unfortunately with states like Alabama and Georgia. So that's got to be fixed if the state wants to avoid that kind of situation.

. . .

(Y)ou can predict after about 20 years of applying a new death sentence (law) . . . you can imagine that you will get one or two executions per year statewide. And over the course of 20 years you will expect perhaps two or three (actual) executions total. The expected cost for the state over that 20 year period will be something like $500 million or about $200 million per execution beyond what it would cost to rely solely on life without parole.

(I)t seems to me that that issue comes down to the answer to this question, which I will simply posit, and that is, if the State thinks of itself as having this sort of discretionary $500 million pot of money that it's going to apply to law enforcement over the next 20 years, is it the best . . . (use) of that $500 million to buy two or three executions. Or, on the other hand, would the State of New York gain more in (the) way of law enforcement, deterrence, (saving) lives, by taking that same money and using it, for example, to fund additional police detectives, prosecutors, judges and corrections officers so that we could arrest, convict and incarcerate the many murderers, rapists . . . robbers in this State, who currently escape any penalty at all because they never get arrested because we don't have sufficient law enforcement resources in place to find them, convict them, and incarcerate them.

Assemblyman Aubry: We had the Detectives' Association President testify earlier. He raised the question of . . . (the accuracy of) the numbers that we have heard . . . about cost of life without parole against having the death penalty. He said he had a degree as an accountant and that you could make numbers do whatever you wanted to do. Do you have a response to that?

Mr. Liebman: There is no question (about the fact of added costs). Nobody, nobody doubts the fact there have been many studies. They've all found the same thing. The numbers have ranged from cheap states where you can get it (an execution) for two million more per death penalty, to more expensive states where it's four or five million more. But there's just no question. You just look at the time and motion of a life without parole case and you look at the time and motion in a capital case, it is infinitely greater in the capital case.

If you ask state supreme court justices across the country, they will tell you, in Florida, for example, they spend 50 percent of their time reviewing capital cases. The rest of the 50 percent is every other kind of case including mostly civil cases. So you know there that life without parole cases certainly aren't anywhere near what they're spending their time on. And the other fact is that the reversal rate in life without parole cases is, in a really liberal state that reverses a lot of cases, maybe 10 percent or 15 percent. In capital cases the reversal rate is upwards of 50, 60, 70, 80 percent. Those reversals cost money because that means in that case there will be two trials instead of one trial. So you know that the costs are just going to be dramatically greater in the capital cases.

You can look at the incarceration costs. Executions themselves are extremely expensive. Entire prisons actually have to be locked down in a very expensive way whenever there's an execution because of the security problems that those create.

So there's just no step along the way where you can find a place where you're actually saving money with the death penalty. And that's particularly true when you keep them in prison for at least, on average, 12 years before you execute them. So you're paying for a very high cost incarceration, which death row is, because everybody is single celled at that point, while you're going through all of those procedures.

Kate Lowenstein, a former United States Congressman's daughter, summarized this topic of excessive costs and "budget busting" as follows.

Ms. Lowenstein: My name is Kate Lowenstein. My father, former Congressman from New York, Al Lowenstein, was shot to death in his office here in the City. Dad agreed to meet with a mentally ill former student who took out a gun and shot him five times in the chest until Dad lay on the floor of his office, bleeding and dying. I miss him desperately.

. . .

(T)he death penalty puts all the focus on a few murderers. It pours millions of dollars into killing one person. Those millions should go to preventing murders, to providing victims with the best help they can get, to helping police solve murders and lock up murderers. One half of all murders go unsolved. One half. Police need the resources to help solve those crimes. I know that the vast majority of victims would rather you take the $175 million New York has put into sentencing a handful of killers to death and put it into solving thousands of unsolved murders.

As noted in the call to Hearings questions presented at the beginning of this Chapter, a number of problems beyond cost arise in the death penalty prosecution process. Some raise potential constitutional issues in terms of the arbitrariness of the system. These fairness problems include prosecutorial discretion, geographic inconsistencies in reliance on capital charges, competence and effectiveness of defense counsel, and jury functioning. The New York Death Penalty Hearings produced impressive testimony on all of these matters.

In most death penalty systems the decision on whether to seek the death penalty in a particular case lies solely with the discretion of the District Attorney. Capital punishment laws are generally very detailed in terms of the types of killings that merit the death sentence. So-called "aggravating factors" - killing a public official, murder for hire, torture killings, acts of terrorism, serial murders – define categories of death eligible crimes. However, these laws, and the systems used to apply them, do not provide standards or guidance for a prosecutor's decision to seek the death penalty in a specific case. This can lead to arbitrary, capricious, or unequal charging decisions. Witnesses commented about vast differences in the use of the death penalty from district attorney to district attorney, and county to county, within the same state.

The testimony of retired New York Judge Stewart Hancock described many of the basic problems.

> One feature of New York's death penalty sentencing scheme virtually guarantees inequality and arbitrariness in its application, the unbridled discretion vested in one person, the district attorney, to make the critical death sentence decision, the most crucial decision, the one that determines whether a defendant will live or face execution . . . the service of the death penalty notice. This decision is within the prosecutor's total and sole discretion. There is no review and no appeal. The district attorney's decision is final.
>
> The marked differences in the cultures, and political, philosophical, and moral views of the populations in the various parts of (N.Y.) state, are reflected in the attitudes of the sixty-two district attorneys toward capital prosecutions.
>
> The political realities of having to run for elective office inevitably lead to situations where a defendant may be subject to the risk of a death sentence, not because of the nature of the

crime, but because of the prosecutor's sensitivity to what may be perceived as a public outcry for retribution and justice.

Not surprisingly, the result of vesting unbridled discretion over the critical prosecutorial decisions in the sixty-two different prosecutors is a jumble of haphazard variations in capital prosecution throughout the state.

Professor Baldus, I understand, has testified already before you as to the disparities on a geographical basis in the state of New York.

Can the system possibly be fair where a defendant who has committed a crime in New York County will assuredly not receive the penalty, the district attorney (in that county) not having filed a single notice in ten years.

But if that defendant commits the identical crime across the East River in Kings County, where District Attorney Hynes has filed the highest number of death notices, he may well face the possibility of execution. (This opens the door to prohibited types of discrimination). It is doubtful that any informed American citizen would deny the regrettable truth that racial prejudice exists today throughout the United States (and can affect the capital charging decision).

There are today scores of statistical studies based on empirical evidence . . . which demonstrate beyond question that discretionary death sentencing statutes discriminate unfairly against minorities, particularly blacks.

While six members of the NY Appeals (Court) have not expressed opinions on the issues of arbitrariness and inequality, one member of the Court has done so, Judge George Bundy Smith. Although stopping short of making a definitive ruling . . . Judge Smith concluded in a separate concurrence in (People v.) Cahill that the arbitrariness argument is a strong one.

Commenting on this issue, Judge Smith wrote: "There is no safeguard to ensure that race plays no role in the decision to seek the death penalty."

And further he wrote: "When the death penalty is sought against a defendant in one county, but not against a similarly-situated defendant in another county, the decision as to who gets the death penalty may be said to be arbitrary. The death penalty statute does not prohibit this kind of arbitrariness."

You know, it's interesting – I didn't mention this before, but in over 40 years (of practice) I (have) participated in the decision making in one way or another in almost 1,200 capital cases. That's a lot of cases (and the basis for this judgment on the issue).

Gerald Kogan, retired Chief Justice of the Supreme Court of Florida, made the same point. (Justice Kogan ruled in 28 death penalty cases while he was on the Court).

Mr. Kogan: But the thing is, you do leave it to the discretion of the individual district attorney. And what one district attorney may consider a capital case, another one does not. And basically, your function is to see to it, and the courts especially, that the laws of the state are equally applied throughout the entire state. And you can't have something, a death penalty in one part of the state that is clearly not a death penalty in the other part of the state.

We (in Florida) can do a better proportionality (fairness) analysis than you (in New York) can because we have so many more cases that the death penalty is the sentence, and so many more people sitting on death row, so we can make comparisons as to which (prisoners) are the least (culpable) and which are the worst (killers).

And it's just a problem whenever you leave a choice of life or death in the hands of . . . sixty-one, apparently, district attorneys that you have in the state of New York, that is a very, very dicey, chancy thing. And that may very well be an issue that can be the cause of a reversal on constitutional grounds of any . . . (conviction under a new death penalty law in N.Y.) by either, you know, your Court of Appeals here, or, eventually by the US Supreme Court.

New York prosecutor William Fitzpatrick and law professor Robert Blecker characterized these alleged flaws in the system as strengths of a democratic society. The fact that between 1995 and 2005 the death penalty was most frequently sought in only three or four of New York's sixty two counties – Kings, Queens, Onandaga, and Monroe – and never invoked in some of the state's most populous ones was, to these witnesses, evidence of the proper functioning of elected officials in a complex political system.

Professor Blecker: The more difficult question is the county by county variability. As was pointed out in the question, of course, that some DA's go for the death penalty routinely and some DA's don't. (Y)ou didn't ask . . . whether that (variability) is skewed by the fact that the New York County District Attorney never goes for the death penalty. So one can say, if we're committed to a uniform application of the penal law and we had a death penalty and he has 35 situations that qualify as murder one and he never goes for it, we can ask whether that particular district attorney is uniformly applying the law.

This is a deep and difficult question because on the one hand, each district attorney is elected by his or her constituents of the county, and to that degree should reflect the values of . . . (those) constituents. On the other hand, they are uniformly applying the New York penal law, at least in theory . . . .

But it's the same question over and over again. To what degree do we want uniformity . . . . To what degree do you want local control of government. To what degree do you want local opinion to count. To what degree do you want to impose uniform standards. We impose . . . state constitutional uniform standards. (B)eyond that, we are leaving it to the good sense and discretion of each prosecutor and the good sense and discretion of each jury drawn from the community.

(I)t turns out that (if there is a) . . . race of victim effect, (it) turns out to be a geography affect. That is, in jurisdictions, principally suburban jurisdictions, (there are more capital cases), and I know the community is interested in this because it's one of the questions you posed, in suburban counties, which tend to be white, with greater budgets and a constituency that has a greater support for the death penalty, and by the way, the polls show that while the overwhelming majority of whites support the death penalty, and while support is much lower in the black community than it is in the white community, it is substantial in the black community. The last Gallup poll showed 46% of the African-American community supports the death penalty. 48% is opposed to it.

So while it is a minority, it is a substantial minority of the black community that supports the death penalty. But it's much lower than the white community and partly because there is this perception of racism, based upon historical legacy.

In white counties, suburban white counties, with a constituency that supports the death penalty to a greater degree, with a budget that can withstand the cost of going for death penalty to a greater degree, with a prosecutor who is likely to reflect the values of the constituents, and (you can) predict to a greater degree of certainty that the cost will have been worth it in a sense that you can get a jury to go to death. (In those counties) you more often find death penalty prosecutions (being brought).

Prosecutor Fitzpatrick

I hope it is obvious to everyone that certain district attorneys will never seek the death penalty .... That dynamic essentially insulates about one-third of the state's murderers (from) the death penalty.

(A) fundamental principle of our American federalist system . . . . (is that) as specific powers were given to the Federal Government with the balance of this power reserved to the individual states, the power to make the prosecutorial decision was left, in our State Constitution, to the countywide elected district attorneys.

It is unreasonable to construct a system that on the one hand constitutionally vests independently elected prosecutors with discretion, and then statutorily invalidate convictions or sentences based on differences in the exercise of that discretion.

That is a classic catch 22. If the system of independent district attorneys functions as it was constitutionally designed, it will . . . (lead to county-by-county differences).

Mr. Benajmin: Mr. Fitzpatrick, good morning.

Mr. Fitzpatrick: Good morning.

Mr. Benjamin: I come from a county where our DA has not sought the death penalty. Would you support a provision prohibiting a Governor from displacing DAs who choose not to seek death, as Govenor Pataki did in a case several years ago?

Mr. Fitzpatrick: I would say it is up to each individual DA to make his or her decision about that. Rob Johnson – is that who you're referring to?

Mr. Benjamin: Yes.

Mr. Fitzpatrick: Rob Johnson is one of the finest people I know. I consider him a close friend. He will never seek the death penalty. I don't know if he would say that publically, but that's the fact. That's for the voters of the Bronx to decide, and that's for him to decide. If the voters of the Bronx accept that, then so be it.

(T)he reality of it is that . . . New York prosecutors who are the pilots of this plane that you built for us, we did a pretty good job with the (1995 death penalty) statute. You know, we put seven people on death row in ten years when there were 2,000 people murdered.

And of the seven people, there isn't one of those seven that had even a colorable claim of innocence at the end of the day. Every one of them was overwhelmingly guilty, they were racially disparate, they had access to DNA, they had access to the finest defense lawyers imaginable.

Mr. Levine: How is the decision made as to who is going to be – receive the death penalty? Is it via committee? Do you do it yourself?

Mr. Fitzpatrick: Sure, good question. There are no guidelines. You didn't give us any guidelines. You told us to rely on our discretion. And what I do in my office is, I have a senior level staff meeting. It's made up of prosecutors, investigators and lay people that work in the office, and I try to make it as diverse as possible.

And then we will discuss – the trial prosecutor will then present the facts of a murder one case. We will then give the opportunity to the Capital Defender's Office or a private retained attorney, depending on the circumstance, to come in, and they can pitch to us as to why this is not a death penalty case. Or why they feel life without parole or some other sentence is more appropriate.

We then seek input from the victim's family. We allow them to come in. Most of the time that's pretty clear-cut. It's a husband and father, a wife or a husband. Sometimes it's a little blurred, but in any event, we allow everybody that feels they need to make input, to come in. Then they will make a nonbinding recommendation to me, and then I will make the decision.

One case we had which was a particularly heinous case, and I won't belabor the point, but the Capital Defender's Office made a very, very risky move by bringing in the defendant's medical records, which convinced me after my expert looked at them, that the defendant was mentally retarded. And despite, you know, heinous, heinous multiple homicides, he pled to life without parole.

So that's how the process works. And I know some of my colleagues follow a similar process.

Chairman Lentol: As a follow-up to what Mr. Levine asked you, and this thought always intrigued me when I considered the death penalty, and that is this proposition. You know, we and you are political animals, and we make (political) determinations all the time, sometimes for the wrong reasons, sometimes for the right reasons.

And what I'm talking about is, you have to make a determination in a short period of time whether or not you're going to file a death notice. And we don't have those kinds of things to do as Assembly members, but we sometimes make judgments based on politics as opposed to what Professor Blecker would call making a judgment about the worst of the worst as to who should receive the death penalty.

Now do you think that that's a flaw in the way we operate, because of who we are, and the political nature of our business, to make determinations that some might consider as political rather than moral judgments, making a determination on life and death as to who is the worst of the worst?

Mr. Fitzpatrick: I don't take the word political as pejorative, and I consider it an honor to be in politics, and I know you do too, Assemblyman.

Chairman Lentol: Yes, I do.

Mr. Fitzpatrick: And if by politics, you know, I sit in my office, and I look out my window and I see that there's a crowd demonstrating for me to hang somebody, and then although I don't think it's morally correct, I seek the death penalty, then that's reprehensible.

But you gave – you and your colleagues in '95, you gave that judgment (about seeking the death penalty) to sixty-two people, most of whom you probably had never met. And I think I can say without equivocation, they did an outstanding job.

I hate for us, as I did earlier almost comically, to compare New York State to Texas or Illinois. Frankly, those cases that death penalty opponents bring out that occurred in those two states, if what prosecutors did there occurred in New York, I can say with a certain degree of assurance, those prosecutors would be disbarred, justifiably so.

You gave sixty-two elected DAs this decision, and we all made various judgments. Some people made decisions based on economics; in small counties (the DA will say) I can't afford a death penalty prosecution. Some people made the decision, I'm never going to seek the death penalty.

I made it – you gave me the law, I put my hand on a bible, I said that I would – to the best of my ability - I would support the laws that you give me, and I would follow them. And it's not in my judgment to say, you know, I can't seek the death penalty ever.

(In the) appropriate case. . . I made the decision (to capitally prosecute) for moral reasons, but at the end of the day I'm still a politician, so are all of you on the panel, and I don't consider that a bad thing.

As noted in this testimony, politics colors much of what happens in state decision-making on capital punishment. An extreme example of this occurred in the case of <u>Johnson v. Pataki</u>[48], referred to by prosecutor Fitzpatrick, in which the N.Y. Court of Appeals upheld an executive order of then Governor Pataki to remove Bronx District Attorney Robert Johnson from a potential death penalty case, and substitute N.Y. Attorney General Dennis Vacco as prosecutor, on the grounds that Mr. Johnson would not seek the death penalty.

The testimony of District Attorney Fitzpatrick and other prosecutors made it clear that the people of the state of New York, and of the vast majority of American states, were represented by competent and committed attorneys in capital cases. The same might not be said for legal representation of capital defendants.

Most Americans have heard stories about defense lawyers "sleeping" through trials. One of the most notorious involved Calvine Burdine. Burdine's defense lawyer, Joe Cannon, slept for "long periods of time" during witness examinations and slept at one point for "at least ten minutes." Burdine ultimately won a new trial on charges that he killed his gay lover, but only after the Texas Court of Criminal Appeals affirmed his conviction and death sentence.[49]

A similar case in New York, <u>People v. Tippins</u>[50], held that N.Y. standards for effective assistance of counsel were not automatically violated by a defense lawyer who napped during portions of a criminal trial. At the time of the N.Y. Hearings, <u>Tippins</u> appeared to be still good law.

Former New York Public Advocate Mark Green asserted that

> (S)o often, as the book by Austin Sarat, WHEN THE STATE KILLS, (points out), there's incompetent counsel and procedural failures (in many capital cases).
>
> Now, examples of incompetent and inexperienced counsel in capital cases abound, which helps explain why so many convicted defendants are later exonerated. That's disgraceful, but not surprising. If, on the one hand, you have an army of experienced prosecutors out to get a conviction up against, often, a lone inexperienced public defender, juggling 70 cases, are we really surprised that this lone reed is blown down by this gale force wind, and that innocent people are executed in the United States. It would seem to be inevitable....
>
> A bipartisan bill now in Congress lauded by Justice Sandra Day O'Connor would create national standards for competent counsel in capital cases and in fact our President Bush lauded (this bill) and urged more funds for just such an effort in his... State of the Union address....
>
> If the Supreme Court could strike down a Florida recount (of the vote in the 2000 Presidential election) in Gore v. Bush[51] because it violated Equal Protection for different counties to have different standards for vote counting, why is it (not) analytically a comparable violation of Equal Protection for 62 counties in New York, effectively, to have 62 different standards for execution? I care about vote counting, but I would assume that when the State is about to execute somebody, that is more important even than vote counting.

(T)estimony presented by the criminal defense Bar in New York challenged the notion of inadequate representation of capital defendants.

> Mr. Goltzer: Good afternoon Mr. Chairman and members of the Legislature. My name is George Goltzer, I'm a member of the Board of Directors of the New York State Association of Criminal Defense Lawyers. Thank you for inviting me to address you on

this most serious issue of public policy, whether the death penalty ought to be reinstated in New York State.

The Association that I represent today is comprised of nearly 800 criminal defense attorneys practicing throughout this state. It is also one of the largest affiliates of the National Association of Criminal Defense Lawyers. We come from all sorts of professional, racial, religious and economic backgrounds, we're diverse, opinionated, and quite vocal on most issues.

On one issue however we are virtually unanimous. There is no place in New York State for the death penalty. Do not reinstate it. The 9 years (that) many of us . . . (have devoted to defending) death eligible defendants has convinced us that no death penalty system instituted and administered by human beings can be fair, even handed, non-discriminatory, and foolproof.

In many cases, death sentences are reversed because the lawyer was constitutionally inadequate, ineffective, lazy, dishonest or asleep at the defense table. We in New York like to think we have a cadre of competent lawyers to defend capital cases. Indeed we do. But even the most experienced and dedicated of us know how imperfect we really are. (W)e can make strategic errors, forget to raise an objection in the heat of battle, miss an issue or just have a bad day.

Maybe we weren't forceful enough with our client to convince him to accept a guilty plea to a life sentence to save his life. Perhaps our personality was abrasive to the prosecutor who had to decide whether to offer that guilty plea to a life term. We know full well that serendipity kills. One defendant gets a new trial because his lawyer objects while another dies because his lawyer did not raise the same issues . . . . (This) death (penalty structure) is not the product of any rational system.

Are you from Syracuse or the Bronx? Brooklyn or Manhattan? Were you born in the United States where your lawyer can retrieve decades old documents proving that you were abused, deprived or retarded. Or are you from the third world where the proof of mitigation evaporated long ago? (This is what can determine whether a killer will live or die).

Most Americans do not understand the jury trial system used to prosecute death penalty cases in the United States. In a typical criminal case, a jury made up of 6 or 12 citizens from the community hears the evidence and lawyers' arguments, receives instructions on the law from the judge, finds the facts "beyond a reasonable doubt", and returns a verdict of "guilty" or "not guilty". The trial judge then sentences the convicted defendant. All of this takes place in one proceeding or "trial".

Death penalty cases are heard under some form of "bifurcated trial" procedure. In the first or "guilt phase" of the case, the jury must determine whether the accused committed capital murder by finding "beyond a reasonable doubt" all of the facts necessary to prove the "elements" or definitional components of the crime. For example, under N.Y. law this might require for first degree death-penalty-eligible murder the existence of an intentional killing of a judge, police officer, or corrections official. Upon a finding of guilt in such a case, the second or "sentencing phase" of the bifurcated trial asks the jury to weigh "aggravating" and "mitigating" circumstances and to then find, unanimously, under the balance of these factors or the stronger weight of "aggravators", that the defendant deserves the death penalty. In some systems the two stages may be technically merged into one proceeding, but a separate determination of sufficient aggravating or mitigating circumstances must still be made.

This is a demanding process for ordinary citizens made more difficult by legal limits on which potential jurors are "qualified" to sit on death penalty juries and which are not. As a general principle, potential jurors who hold strong beliefs about capital punishment, either in favor or against, are eliminated from the jury pool "for cause" (as compared to "preemptive strikes" of jurors by which jurors are eliminated without any need for explanation).

The New York Death Penalty Hearings presented testimony on
several aspects of jury selection and competence. Matters relating to race
and the potential racism of jurors are considered in Chapter Five.

Issues relating to effective jury functioning were raised by Professor
James R. Acker of the Criminal Justice School at SUNY – Albany in response
to questions from Assemblyman Daniel J. O'Donnell.

> Chairman Lentol: Mr. O'Donnell.
>
> Mr. O'Donnell: Professor Acker. Among the most
> entertaining of the testimony we received I would say would be
> Professor Blecker who testified in December – he had a very
> interesting view of the world that included expanding the death
> penalty to include a whole variety of people that no one ever
> contemplated (being covered by it) . . . as well as (imposing)
> certain limitations . . . upon it.
>
> And I am not an academic. I don't think any academic
> institution worth its salt would want to hear what I have to say.
> But I was a practitioner, and . . . for seven years I was a public
> defender in Kings County, and I represented people who were
> accused of all (kinds) crimes, including homicide cases.
>
> And I would like you to just briefly address, if you can, the
> problem that we have. Let me sort of backtrack for one second.
> When, after a trial was over, you would speak to juries, and you
> would see this even in major cases that get covered on the
> tabloid news, jurors often reflect some degree of anger at
> defendants for their inability (to display remorse), or (the
> juror's) perception that they have no remorse for the crime.
>
> And yet, we have set up the system here in New York where,
> one, we eliminate all people who are opposed to the death
> penalty from a jury pool. So now you take the 40 percent of the
> people, just as a hypothetical, in New York who don't believe in
> it, take them out of the selection process. Then you put – you're
> left with the 60 percent.
>
> And then the same group of people who are sitting in
> judgment and making a determination as to the facts and the

guilt or innocence have to make a decision about the penalty (in a bifurcated trial). Well, I mean, it sounds like a good idea. The problem, though, is that, how can one argue as a defense lawyer . . . that . . . (your client) did not commit a crime and then turn around and (expect the client to) act remorseful.

So I mean, it's a very difficult position. Most of my – in fact, none of my - clients ever testified because they shouldn't have. And most of them were convicted.

So . . . if you can sort of just from an academic perspective share with us a little bit about the problems of the human . . . desire to see remorse and sorrow (from the defendant) about a person who is no longer alive, . . . (and) . . . the contradiction of (jurors) having sat through three to six months of grizzly testimony and somebody (the accused) maintaining that they, in fact, did not commit the crime.

Mr. Acker: Sometimes we border on fooling ourselves that the very elaborate legal rules that have been designed to govern death penalty cases in fact are effective. Because as you've pointed out, these are very, very emotionally charged cases.

It's doubtful that jurors can follow all of the rigorous instructions that they get from the bench. It's natural that their emotions will take over. As humans, they are searching for signs of remorse. We know that from empirical studies. We know that despite the way that laws are constructed, jurors often will go back into the jury room and begin to discuss issues that are not properly before them, such as future dangerousness, is this person going to kill again.

And there is a very difficult structural problem that was designed to respond to other constitutional problems that involve separating the guilty phase of the trial from the punishment phase. And you've identified a problem that has vexed defense attorneys for a long, long time. How do I plead not guilty? I didn't do it. Mount a defense, and then in the face of a conviction, ask this same jury to share the sentiment that I am truly sorry for doing what I denied doing in that other phase of the trial.

If we were looking exclusively at procedural devices, to try to circumvent that undoubtable problem, it would come in the form of, for separate phases of a capital trial, impaneling separate juries.

I know this was discussed back in 1965 – or '95. It was. (And) it is true, as you point out, that people with very strong convictions against capital punishment are not allowed to participate in any aspect of a capital trial. They are excluded. They are not "death qualified".

One possible solution is to dispense with the requirement for a death-qualified jury at the guilty phase. Let everybody in this room, pro, con, indifferent about the death penalty, decide guilt or innocence. You'll see a much more representative segment of the community deciding difficult questions of guilt or innocence.

If and only if there is a capital conviction, (then) impanel a separate jury that's comprised of people who can and will follow the law, including enforcing the death penalty if appropriate. (These jurors will be) . . . responsive to the difficulty of the contradictory faces that are presented (at trial) – I didn't do it, or I'm sorry – because it will be, after a fair trial on guilt or innocence, where the accused doesn't have to say a word and can deny responsibility. Now that responsibility has been determined, (and the defendant will now) come before a new jury, a different jury, that would . . . be more receptive to (mitigating and aggravating) evidence that is . . . admissible at the punishment phase.

Mr. O'Donnell: Thank you, very much.

Pace Law School Professor Bennett Gershman added that the striking of fair-minded jurors who generally oppose capital punishment could "skew" or influence the guilt or innocence phase of a capital trial in favor of the prosecution.

In many ways, the testimony of Professor William Bowers of Northeastern University's Capital Jury Project presented the most disturbing challenges to the reliability and trustworthiness of jury decision-making in capital punishment trials.

Professor William Bowers, Capital Jury Project, Northeastern University: I'm a principal research scientist at Northeastern University in Boston. I have a long history of researching capital punishment. I've written a couple of books, EXECUTIONS IN AMERICA (1977), and, LEGAL HOMICIDE: DEATH AS PUNISHMENT IN AMERICA (1984), that are based on statistical kinds of evidence about the death penalty.

I became involved in this research shortly after the Supreme Court handed down the <u>Furman</u> decision declaring the death penalty unconstitutional as it was being performed. And so, I've been working on capital punishment in its modern form, so to speak . . . .

Well, the project I want to tell you about today is a study that was actually, I might say, inspired by the Court's decision (in <u>McCleskey v. Kemp</u>) because the Court said it wouldn't impeach the work of the jury on the strength of statistical evidence about (racial) disparities in sentencing outcomes. That it would have to know about the process, the decision process. It didn't want to impeach the jurors, the jury. It held too much reverence for the jury.

So, I sat down with others I had come to know in working on this issue, who were from other states where the death penalty was, you know, being renewed. And we formulated a proposal to the National Science Foundation for a study, which has come to be known as the Capital Jury Project (C.J.P), which now encompasses 14 states. There were 14 states in which C.J.P. investigators interviewed 1200 jurors from 353 capital cases . . . .

This is a project that was essentially operated as a consortium of these investigators, working together to design the research interview structure, the protocol. The interviews took three and a half hours, on the average, of these jurors. We targeted four jurors in each case, each trial, that was our target. Some cases we got a few more, others we didn't reach the target of four, but that was how we developed the sample.

And we had equal numbers of life and death cases so we could compare the results for . . . how jurors were . . . making a decision for these two kinds of different outcome situations.

There have now been some 40 published articles in the scholarly journals, law reviews, based on the research we've conducted. I want to talk about – naturally I can't try to summarize all of the detail of it, but there's one recent publication[52] that brings together these results more succinctly than, I think, any other, and I want to talk about that one briefly now. . . .

This report essentially identifies seven areas in which the death penalty is failing to meet the constitutional mandates of the Supreme Court about the way jurors are supposed to deal with or handle the (death penalty) decision process. . . .

(T)he question of how the jury makes its decision is – it's been under a veil (of secrecy). . . . (N)obody has access. You know, the veil is drawn, so that the jury room is a private, privileged, locus for the decision process. The only way to find out about it is to ask jurors and that's what we did.

Number one: We found that half of the jurors reported that they believed they knew what the punishment should be during the guilty stage of the trial. Now, the Supreme Court endorsed the return to capital punishment under a bifurcated trial system where the guilt stage and the punishment (stage) – there would be a separate punishment stage of the trial.

And they would separate them so that the punishment stage could be guided by statutory aggravating and mitigating considerations, and that's – the jurors were supposed to make the punishment decision at the second, penalty, stage of the trial.

This research reveals unambiguously that half of the jurors say they thought they knew what the punishment should be (at the guilt phase). Seven out of ten thought they knew what it should be, said they were absolutely convinced. And all the remaining (interviewed jurors) except for a couple percent say they were pretty sure what the punishment should be during the guilty stage of the trial.

So, the law might prescribe a separation of this decision, the same way you can, maybe, in a math class, cut the problem into two parts or something. But it seems quite evident from these data that human beings, when they are asked to make the guilt and the punishment decision separately, find that very difficult to do and are not doing it.

We found that they talk about what the punishment should be during the guilt stage of the trial. We found that (in) the guilt stage . . . decisions are (influenced by what punishment should be imposed) – not only did (jurors) say they were absolutely convinced (of the sentence), seven out of ten, but they say – they stick to those positions. We had (jurors) . . . saying yeah, they thought (the) punishment should be death . . . they stuck to that . . . . (I)t was remarkably consistent – we have every indication of this violation of the great inspired bifurcation of a trial.

The second and related point is we asked them a question that said: "For the following types of murder, do you believe the punishment – the death penalty - is the only acceptable punishment, is sometimes acceptable, or is unacceptable?"

We listed typically aggravated murders, someone killing in prison, a previous (or prior) killing, somebody who killed a police officer, a prison guard. . . .

Of those . . . things I've described, the kinds of killings, half or more (jurors who sat on capital cases) said that death was the only acceptable punishment, instead of (saying) that it's sometimes acceptable or unacceptable.

Now, there's law in <u>Morgan v. Illinois</u>[53] where the (Supreme) Court says that death penalty jurors are not qualified if they cannot give effect to mitigation. But if someone tells you that death is the only acceptable sentence... (it is not) hard to imagine how unsuccessful the jury selection procedure is. There was discussion earlier about the question of, well, do we have people who automatically mete out death or who automatically wouldn't. Here what we find is (that) they're all ... (very certain about what the sentence should be).

Let me go on to the third point. The third point is about understanding jury instructions. We asked them about the (legal) guidelines and rules (they received) for consideration of aggravation and mitigation. It's decidedly different rules that govern aggravation and mitigation. The rules for mitigation, someone earlier mentioned, mean that the individual jurors (make) a decision, each juror decides what ... mitigating consideration ... matters.

And the (standard) of true beyond a reasonable doubt is not the standard. In a couple of states it's preponderance of evidence; and elsewhere it's to the satisfaction of the individual juror.

These are contrary to notions that we get from television about how trials go. People, these jurors, 50 percent or more, fail to understand the rules, the guidelines for how mitigation should be considered. The gist of these ... misunderstandings was to impose on mitigation a stricter standard that tilts the death decision, the sentencing decision, towards death. In other words, they impose standards ... (for) mitigation ... (that were) the same standards as (those for) aggravation, and that works against the consideration of mitigation.

I'll move on here to number four. (T)here were some decisions of the Court at the same time as the <u>Gregg</u> decision that made it clear that the law could not require that the death sentence be imposed. The Court rejected the mandatory death sentence, essentially, and said that (the) judgment, that (the) sentencing decision, must entail a consideration of the character of the defendant, and the nature of the crime, and couldn't – under no circumstance did the law require the death penalty be imposed.

We asked them, did the evidence (in the case they heard) prove, when we asked them, that the crime was heinous, vile, or depraved. About eighty percent said it did. We asked them, did it prove the defendant would be dangerous in the future, and nearly as many said that was so.

And the next set of questions, if the law proved that, and if that evidence proved that, did the law require you to impose the death sentence? 40-three percent said that if the defendant – if the crime was heinous (and) vile - that a death penalty was required by law; and 37 (percent) said it was required by law if the defendant was dangerous, would be dangerous in the future. . . .

So, yet again, there is an utter failure to recognize or understand (the law) on the part of jurors. That under no circumstances does the law require a death sentence.

We then asked them a question about who is responsible (for the death sentence). This is point number five.

The questions read: Which of the following is most responsible? And it listed (those who could be) responsible for the defendant's punishment: the law that provides for the death penalty; the judge who imposes it; the jury, because, you know, it has to vote for the death sentence; (the) individual juror because the vote needs to be unanimous for a death sentence; and the defendant, because he's the one that, after all, committed the crime.

The picture here is of people scurrying every which way to evade responsibility, foremost, responsibility for the punishment. Now, sure, if we didn't have the law we wouldn't have a death sentence, and then, sure, if the guy hadn't committed a crime (there would be no sentence). But, the question is about the punishment; who is responsible for the punishment?

Well, I can talk a lot further on this topic, but I think it should be clear that the punishment decision, it (is) the decision of the jurors. It's not their responsibility for making the law, but . . . (only) about six percent of the jurors said the individual juror (was responsible), another eight percent said (it was) the law . . .

15 percent, less than 20 percent of these folks, could see themselves individually, or as jurors, as foremost responsible for the punishment.

Number six; a question of what the alternative would be. In all 14 of these states we asked them, . . . how long would a defendant not given the death sentence usually spend in prison before returning to society? In every state the jurors said the defendant would usually be back in society sooner than the law permits, . . . (sooner than when they would) become eligible for parole consideration.

So they imagine that the defendant would be, you know, (out) far sooner. (Y)ou can see how this mistaken view about returning, about getting back in society early, . . . became a . . . critical . . . (factor in) a life and death vote. As the death (penalty decision-making) process is continued we can see that this misunderstanding becomes a critical point in the decision process, especially towards the end. It seemed to be one thing they argue(d) about at the end.

But . . . they're making what the Supreme Court has called a false choice between the death penalty and a mistaken view about the alternative . . . . (S)uppose the law does prescribe life without parole, then they must understand that that's the alternative. Four of these states had (the) death penalty (and) the alternative to death penalty was life in prison without the possibility of parole. You'll see that (in) those states jurors would call it folk wisdom. They bring with them to these trials folk wisdom. Competent, informed, responsible jury functioning (is a) legal fiction. (It is a myth) that the instructions we give them (are understood), written often in legalese language so that the judge can't be reversed and the attorneys – usually the judge will read the instructions and then ask the attorneys is that okay? And you know, when the instructions are supposed to be, somehow or other, you know, supposed to instruct the jurors. (This doesn't happen). Let me go to point seven. Point seven is race and racism. . . .

Mr. Lentol: Professor Bowers, you were quoted in the LaValle decision (from a) Texas law review article regarding the issue of capital jurors, actually, most of whom believe that the defendant, at some point in time, is going to get out on the street. ... I wonder if you think, in view of that, whether or not it's possible for us to come up with a deadlock jury instruction that could meet constitutional muster.

Professor Bowers: (I)n response to your question, you know, it's my feeling, from this work I've done, that the guidelines, instructions, and choices that are being given to jurors are not functioning as the drafters of these statutes had hoped or thought they would.

It might be possible to change the deadlock phrasing . . . .

I guess what I'm wanting to say is that even if you could rewrite that particular provision and all the jurors got it real clear, I feel that the evidence we have suggests that you haven't begun to remedy the problems that death penalty statutes have, because you're not making or enabling jurors to do what I think the Supreme Court and what probably the New York constitution would insist has to happen.

Mr. Lentol: I guess the question that ought to be asked, that hasn't been asked yet, is this one: No matter what you do, if the choice is death and something else, are juries always going to think that the defendant is going to get out at some point, even if you tell them that it's life without parole?

Professor Bowers: That was the biggest surprise that we found . . . . that in Georgia, 60-some-odd percent of the jurors thought the defendant would be out in seven years. We went back, and we found out that back in 1939 Georgia enacted some very progressive things which meant that the (capital) defendant would be eligible for parole consideration, . . . all defendants, you know, death and everybody - and (there developed a 7 year time period that) was translated in politics and in campaigning, in the media, in jurors minds, (into) a likely release time.

Now, we found out, when we checked with the corrections folks there, that nobody who had got a death sentence would be even considered for (parole for at least) fifteen years, (and) that (in) gubernatorial campaigns, and (in) the judge elections, you know, the death penalty... and the crimes (involved) generate so much fear in the public, and so much hatred and vengeful feelings, that myths (such as the 7 years and out) become reality in terms of which jurors work.

This is not a very happy situation for those of us who believe in the rule of the law, but it does say that when you can discover that the rule of law is not working the way it's supposed to, you know, you don't want to put your head in the sand and declare, oh ... we've done our job, because we've told them how they should behave, especially now that we can see they don't do it that way.

A final word on the reliability of death penalty jury verdicts came from Attorney John Dunne who served in the New York State Senate for many years, was Assistant Attorney General in the Civil Rights Division of the U.S. Justice Department from 1990-1993, chaired the N.Y. State Capital Defenders Office from 1997-1999, and was, at the time of the Hearings, in private practice.

Is it possible for jurors to genuinely keep an open mind after a guilty verdict? While life imprisonment without parole verdicts seem to indicate that the answer may be, in some cases, yes, I now have profound doubts about how the death penalty itself interferes with our jury system: the stress on capital jurors, their empirically documented confusion with court instructions, and the pressure on them from media clamor, (these) all lead me to conclude that the problems of death penalty decision-making, and the hidden juror miscalculations associated with constitutionally-required capital jury instructions . . . (are) intractable, randomly generated, and frequently unobserved.

In concluding this Chapter, it should be noted again that the N.Y. Hearings were held because of a decision on jury instructions, People v. LaValle. The New York Court of Appeals ruled in 2004 that it was unconstitutional under state law to instruct a capital jury during the sentencing phase of a case that if the jury did not agree unanimously on a sentence of death or LWOP, the judge would be required to sentence the defendant to life in prison with parole eligibility after a minimum of 20 - 25 years. In light of the testimony presented in this Chapter that capital jurors are strongly influenced by emotion, that they make up their minds on a sentence early in the trial, and that they fail to understand or follow the court's instructions, it is not surprising that the Court of Appeals found this instruction to be potentially coercive. From this Chapter's testimony, one can see that jurors might agree to a death sentence that they don't believe in based on a fear that a judge's sentence with parole availability could lead to the release of a dangerous and depraved killer. As the Court observed, jury decision-making of this kind carries an "unacceptable risk . . . (of an) arbitrary and unreliable sentence." This problem seems to permeate the jury trial system in capital cases.

CHAPTER FIVE: SPECIAL PROBLEMS - RACE AND MENTAL ILLNESS

Recent decisions of the United States Supreme Court have recognized three types of crimes and criminals that are categorically ineligible for the death penalty: the mentally retarded; juveniles; and child rapists who do not kill. [54] In each of these categories, the Court found that the justifications for capital punishment set forth in Chapter Three of this book did not apply and that the state death sentence imposed in each case was unconstitutional under the Eighth Amendment.

The New York Death Penalty Hearings addressed two other areas of death penalty controversy – race and mental illness – that have yet to be conclusively settled by the Court. Significant legal and policy issues exist in these areas. Two Hearings questions focused witness testimony.

> II. 3. Did the 1995 (death penalty) statues provide appropriate protections against convictions and imposition of the death penalty by virtue of bias applicable to the race or ethnicity of death penalty defendants or murder victims? If not, what additional steps would be necessary to achieve that goal?

> II. 13. The 1995 statute contained extensive provisions related to a jury's consideration of a defendant's possible mental impairment when determining whether the death penalty should be imposed. How well did these provisions operate? Would these provisions need to be revised if the death penalty in New York were reinstated?

Race

The history of American capital punishment is inextricably bound up with the history of race relations in the United States. Our death penalty experience originates with slavery, the lynch mob, and hangings of African Americans. When it comes to race, many critics of the death penalty continue to equate it with the "legal lynchings" that marred decades of treatment of racial minorities in this country. Chapter Five begins with Hearings testimony on this sensitive topic.

Kathryn Kase, Staff Attorney for the Texas Defender Service, represented five death row inmates in Texas prisons at the time of her testimony, and made some critical initial points.

> Ms. Kase: (T)he thing that I want to point out is that one of the things that we see, and it's a comparison here as well, is that around the nation, but particularly in places like Texas, but I think it's also true in New York, (is that) if you kill a white victim, you're more likely to get the death penalty no matter what your race or gender is.
>
> And until last year, until February of last year, Texas had not executed anyone since reinstituting the death penalty in 1974 who had killed a non-white victim.
>
> So you know, we went . . . through more than 300 people that we executed who had only killed white victims, which said that non-white victims basically, you know, sorry, you're lives are worth less . . . .
>
> But you also see that (same white victim phenomenon) in the northeast. (T)he explanation I hear the most in the south is that the use of capital punishment mirrors the use of lynching in the non-white population. And I've read studies about that, and I've heard scholars talk about it.

One of the best known of these scholars is David Baldus. Professor Baldus, of the University of Iowa College of Law, co-authored one of the most famous studies on race and the death penalty, D. Baldus and G. Woodworth, "Race Discrimination in America's Capital Punishment System Since <u>Furman v. Georgia</u> (1972): The Evidence of Race Disparities and the Record of Our Courts and Legislatures in Addressing This Issue" (1977). [55] A later, 1983, study by Professors Baldus and others, "Comparative Review of Death Sentences: An Empirical Study of the Georgia Experience" [56], became the focus of the United States Supreme Court's 1987 decision in the case of

<u>McCleskey v. Kemp</u> .[57] The Court determined in that case that general patterns of racial discrimination in a death penalty system, without proof of specific discrimination against the accused defendant, did not require the setting aside of an otherwise valid death sentence. <u>McCleskey</u> remains the rule today.

> Mr. Baldus: Mr. Chairman and members of the Committee, I'm pleased to have the invitation to appear here today. My name is David Baldus, and I'm a law professor at the University of Iowa College of Law. My specialty is law and social science, and within that area, I have conducted studies of the capital sentencing systems in the various states of the nation for the last 25 years. I've done, myself, (and) with my colleague, George Woodworth, extensive empirical studies in Georgia, Colorado, Maryland, Philadelphia and New Jersey, and I'm also familiar with the findings of other studies that have been done by other scholars in California, Illinois, Kentucky and Florida.
>
> And that's the basis on which I'm making my statements here today, about how our systems work in terms of the arbitrariness and discrimination that are produced by contemporary capital sentencing systems.
>
> In addition to focusing on the evidence of arbitrariness and discrimination, our work is concentrated on various legal procedures that have been adopted in other jurisdictions to reduce the risk of arbitrariness and discrimination. In that regard, for three years, between 1988 and 1991, I served as a special master for the New Jersey Supreme Court to help them establish a system of proportionality review, which allows them to monitor the actual fact-finding patterns (of capital juries) in their system and adjudicate claims of excessiveness and racial discrimination.
>
> And it's against this background that I examined the available data on the operations of the New York death penalty system since it was reinstituted in 1995.
>
> I'm going to speak about four aspects of my empirical findings, which are based on the database maintained by the

(New York) Capital Defender's Office.... This analysis raises a number of concerns about the fairness and the operation of the New York death penalty system . ... (F)irst (please note) ... how infrequently the death sentence is used in this state. In addition to no executions thus far, there have only been seven death sentences imposed. It's interesting to note that (in terms of) the frequency of death sentencing here among murder one indicted cases, an important subclass of death eligible cases, the death sentencing rate has been one percent. The United States Supreme Court, in <u>Furman v. Georgia</u> (1972), expressed great concern about infrequent death sentencing because it raised the risk of inconsistency and arbitrariness in the system.

And I think this evidence presents a prima facie suggestion that there may be a problem in your system in that regard.

(The) analysis ... focuses on race of victim discrimination in this system. Now, I want to emphasize, unadjusted numbers, like I'm presenting here, are not a basis to infer whether discrimination does or does not exist. To do that you need to have a thorough empirical study that takes into account the severity of the offenses that are involved.

But what is interesting about this is the consistency of these findings with what we found in many other jurisdictions .... I'll give you an example .... (A)mong murder one indicted cases, 31 percent of those cases involved white victim cases. However, if you look at the people who received death sentences ... you can see that 71 percent of those people had white victims in their cases, one or more white victims.

That tells us that having a white victim keeps you at risk of receiving the death sentence longer than if your victim was non-white. And that's the same pattern we see nationwide. About 55 percent of the victims of homicide are white. If you look at the people who are on death row, 80 percent of (their) victims are Caucasian. Now, to get more focused ... (look at) where these race effects are coming into the system. The most prominent source of them is at the stage where the M1 (first degree murder) case (has) been indicted (and a) death notice (issued).

That is, the government sends a notice that they intend to seek a death sentence.

The rate at which death notices are served is about three-and-a-half times higher (with) white victim cases. . . . So that you can say that the risk of having your case death noticed is much higher in a white victim case, and also, if you look at the actual outcomes of the penalty trial, (with) death sentencing decisions . . . you can see that it is a much greater risk of receiving a death sentence (with white victim cases).

The consequence of that is, if you look at death sentencing among all (first degree murder) indicted cases, (that) white victim cases are five times more likely to result in a death sentence. And that's a statistically significant difference.

Professor Blecker mentioned here this morning that the explanation for this is the fact that in counties where you have a (large) . . .white population, prosecutors are more willing to seek a death sentence. That may have an effect, but that's an empirical question.

One of the suggestions that I'm going to make to you as a legislative body is that you conduct a thorough-going empirical study of your system, to make a reliable estimate of what race affects there are in the system and what the sources of them may be.

Now, . . . in contrast to what is generally the understanding of race discrimination and the death sentence, black offenders here in New York are at lower risk of receiving a death sentence once they get in the system. And that's all we're looking at, the decisions made in the system. They're at lower risk of receiving a death sentence than non-black offenders. This is not to suggest that there may not be discrimination against black defendants in individual cases, but there's no evidence in this state that we're seeing any systemic bias against black defendants in the way we're seeing evidence of systemic bias against people who have white victims.

And you'll notice (that) the rate (or number) of the death sentences being served is lower in the black defendant cases

than in the other cases. The rate of death sentencing is lower.
And as a consequence, the overall rate of death sentencing
among M1 indicted cases is lower in the black defendant cases
than in the other defendant's cases.

People might say how can that be. The explanation for that
odd finding, in the face of what the general understanding is, is
that what it's reflecting is the race of victim affect that you're
seeing in the system. As has been pointed out, most homicide is
intraracial. Most black defendants have killed other blacks, and
the system is less punitive to those who have black victims than
it is to have those that have white victims. The beneficiaries of
that less punitive treatment of the black victim cases are the
black defendants themselves. So that's what produces this
curious result of . . . less punitive . . . (consequences) overall for
the black defendants; it's a product of the victim race affects that
are operating in the system.

But again, as I'm indicating to you, I don't have any controls
here for the severity of these offenses, therefore, it's important
for you to consider as a legislative body in my judgment, the
prospect of commissioning a study to examine how the system
works.

Assemblyman Lentol: What about white defendants who kill
white victims, as opposed to white defendants who kill black
victims?

Mr. Baldus: Well, there are very few of the latter, sir, but
basically what it appears here to be is that it's mainly the race of
the victim, regardless of who the defendant is in the case, it
seems to have the biggest affect.

Finally, . . . (there is) the question of geographic disparities in
the use of the death penalty. There are many ways you can slice
up the counties in New York, and I'm kind of a novice being from
out in the mid-west, so I took kind of a standard breakdown I see
used in the New York Times, upstate and downstate, and I've
indicated here which are the downstate counties, Bronx, Queens,

New York, Kings, Richmond, Nassau, Suffolk, Rockland and Westchester. What you see is a very interesting pattern here. That if you're upstate, the prosecutors are much more prone to file a death notice, to charge a case capitally in the first place, and to file a death notice in the case, than they are downstate.

But on the other hand, in the cases that are death noticed, downstate, the prosecutors are more likely to take those cases to a penalty trial and the juries are more likely to return a death sentence. So we have higher capital charging patterns upstate, but higher penalty trial rates and death sentencing rates downstate. So, . . . (that appears to result) in basically a parity in the death sentencing rates in the two parts of the state. Nevertheless, these disparities and the use of death sentencing upstate are statistically significant and it puts people in upstate situations at a much higher risk of being exposed to a capital punishment.

Now, the other thing that I've indicated that you should look at is, what are states doing when they have concerns about fairness and the possible affects of race in a system. One of the things they do is a study of a system. There are over 10 jurisdictions that have commissioned empirical studies by one institution or another of their system.

And that's one of the things that I would recommend that you might want to consider doing. Or, appoint a commissioner and just commission a study . . . .

(A)n . . . alternative that I'd like to recommend to you to consider is the Racial Justice Act. The Racial Justice Act basically says that a defendant may raise a claim in a trial court asserting race discrimination in the charging decision or in the sentencing decision in his or her case, and present evidence to that affect. We have experience in the State of Kentucky, which has such a statute, that it has a desirable affect. It has made people, made the prosecutors, much more sensitive to the racial consequences of what they have done. It's allowed defendants to bring claims and to do discovery and to be able to look at the pattern of decision making in cases by prosecutors, and in my estimation, having examined the empirical evidence in Kentucky, before and after that statute, it does have desirable affects.

The final Hearings report referred to the following data from Professor Baldus's study of the New York death penalty experience:

- Seven of the 500, or one percent, of first degree murder case defendants were sentenced to death;
- Death notices were filed in 58 of these 500 cases;
- Of the 58 cases in which prosecutors filed a death notice, 12 percent of the defendants were sentenced to death (seven cases);
- The first degree murder cases involving white victims were 3.3 times more likely to receive a death notice than those where the victim was non-white;
- Among the seven defendants who received the death penalty, white victim cases outnumbered non-white victim cases by a two to one margin (62 percent vs. 29 percent);
- Black defendants were 59 percent of first degree murder cases and 43 percent of those sentenced to death.[58]

The Hearings report provided additional race-based data and noted that "Several witnesses introduced similar statistics (to those cited above) compiled by the New York State Captial Defender's Office."

Of 459 defendants indicted for first degree murder, 59% were Black, 19% were White, and 21% were Hispanic. Death notices were filed in 50 cases; 48% were Black, 40% were White, and 10% were Hispanic. Race of the victim was known in 446 cases; 42% were Black, 31% were White, and 20% were Hispanic (the remaining victims were of multiple races). Race of the victim in the death-noticed cases equaled 30% Black, 48% White, and 14% Hispanic.

According to the report, "Based on these records, Ann Brandon of the League of Women Voters reported that of the seven defendants sentenced to death under the 1995 New York law, three are black, three are white and one is Hispanic."

Remarks similar to those made by Professor Baldus were made by Attorney Christina Swarns of the NAACP Legal Defense fund.

> (U.S. Supreme Court) Justice William Douglas . . . eloquently explained the reasons why (a death penalty) statute, even though it was racially neutral on its face, (could be) unconstitutional. He explained that any law that stated that anyone making more than $50,000 would be exempt from the death penalty would plainly fall, as would a law that in terms said that blacks, those who never went beyond the fifth grade in school, those who made less than $3,000 a year, or those who were unpopular or unstable should be the only people executed. A law which in the overall view reaches the same results in practice has no (greater) sanctity than a law which in (explicit) terms provides the same.
>
> So, the fact that it was racially neutral on its face was not enough to protect the death penalty statute . . . from being found unconstitutional. . . (in <u>Furman v. Georgia</u>).
>
> Unfortunately, we now know that (modern) guided discretion statutes have not removed race from the death penalty calculus. Race remains a critical factor in who lives and who dies. As described by other people who have testified today, race plays a significant role in which defendants are actually sentenced to death, in which victims for whom (the) death (penalty) is sought, and in which jurors . . . make the death penalty decision.
>
> Across the country, nationwide, although 12% of the U.S. population is . . . African American, 42% of the inmates on death row are African American and 34% of the inmates who have been executed since the reinstatement of the death penalty have been African American. With respect to the issue of victims, although 47% of homicide victims, nationwide, are African

American, only 13% of the (killers) of (these) victims ... were black.

Clearly, race is determining which defendants are being sentenced to death and ... the defendants with white victims are the ones for whom death is being sought. As Professor Baldus has already described, this is not a phenomenon that is only outside of New York, that is only in the south. Professor Baldus has done extensive research in lots of northern jurisdictions, he talked about New Jersey, he's also done research in Pennsylvania and Philadelphia, and he has obviously submitted data to this body about the early preliminary results of his analysis of this data in New York and that data reflects the same disparities as we find across the country.

So, with even all the protections that this body attempted to implement in (the) 1995 (death penalty law), it has not been successful in removing race from the decision of who is and who is not executed. A lot of people will say that the statistics don't mean anything, that there are lots of possible reasons for those kinds of disparities, that it's not race that's informing these (decisions on) who lives and who dies, and which victim's (killers) get death and which victim's (killers) don't get death.

Well, there has been a lot of studies ... looking into that question ... And I can tell you that there is not one study that has found a non-racial answer to that question. In fact, to the contrary, the United States General Accounting Office in 1990 issued a report to the Senate and House Committees on Judiciary, (and) that report evaluated 28 separate studies of the death penalty from various regions of the country. And that report concluded that those studies all show a pattern of ... racial disparities in the charging, sentencing and imposition of the death penalty after the Furman decision.[59]

So, ... all the studies that have been conducted have found some form of racial disparity and racial bias in the administration of the death penalty. Because (even with) all of our work ... to create a statute that removes race from the death penalty calculus, despite the fact that we have endeavored, judges, legislators, attorneys, all throughout this country, have tried very hard to come up with a statute that prevents race from playing a role, we have been unsuccessful.

And because we cannot create a statute that completely removes race from the sentencing calculation I think that this body should . . . not reinstate the death penalty in New York and we should just go forward without a death penalty. Thank you.

Now, consider the lengthy testimony of Attorney George Kendall:

Mr. George Kendall, Esq., Holland & Knight: Thank you very much. My name is George Kendall. I'm an attorney. For 25 years I have represented capitally charged clients in trial courts, and represented them through direct appeals and into state post-conviction and federal habeas proceedings, and at the Supreme Court.

(T)here's a real historical pedigree for . . . (these hearings) . . . (because) our country has been trying to get the death penalty right for over two hundred years.

And we try and we try and we try, and each time we have major reform we think, we hope, we've solved the problem(s), and after 20 years goes by and there's a rich body of evidence, we see that once again we failed.

The last time we did this, the last time that your former colleagues in legislatures around the country did what you are doing, was in the wake of the Furman decision from the Supreme Court in 1972 . . . .

(In Furman) the Court looked at how the (death penalty) statutes worked and saw that poverty was playing too large a role in deciding who was selected for capital trial and who was actually getting the death penalty and who was not; and also race, that the evidence showed quite clearly that when the death penalty could have been imposed for crimes other than homicide, in a rape case, for example, 90 percent of the defendants who had been put to death for rape in the 30 years before Furman had been African-American.

(The Court required) three protections.

For the first time in our history criminal trials were bifurcated. There was a guilt phase and there was a sentencing phase, very formally done. (Second), at the sentencing phase, for the first time in our history, there were factors that were designated aggravating factors and mitigating factors. And the whole point of this was to focus the sentencers, in most states juries, in some states judges, on the only relevant factors that should be considered when making a responsible choice between death and a life sentence.

And thirdly, what all these statutes had was the command of (a) hands (-on) penalty (re)view, that the state supreme courts have to really step up to the plate and look very carefully at these trials, . . . (from) conviction to death sentence, and make sure that no arbitrary factor affected the scale of justice, and might have been responsible for a sentence of death being imposed.

(What) I want to talk some about (today is) race, (and how) it continues to play a very significant role (in death penalty cases), not just in a few places, but in most places.

And what we see overall is that white-victim cases are the cases that get the most attention from the D.A.s, and are the ones more often than not where juries impose the death penalty. I'm going to talk a little about that in a minute.

There has been a link between the death penalty and racism since the beginning of our country, from the slave codes to the black codes to Jim Crow, to a period in time in the '20s and '30s . . . when all the capital jurors would never leave the courtroom. They'd hear evidence in a case involving a black defendant and white victim, and they would vote to convict and impose a death sentence without even leaving the courtroom.

Let me tell you, in my experience in the last 25 years, how race gets into the process. It starts up oftentimes with the news media. Now, I think the world of the First Amendment. Our country would be a far worse place to live in if we did not have a vital First Amendment. But there are times when the media acts irresponsibly, and in its coverage of crime oftentimes it acts very irresponsibly.

We're seeing it play out again in New York City now, with the tragic homicide of . . . (a) young white actress. There have been other murders in New York City during the past two weeks. The editors of newspapers have decided to focus on that crime. There have been individuals arrested; they are minority. They have been villainized, and in many parts of this country, and including New York, that puts tremendous pressure on the prosecution to be tough. And it puts even horrible pressure on the victim's family to also be tough.

And one of the ways you have to be tough now in America is that when something horrible like this happens, you have to support the efforts of the prosecutor to seek the death penalty. But others have spoken more eloquent(ly) than I ever could about this, but it's very real.

The media oftentimes flags these cases, and it puts pressure on the prosecutor and the system to see that the harshest sentence is returned, even though the offenders in those cases are oftentimes way far from the worst of the worst, who we're supposed to reserve the death penalty for.

This kind of coverage affects the prosecutors. In most parts of our country prosecutors are elected. And in too many places they can be elected without one minority vote. And I would have never thought this was the case when I started to do capital work, but it is not surprising that there is intense pressure to win these cases, and by win, the only way you win a capital case is by giving a death sentence.

But what we're seeing in these cases is an enormous amount of misconduct, that some prosecutors are willing to cheat in these cases so that they can win, when I think in noncapital cases, and some of these cases, they would not. And the reason why they do it is because of little or no sanctions. There have been hundreds of instances now in the last 25 years, quarter of a century, where there's been horrific misconduct in cases by prosecutors, by law enforcement officials, and there are very few cases where there's been anything more than the most mild of sanctions.

Race also affects the delivery (and effectiveness) of defense services. Imagine my surprise when I met my client Eddie Lee Ross in Georgia in 1984. He's African-American, been charged with the homicide of two elderly white females. He had been on death row for three years. His lead lawyer at trial was the former imperial wizard of the Ku Klux Klan in Georgia, who made no effort to do any investigation on this case, and advised his client to take the stand to testify that he had not committed the crime after co-counsel had put on an insanity defense.

Or when I met Nathan Brown, another African-American defendant whose lawyer, the public defender, referred to him when I went to see him as a – excuse the language – a nigger. And through my hour-long meeting with the trial lawyer, that's how he referred to his client, who was on death row.

Or when I met Victor Roberts, another African-American defendant, who also had been convicted of killing a white female. The entire time I talked to his lawyer, the only way he referred to Mr. Roberts was to call him "boy." Mr. Roberts was 24 years old at the time that he and his lawyer worked together.

Well, there's no way these individuals ever trusted the lawyers who had their life in their hands at trial. And in fact, in the Roberts case, after we won full habeas corpus relief for him, and went back to the trial court – I'd known Vic for eight years at that point, and he said to me, he said, "You know, George, I think you're a good lawyer; you've gotten me relief, but the last time I was tried I was the only black person in the courtroom. Do you think that maybe we could have an African-American lawyer on the defense team when we go back to trial?"

Okay. I'm glad Mr. Roberts told me that, because that taught me a great lesson, that in these cases – I will never do another case involving a minority defendant with an all-white defense team, because there's information, there's things that I'm never going to learn about that client in that case, (but) that I will (learn) if I have an integrated, mixed-race team.

How else does race come into the system? With jury selection. There are hundreds of African-American defendants who were tried in communities with substantial minority populations, who were tried before all white juries, hundreds of them.

Now, the problem is not in the (composition), so much, of the pools, the jury pools. 30 years ago that was a huge problem. (In) some states women were not in the pools. That's not the problem any more. In a lot of places minorities were very thinly represented. Speaking generally, that is not a huge problem any more, but (today), the problem comes with the peremptory strikes that are used in capital cases by the prosecution. Now, if you don't believe me, just look at the record in the Miller-E1[60] cases presently before the United States Supreme Court. It's from Dallas, not a backwater place. The case was tried in 1986 and there's a horrific record of racial discrimination by that district attorney's office. Not simply in the Miller-El case, but in scores of cases before it.

And what's deeply troubling about that case is that Mr. Miller-El came within a day of being executed before the stay was imposed. Every lower court, state and federal, had found insufficient evidence of discrimination to stop that execution. And just, if you go back and read the Supreme Court appeal in that case, from 2003, it's unthinkable that (legally) there wasn't enough evidence to show that there was a likelihood that racial bias affected the impaneling of that jury. There were four very qualified, very conservative African-American jurors who were struck (eliminated from the jury). They were struck because they were African-American.

There's another case you're going to be hearing a lot about. (T)he so-called great liberal Ninth Circuit Court of Appeals in San Francisco earlier this week just denied rehearing it in the Stanley Williams case.[61] Mr. Williams was a gang banger from Los Angeles, tried before an all-white jury, where several persons of color were struck by a D.A. who had been sanctioned previously for this kind of misconduct in other cases.

This is a problem that existed a hundred years ago; it continues to haunt our system that the juries are being manipulated by this kind of misconduct.

At best I think there's a question (whether) . . . if the system works perfectly, are we going to get it right 85 percent of the time? On race, if the system acts perfectly, it's going to be far less than that. This is the problem that's haunted our history and is going to continue to do so.

Lastly, let me end with sort of a case in point. I just completed a case, a capital case in Louisiana, involving a man who was three times death-sentenced in Louisiana. His name is Wilbert Rideau. He was charged with a – he's African-American, and the victim in this case was white.

It was a failed bank robbery and one of the tellers was killed in the process. And in '61, in '64, and in 1970, he was tried before all-white, all-male juries. In '61 his trial took the jury 55 minutes to convict him and impose the death penalty. In '64 it took the jury 15 minutes. And in 1970 it took the jury eight minutes to convict and impose a death sentence.

He spent 12 years in solitary confinement. During that time he decided that he wanted his life to stand for more than the worst thing he had ever done, and with the aid of white prison guards who risked their job to smuggle in reading material, he taught himself to read and write.

In the wake of the Furman decision, in 1973 his death sentence was changed to a life sentence. And after bloody prison riots that took place in Angola prison a new administration came to that prison and decided that for the first time in the history of that state that institution was going to be integrated; before it had been strictly segregated. And before (that) there had been this fledgling little mimeographed newsletter called the Angolite, which only white prisoners could work on.

Well, the new warden came in and had heard the Mr. Rideau had turned himself into a very good writer and named him as the editor. In the next 25 years he turned that little publication into the best piece of journalism anywhere in the country or the world coming out of a prison.

To the great credit of the administration they allowed (the prisoners) to write about anything that they could prove was true, and so they explored some of the most difficult issues within the prison setting. He won journalism awards some of our best journalists in the free world have never won and will never win.

And for 23 years he was allowed to go out with an unarmed guard and speak to juveniles, at the Kiwanis Club, to all kinds of groups about what works about prison and what doesn't. And four times during this period of time, while hundreds of other people convicted of murder during the '60s had been released, because the life sentence in Louisiana in 1961 required only 10 and half years of servitude, and then unless you had done something horrible in prison, you were released. Four times the board of pardons and parole, after he served more than 20 years, recommended that he be released. Four times the governors said no.

Now, there's no way that anyone is going to believe that Wilbert Rideau, had his victim in the case have been black as opposed to white, would have . . . gotten the death penalty in 1961 or '64 or '70, and he surely would have never spent more than 10 and a half years in prison. And if Mr. Rideau was white instead of African-American, he would have been released a long time ago, and he would have been celebrated. This is really a great example of the prison system reforming somebody, as the prison system ought to try to do.

It finally became clear to him that the political process would not release him and so he filed a challenge to his third conviction, and in 2000 he was – his third conviction was overturned because of a claim involving racial discrimination.

I had thought that after this man served all this time, more than 40 years, and had done so with having only one infraction in his record (one night late he brought a bottle of white-out back to the cell) that we could negotiate a settlement where he would plead guilty and he'd be released, but that was not the case.

We had almost four years of very, very tough litigation in this case, and to my utter surprise the community in Louisiana was as divided racially in 2005 as it was in 1961. Then when we actually tried this case last month in Lake Charles, Louisiana, you could have painted a color line right down the middle of the court. (L)iterally everyone who was sitting behind the prosecution was white, and . . . the overwhelming number of folks who sat behind the defense were a mixed-race group.

There were two times where black judges were appointed in this case. Those judges were removed, both for very, very insufficient reasons. We had to fight tooth and nail to have a mixed-race jury in this case. And finally when the dust was settled we did get a mixed-race jury. There were eight whites, three blacks, and one woman who was mixed race.

And for the first time he finally had a defense and that defense showed that some of the most horrific facts which the state had introduced in the prior trials, which had become lore, simply were not true. And that when you finally broke this crime down to what it was, it took the jury only five hours to conclude unanimously that the crime was not murder, it was manslaughter.

And the lessons of all this, I think, are these for you; (Justice) Lewis Powell came to the Supreme Court a strong supporter of the death penalty, and in his 15 years on the Court (he) affirmed many death sentences, (but) in retirement he stunned his biographer when he asked him "What votes would you change?" And Justice Powell said, "Well, I would change a couple, but the key one would be the one in <u>McCleskey v. Kemp</u>.[62]" And why was that? And he (Powell) said, "We just can't get this right."

Justice Blackmun, similarly, while not in support of the death penalty, also came to the Court and in his early years affirmed almost every death penalty case he saw. But over time he got to see that this – the <u>Furman</u> experiment - was not delivering the promises that the states had made, that they could reliably get out these arbitrary factors of race and poverty and other things. And in his last year on the Court he issued this opinion where he said he would no longer tinker with the death penalty.

And finally Governor Ryan, lifelong Republican, lifelong supporter of the death penalty, a pharmacist, who found himself as the governor at an extraordinary time in Illinois when there was exoneration after exoneration after exoneration. And I remember I had the privilege of being at dinner with him one day in Washington, D.C. a few years ago, and he said, "You know, I'm a pharmacist. If I filled, and continued to fill, prescriptions that nearly led, or could have led, to the deaths of the people who got those prescriptions, I wouldn't be a pharmacist. (That is what is happening with the death penalty), (a)nd no one has been able to persuade me that we can fix this." And that in large part, I think, was responsible for why he took the action he took (imposing a moratorium on executions) just before he left office.

I think there are lessons to be learned from what Justices Powell and Blackmun said, as well as Governor Ryan, and I appreciate very much the opportunity to speak to you today.

Thank you.[63]

Discrimination on the basis of race is not limited to African-Americans. The testimony of Professor Edward Rodriguez of New Jersey's Seton Hall University School of Law emphasized how this discrimination has impacted Latino criminal and death penalty defendants.

Mr. Rodriguez: Good evening. My name is Edward Rodriguez. I'm an associate professor at Seton Hall University School of Law.... (Our) inability (to design) a death penalty law that is fairly administered and consistently applied and free from impermissible racial and ethnic bias is of great concern to the Latino community and the organizations that support Latino and immigrant communities.

Professor Charles Ogletree (of the Harvard Law School) has aptly noted "The struggle for racial equality is inextricably tied to the struggle for fairness in the criminal justice system." Indeed, there is ample empirical data of racial disparities in the criminal justice system. I will not detail these here, as the death penalty experts in the prior testimony have presented much of this work.

(But), (n)otably, in 2002, Human Rights Watch released an analysis of the 2000 Census data reporting a number of troubling findings, particularly as they related to Latinos. For instance, African Americans and Latinos make up 62 percent of the incarcerated population, though compromising only 25 percent of the nation's population. In some states Latino youths are incarcerated at seven to seventeen times the rate of white youths, and African American youths are incarcerated 12 to 25 times the rate of whites.

Why are these facts important to the discussion about the death penalty? Scholars have noted the disproportionate imposition of capital punishment in our society on people of color. One of the considerations that the legislature must bear in mind in its deliberations is that, as an empirical matter, race and ethnicity still predominate in the American criminal justice system.

Nowhere is this more apparent than in the jury selection process. Indeed, legal commentators have explained (that) "the discriminatory use of peremptory challenges is the single most significant means by which racial prejudice and bias are injected into the jury selection system."

Before the United States Supreme Court's seminal 1986 decision (in) Batson v. Kentucky,[64] prosecutors in this country routinely struck jurors based purely on racism or gross racial prejudice .... For example, one prosecutor's office prepared a jury selection instruction book that included the following instruction: "Do not take Jews, Negroes, Dagos, Mexicans or a member of any minority race on a jury no matter how right or well educated." While such blatant and outrageous instructions now seem to be a relic of the past, existing statistical evidence reveals the continuing disproportionate use of peremptory challenges to remove African Americans and Latinos from juries.

The discriminatory use of peremptory challenges and the failure of courts to curb such abuses is not banished to the dust of history. Just this past September, the New York Appellate Court, First Department, had to intercede and reverse the decision of a prominent jurist, Justice Leslie Crocker Snyder, when the trial court failed to apply . . . Batson . . . properly. In that case, People v. Claudio,[65] which went to trial in 1992, the prosecutor challenged practically every potential Latino juror. The grounds for these challenges included: two Latinos who were secretaries who the prosecutor "didn't get a strong feeling for either one way or the other." As for a Latino male, the prosecutor stated, "I didn't get a strong feel whether he had roots in the community. And, therefore, he wasn't very verbal. I felt – I didn't get a very strong impression of him one way or the other. That is my challenge to him." Based on these grounds, the prosecutor concluded, "It is clear that there is no pattern of racial discrimination in my peremptory challenges."

These flimsy reasons were put to the test when defense counsel objected during the jury selection process. First, counsel noted (that) the prosecutor had challenged every Latino and argued that the submitted reasons were pretext. He pointed out that all three Latino jurors who were struck had lived in the community for a significant number of years and had the same employment during the same period. Counsel further argued that although the prosecutor claimed he challenged the female Latinos because they were secretaries and he did not want secretaries on the jury, a non-Hispanic secretary was selected and seated on the jury.

After observing that the prosecutor's peremptory challenges were exercised "primarily on instinct," which is legally permissible and something I think we really need to look at, the trial court concluded that she did not believe there was any intended (racially discriminatory) pattern made out by the prosecutor. However, the court went on to state that since the prosecutor had struck all three Hispanics who had been in issue "I am striking the challenge to Ms. Arroyo and sitting Ms. Arroyo on the jury. As to the other two challenges, I am not. I feel this is a fair exercise of attempting to avoid any kind of racially motivated peremptory challenge. I think this is a fair exercise of resolving the issue." It was not.

The Appellate Court found this independently constructed procedure to resolve the issue of . . . discrimination . . . to be arbitrary and clearly outside the <u>Batson</u> protocol. The court then remanded the case for a new trial.

It is precisely this level of arbitrariness and unfairness, the lack of guidance by the Supreme Court, and the often times random application of the law, that concerns the Latino community. How can a system be trusted where no guidelines can ever be drawn to account for the latent racism that underpins our criminal justice system and its processes? Indeed, as suggested earlier, despite <u>Batson</u> and the host of other purported procedural protections that pretend to bring us to a place where there is "error-free capital punishment", the discriminatory use of peremptory challenges and the disproportionate imposition of capital punishment on people of color remain indelibly as fixtures, ensuring that one day society will make the mistake of taking the life of an innocent human being, wrongfully convicted. Indeed, for Latinos, who view the death penalty as a mere justification for vengeance . . . such injustice in the construction and application of the law cannot stand.

Death is different. As (Supreme Court) Justice Harry Blackmun wrote in his dissenting opinion in <u>Callins v. Collins</u>[66] just months before stepping down from the Supreme Court, I quote.

"From this day forward, I no longer shall tinker with the machinery of death. For more than 20 years I have endeavored – indeed, I have struggled – along with a majority of this Court, to develop procedural and substantive rules that would lend more than the mere appearance of fairness to the death penalty endeavor. Rather than to continue to coddle the Court's delusion that the desired level of fairness has been achieved and the need for regulation eviscerated, I feel morally and intellectually obligated simply to concede that the death penalty experiment has failed."[67]

As occurred throughout these Hearings, contrary testimony was presented by those who asserted that there has been little or no direct racial discrimination in the death penalty systems of New York and the nation as a whole.

In his written statement, Sean Byrne, Executive Director of the New York Prosecutors Training Institute, commented on the existence of racial or ethnic bias.

> Several recent studies demonstrate that there is no evidence of racial or ethnic bias in the death penalty system. For example, a Justice Department report in June . . . analyzed more than 900 federal death penalty cases, concluding there were no racial biases.[68] A study of proportionality review in New York's sister state, New Jersey, concluded there was no evidence of bias against black defendants, despite arguments of civil libertarians to the contrary – (the study indicated) that the race of neither the defendant nor the victim affects the likelihood that a capital sentence will be imposed. The 2002 report by New Jersey Supreme Court Special Master David Baime found no evidence of bias during the period studied, August 1982 through May 2000, confirming two earlier proportionality reports also finding no racial biases in New Jersey.[69] A recently concluded Nebraska study found that race is not a factor in death penalty cases. The report also found Nebraska is consistent in condemning only the most culpable killers.[70]

> While various studies are interesting, the most compelling information can be found simply by looking at death row. According to the Bureau of Justice Statistics report *Capital Punishment 2003*, of those under a sentence of death throughout the United States, 56%

are white, 42% are black, and 2% are other races. These
findings are consistent year after year. In addition the
2003 report demonstrates that prosecutors are using the
death penalty with great caution. In 2003, 144 inmates
received a sentence of death. This is the lowest number
of death row admissions since 1973.

In 2007 there were 1804 white death row inmates, 1345
were black, 26 were American Indian, 35 were Asia, and 10 were of
unknown race. Therefore, of the total of 3220 death row prisoners,
56% were white and 41.8% were black.

Professor Robert Blecker of New York Law School offered
conclusions on the influence of race that differed from the views of many
witnesses.

Assemblyman Wright: How do you in fact reconcile the
racial disparities of those that are on death row, number one,
and the racial disparities of those that are in fact executed.

Mr. Blecker: The fundamental question about race at first is,
in a similar set of circumstances, is a white defendant more or
less likely to be executed than a black one?

Assemblyman Wright: Let me just ask you this, if you could
limit your answer to the State of New York, because that's where
we are right now, as much has you're able.

Mr. Blecker: As much as I'm able to, it understates the
seriousness of the question to limit it to New York because the
problem, at least temporarily, I don't think there is much of a
race problem in the death penalty in New York, though there is
always the potential for it and we have much more evidence of
the problem nationally.

We have such a small snippet to work with. I'll try to be, I
really will be brief, but it doesn't allow for a sound bite here.
This is a fundamentally disturbing question because if the death
penalty is racially discriminatory, it must be . . . rejected on that
basis alone. Now, the primary question of race is the race of the

defendant. Do black defendants, and by the way, let me acknowledge something that we must never forget, which is that historically in the United States of America, the death penalty has been used as an instrument of oppression, principally of black males.

That is undeniable. We have a legacy of racism that is despicable and a prime instrument of that was the death penalty. So we've got to be very careful.

Assemblyman Wright: Will it continue, do you think?

Mr. Blecker: No. I'm convinced it will not and I'm convinced the news is really very good, that it has largely ended, almost exclusively ended.

Okay. The primary question of race, the race of the defendant first. Do black defendants fair worse than white defendants in similar sets of circumstances?

The studies show virtually uniformly not. (Professor) Baldus himself analyzed the post 1990 studies, 18 of them, and showed that except for Philadelphia in 1997, in one phase of the death penalty process, that was where the juries weighed the aggravators against the mitigators, except for one phase in one place (out of) 18, there was no discrimination against black defendants as such. That is in a similar set of circumstances. If anything, a white defendant was slightly more likely to get the death penalty than a black defendant was.

The focus therefore shifted from the race of the defendant. But again let that sink in. This is very good news.

Generally we only face bad news. We're a culture right now (in which) we face good news, which is that there is less racism in the death penalty system than there is racism throughout society.

The focus shifted to the race of the victim. That's what we discussed briefly, which is, does a white victim killing result in the death penalty more frequently than a black victim killing. The answer so far appears clearly, yes, it does. Now, why is that and what does it mean? It gets more complex than is usually reported. The standard answer is, that's because we devalue black life.

That shows it. That is the fact that you're more likely to get a death sentence if you kill a white than you are if you kill a black, (and that) show(s) that we don't care about it, if you kill black. We say it's not so bad. So we don't go after you for the death penalty. That is not what this means at all.

It means a few things. Number one, principally what the most contemporary studies seem to reveal to us is (that) we know that almost all killings are same race killings. That is, whites kill whites and blacks kill blacks.

There are some mixed, but they are relatively small in number. But it turns out that the race of victim effect turns out to be a geography affect. That is, in jurisdictions, principally suburban jurisdictions, and I know the community is interested in this because it's one of the questions you posed, in suburban counties, which tend to be white with greater budgets and a constituency that has a greater support for the death penalty . . . and by the way, the polls show that while the overwhelming majority of whites support the death penalty, and while support is much lower in the black community than it is in the white community, it is substantial in the black community. The last Gallup poll showed 46% of the African-American community supports the death penalty. 48% is opposed to it.

So while it is a minority, it is a substantial minority of the black community that supports the death penalty. But it's much lower than the white community and partly because there is this perception of racism, based upon historical legacy.

In white counties, suburban white counties, with a constituency that supports the death penalty to a greater degree, with a budget that can withstand the cost of going for the death penalty to a greater degree, with a prosecutor who is likely to reflect the values of the constituents, and to predict to a greater degree of certainty that the cost will have been worth it in a sense that you can get a jury to go to death, you more nearly and often find death penalty prosecutions.

That's not – and because it's a white county, largely, the victim will be white –

Assemblyman Wright: I just want you to stay with the answer to my question.

How do you reconcile the disparity between those on death row and those that are in fact executed?

Mr. Blecker: The latest pool of Justice (Department) statistics shows . . . (that) we have executed, I think, 10% of the black population on death row and 14.8%, I'm close, but maybe not exact, something like 15% of the white population.

We have more frequently executed whites on death row than we have executed blacks on death row. On average, it takes us

[...] on death row than [...] ugh that trend has

[...] geography . . . [...] aryland, show that [...] no race of victim

[...] ing else, which is [...] fe. Where there is a [...] killer. Where the [...] ick victim's families, [...] more sensitive to the [...] ditions on the street [...] ly that the victim's [...] is spiral of violence; [...] sily been on the other [...]) defendant instead of

[...] frican-American [...] om the retributivist

point, which I embrace, is reflected cruelly in those polls, for example, that say, are you in favor of the death penalty for murder. Of course I'm asked that question. What's my answer, my answer has got to be no, because 95% of the time I'm not in favor for the death penalty for murder.

Well, people spontaneously sometimes add, it depends. And when they did the breakdown, the racial breakdown of who refused to go yes or no, but rather the nuanced, only correct answer, it depends, it turned out that 14% of African-Americans answered it depends and only 7% of white's responded it depends.

And finally, to the major point, the one that's rejected even by abolitionists, which is why is 12% of the population (blacks) 44% of death row? Proponents say that's because 12% of the population is committing 50% of the murders and still there's only 44% on death row. And they dismiss the argument as naive.

Ironically, I think they're wrong, and abolitionist(s) also dismiss that as superficial. What you really have to look at is the population of murderers, it's 50% minority and death row is only 44% minority, therefore they're not over represented, they're under represented. In my view, that's wrong. The reason why, and this is where there is race in the death penalty, this is the primary place that there's race in the death penalty, it's not in the administration, it's in the definition.

African-Americans are committing 50% of the murders because we are defining felony murder as murder, even when there is no intent to kill. That is a crime of the underclass. That is an economically motivated crime. If you restricted the death penalty and eliminated the felony murder aggravator, the robbery murder aggravator, the burglary murder aggravator[71], and drugs, which we don't have now in this state and we should never embrace as an aggravator, if you restricted and eliminated the felony murder aggravator and confined the death penalty to the worst of the worst and not the mid-range of cases, both the Columbia study and the Liebman study have shown (that) . . . the racial disparity on death row will significantly drop.

The problem of race is in the definition. It (capital murder) is defined to discriminate, and I'm not saying intentionally or conscientiously, but it is discriminatory and it is also retributively unjust.

So, eliminate the mid range of cases, eliminate the felony murder aggravator, the robbery murder, the burglary murder aggravator, and you will see that disparity of 44%, 12% of the population, 44% of death row, that's going to change radically.

Professor Blecker added these further observations about race and capital punishment.

Does a black killer stand a better chance of being executed because s/he's black? . . . Another way of asking it – if you're black, is society more ready to execute you than if you're white? Happily the answer is clearly and unequivocally no! In the modern era (1977-2003), 510 (of the) 3451 whites sentenced to death have been executed; 301 (of) 2903 blacks sentenced to death have been executed. In other words, we have executed 14.8 percent of our white condemned, but only 10.4 percent of our black condemned. On average, during the modern era, it has taken us 8 months longer to execute a black, although this disparity has reversed the past two years. (Bureau of Justice Statistics, Nov. 2004) . . . .

(E)xcept to score debating points, rarely do informed abolitionists claim primary racism, i.e., a systemic race-of-defendant bias or impact. Now the attack is almost exclusively directed to the race-of-victim bias, or effect: Those who kill whites are sentenced to die more frequently than those who kill blacks, the evidence does consistently show. Why is that, and what does it mean? . . . . [T]he Maryland study shows [the answer is] primarily found in the likelihood of a prosecutor seeking the death penalty. After that, there is no additional racial effect.

Why do prosecutors more frequently seek death where there are white victims than where there are black victims? The Maryland study, Baldus' Nebraska study, and Judge Baime's recent New Jersey study all show the same thing: [t]he county –

the jurisdiction – in which the murder is committed, and thus the particular prosecutor's office, primarily accounts for the disparity. In populous states, suburban prosecutors tend to seek death more frequently than urban prosecutors. Capital murders are more frequently of white victims in suburban counties; more frequently (there are) minority victims in urban counties. Thus white victim cases more frequently get prosecuted capitally than black victim cases.

Professor William Bowers of Northeastern University's Capital Jury Project testified to his extensive research on the impact of race in the system.

Professor Bowers: I'm a principal research scientist at Northeastern University in Boston. I have a long history of researching capital punishment . . . .

Let me go to point seven (of one of the Capital Jury Project's reports on jury functioning). Point seven is race and racism. And it returns to an issue that I – that began in my early work with this material. We found that the Supreme Court had ruled in a case called Turner v. Murray[72] that in cases where the defendant is black and the victim is white, there's . . . especially likely to be . . . racial bias. (S)o, special provision (must be made) in questioning jurors about their racial bias . . . that unconscious risks (of racism) might be present . . . (and the jurors must be examined on potential racial prejudice).

We had at least 353 cases; 74 of them are black-on-white killings . . . . (W)e knew what the racial composition of the jury was, because we asked each of the jurors . . . at a certain point, to tell us how many blacks, whites, men, women. We found that when the jury – we called it white male dominate - was white male dominated, with five or more white males in the jury, death sentences were about three times higher than when there were less. That's a big ratio, when just white males dominated juries.

We also found that when there was a black male on the jury, that . . . lowered the likelihood that the death sentence would be imposed. These are pretty remarkable differences that appear to be due to – what? To race and to the (racial) composition (of the jury).

Well, the final point we have to relate on this is that we took those cases (that were) not only black or white killings, but . . . (where we) interviewed black jurors and white jurors in the same cases, so we could be absolutely sure that these folks were exposed to the same evidence, same witnesses, in the course of trial, and we compared the black and the white jurors.

On three very – there were three areas in which their perceptions differed drastically. And by the way, the most drastic difference was between white males and black males with women of either race being sort of a little bit in between. (First, we asked whether there was any) (l)ingering doubt about the defendant's conviction, guilt . . . whether he was the principal person (the killer)?

That separated black and white jurors in these very same cases. Differences where in the blacks – where half of the black males had lingering doubt; five percent of the white males (had such doubt). Huge, huge differences.

Another one was remorse, (whether) . . . the defendant was remorseful . . . . Very few of the whites saw the defendant as remorseful. The blacks, contrary, a great many did. Huge differences.

And then dangerousness; whether he (the accused) would be dangerous in the future. Again, the whites all saw the defendant as going to be dangerous in the future, and far fewer of the blacks . . . . We're looking at the process, the thinking of the jurors. We're looking at what people have been talking about here . . . – the fact that these are human decisions that are being made. And we're seeing, you know . . . deeply rooted evidence of racial disparity in the way they look at these things.

Professor John Blume of the Cornell Death Penalty Project challenged Professor Blecker's analysis.

On the issue of race, Professor Johnson will do the heavy lifting. I only wanted to comment briefly because during prior testimony before this Committee, Professor Blecker talked about a study in an article that my colleague Theodore Eisenberg and I had done, and basically represented that African Americans were not, in fact, discriminated against in the capital charging process .
. . .

I just wanted to say that that was a gross distortion of our findings. And in fact, what we found was that an African-American who is charged with killing someone who is white, no matter what statistical formula or analysis you do, is substantially more likely, at least three to four times more likely, to be sentenced to death than any other race of victim, race of defendant combination.

We of course are not the only scholars to have ever found this, or the only academics to have noticed this. I think the unique contribution we make is that we look at murder data from a number of different jurisdictions in a number of different regions of the country.

And what we can emphatically say is (that) discrimination in capital sentencing is not a Southern phenomen(on), it is not a former slave state phenomen(on), and I can say that as someone who was born and raised in the South, who is now happy to be a New Yorker, that if this Committee – if this legislative body re-enacts the death penalty, there will certainly be racial discrimination in the system. There is nothing that can be done to eliminate it.

Certainly there are things that can be done to minimize it, but it cannot be eliminated. It is inevitable that at least some of the people . . . will receive it (capital punishment) because of their race and the race of the victim.

Professor Blume's colleague at Cornell, Professor Sherri Johnson, continued this challenge.

Ms. Johnson: Mr. Chairman and Committee members. Thank you for permitting me to appear today. I'm a professor at the Cornell Law School, and my testimony today reflects both my own work as a scholar of race in the criminal process, and my familiarity with an enormous body of relevant scholarship done by others in the fields of law and psychology.

In part, because I know that Professor Blecker, a witness at the earlier hearings in New York City, has disparagingly referred to Cornell University as a leading abolitionist center, I would like to note that my own primary scholarly interest is and always has been race, and that my work tracing the influence of race on the criminal process predates my interest in the death penalty by more than fifteen years.

I have spent nearly a quarter of a century studying the influence of race upon the criminal justice system, and while it is undoubtedly true that my expertise on race in the criminal process has contributed to my opposition to the death penalty, I am confident that my views on capital punishment have little or no impact on my opinions on the role of race in capital proceedings.

I would like to talk about two different, albeit related, issues. First is the question of systemic racial disparities in the administration of the death penalty, a topic I know that both Professors Baldus and Blecker have already addressed, and about which I will try not to repeat prior testimony.

Here, my main point is that race of victim disparities are likely, though the size of those disparities can be minimized by narrowing the range of death eligible offenses. I will then speak at slightly greater length about the question of the influence of racial bias in individual cases, which in my own estimation is both inevitable and a more compelling argument against reinstatement of the death penalty in New York than are statistical disparities.

With respect to systemic disparities, there is widespread agreement that most capital punishment regimes over time reveal substantial race of victim disparities, with the death penalty being sought significantly more often, even three or four times more often, when the victim is white.

The General Accounting Office of the federal government, not known as a leading abolitionist center, after viewing both reliable and unreliable studies, has come to this conclusion. I must also find that studies with respect to race of defendant effects are much more variable, with most studies finding no race of defendant effects, but a smaller number of studies finding that African-American defendants are disadvantaged as a group, at least at some stages in the process, or at least when victims are white.

Are race of victim effects a spurious correlation, perhaps one caused by rural-urban differences? This is a suggestion that Professor Blecker has made. And a few studies support this interpretation, but most do not. In fact, the Cornell Death Penalty Project has done empirical studies of several judicial districts in South Carolina, and in every one has found a significant and substantial preference for seeking death in white victim cases.[73]

These are studies that isolate out the effects of a single prosecutor's office in decision making, and therefore make it clear that rural-urban differences are not the cause of race-of-victim disparities.

Professor Blecker's testimony hypothesized a second possible non-invidious explanation for race-of-victim disparities, that black victim family members just do not want the prosecutor to seek the death penalty.

After having personally talked to numerous black victim family members, I found no evidence of this hypothesis. Indeed, what I heard over and over again were stories of black victim family members who were not consulted at all as to what they wanted.

Moreover, in none of the cases we have litigated using this data has the state presented actual evidence of as opposed to speculation about the reluctance on the part of black victim families.

It is not possible with the limited data we now have to determine with certainty whether New York will follow this predominant pattern of valuing white lives more than black lives. In part, this is because we still have a very small number of cases, and statistically significant results require larger sample sizes.

In part, though, it is also because we do not have the right data about the cases that have already gone through the system; no information about all death eligible cases instead of simply cases that have been charged as Murder 1.

Surely it would be a tragic mistake to seek death and execute in a racially skewed way, waiting until the numbers were large enough to reveal the pattern that has been seen in virtually every other state.

So what might we do about race of victim disparities, other than abolishing the death penalty? Some have proposed creating a centralized review of decisions to seek the death penalty, but ironically it might even exacerbate the problem. The federal experience is that centralized review does diminish geographic disparities, but has not diminished racial disparities.

Indeed, the federal system, unlike most state systems, at times reflects race of defendant disparities; that is that black and latino defendants are far more likely to have death sought in . . . (their) cases, as well as the race of victim disparities found in decentralized state systems. Moreover, it is my understanding that at least the apparent race of victim disparities were actually increased by centralized review under (U.S.) Attorney General Ashcroft.

If the legislature determines that it wishes to reinstate the death penalty, a much more promising avenue for decreasing, though likely not eliminating, race of victim disparities is to narrow the range of cases in which the death penalty is available. And this is because it is in the least aggravated cases in which the greatest disparities are generally observed.

Thus, it seems to me that the wealth of experience from other death penalty jurisdictions argues that race of victim disparities are likely to develop in New York, should we reinstate the death penalty, and that it is unwise to choose to do so in the face of that likelihood.

More compelling, however, and I think even less retractable than the probability of statistical disparities, is the virtual inevitability that racial bias will alter the outcome of some individual cases. In the 1990s, the mid '90s, I studied reported cases in which prosecutors made racially inflammatory arguments in criminal cases, and I am currently updating that research.

It is extraordinarily disheartening to see how often, and in how many disgusting ways, prosecutors have called upon the worst prejudices to secure convictions and death sentences, arguing that black witnesses are not credible because of their race, or even that a black defendant more deserved death because he had slept with a white woman. I do think that New York courts are better than most at restraining such arguments.

But what is powerful about the frequency of these arguments is not whether or not they are corrected, but (that) prosecutors believe that jurors will be receptive to these arguments. And indeed the limited information that comes out of capital jury rooms is that jurors are influenced by race in life and death decisions.

Given the confidentiality of the jury room, and the rule against impeachment of juror verdicts, we don't usually hear what jurors say, but now and then, the very ugly terms that jurors have used in describing defendants of a different race than their own are revealed. It might be argued that cases where jurors actually use racial epithets are the exception, and I think they might be the exception, but cases where jurors are consciously or unconsciously influenced by race are not the exception, but the rule.

The evidence that many white jurors will be swayed by race in assessing the death-worthiness of an African-American defendant is both varied and extensive. Let me just scratch the surface of that evidence. First, mock jury studies show that white jurors are more likely to find a mitigating fact, such as mental illness, (is) instead (an) aggravating (fact) in a case where the defendant is African-American. And this is a fact that's corroborated by Professor Baldus' Philadelphia study.

Second, to mention something I'm involved in myself, my study with Jennifer Eberhardt, a professor of Psychology at Stanford, has revealed that in Pennsylvania capital cases, the more stereotypically black a defendant appears, that is, the darker his skin and the more African his features, the more likely he is to receive the death penalty. This is in Pennsylvania, not in the south, and this is controlling for both aggravating and mitigating factors that have been identified.

Third, and most importantly, there is a huge and growing body of psychological literature that reflects an automatic association of white with good, and black with bad, for about 80 percent of white Americans.

Moreover, when primed with images of African-Americans, or names or words associated with African-Americans, white observers, the majority of white observers, are more likely to deem an ambiguous interaction violent, are more likely to deem an adolescent offender culpable, are more likely to deem a crime especially heinous (when the offender is an African-American).

Most people are unaware of these biases. Most people exhibit these racial effects without hostility. Indeed, I will report that I have found these same patterns of associating white with good and black with bad among my law students, who have been shocked and dismayed to find this in themselves. And indeed, not only among law students, but among capital defense lawyers. This is not something that someone can control.

In one sense, it is a measure of racial progress that conscious hostility and endorsement of stereotypes is waning. But as the effects of stereotypes become unconscious, and less morally blameworthy, they also become harder to prevent. Jurors who are influenced by race but who lack hostility and awareness of the biases in their thinking cannot be screened out by voir dire. They will answer questions honestly that they can be neutral, but they cannot.

Jurors also cannot be successfully instructed to disregard race in their deliberations. Most of the literature on instructions suggests that in complex decision - making areas, a juror . . . is incapable of screening out the influence of impermissible factors.

In a factual and moral judgment as complex as whether to impose the death penalty, with respect to an issue so closely tied to the worth of a human being, at a proceeding where stereotypes of violence and animality will be made salient by the facts of a crime, it is inevitable that race will influence the thinking of decision makers.

It will not, of course, always change the outcome, but it will sometimes change the outcome. Perhaps sometimes those stereotypes may even benefit a black defendant. The point, however, is not the systemic, detectable skewing.

The point is rather the knowledge that race will sometimes determine whom the state executes, even, or especially even, when we do not know it. But anyone familiar with this literature knows that it will happen. And in the face of that knowledge, reinstatement of the death penalty is wrong. Thank you.

Mr. O'Donnell: Professor Johnson and Professor Blume, are you suggesting to this panel that Professor Blecker in his hearing testimony in December misrepresented what your findings and conclusions were.

Ms. Johnson: Yes.

Mr. O'Donnell: Thank you, very much.

The Hearings produced some recommendations to lessen the asserted influences of race in death penalty cases. These included:

- Improving trial and appellate procedures for reviewing claims of racial discrimination. (Professor Baldus cited Kentucky's Racial Justice Act and noted that it had "made people, prosecutors, much more sensitive to the racial consequences of what they have done").

-   Eliminating the requirement of proof of discriminatory intent in cases in which the evidence shows disparity in the race of the defendant and the victim.
-   Developing stronger express anti-discrimination jury instructions.
-   Strengthening voir dire procedures to permit private questioning of potential jurors on their racial attitudes.
-   And, most importantly, broadening jury pools to obtain greater diversity along racial and ethnic lines.

Sean Byrne's written testimony on the racial makeup of death-noticed cases since enactment of the 1995 New York capital punishment law provides a closing snapshot for this section of Chapter Five: 55 death notices (the prosecutor's statement that the death penalty will be sought in a case) were filed; of the 47 cases for which data on race was available, 45% of these notices were for African-Americans, 43% were for Whites, and 11% were for the Hispanics. Does that show a racial bias?[74]

Mental Illness

In striking down the death penalty for the mentally retarded,[75] the U.S. Supreme Court in Atkins v. Virginia[76] gave four basic reasons why such a practice violated the Eighth Amendment: a national consensus against such executions existed based on state laws manifesting "evolving standards of decency"; the mentally retarded are less blameworthy and cannot be considered "the worst of the worst"; the goals of deterrence cannot be achieved with this category of defendants; and execution as a criminal penalty was, therefore, disproportionate to the crime of murder committed by a mentally retarded person.

The New York Hearings produced testimony asserting that similar arguments compel invalidation of capital punishment in cases involving the severely mentally ill. New York law defined mental illness as "an affliction with a mental disease or mental condition which is manifested by a disorder or disturbance in behavior, feeling, thinking, or judgment to such an extent that the person afflicted requires care, treatment and rehabilitation."[77]

Estimates vary, but approximately 300,000 mentally ill prisoners are incarcerated in the United States. In 2003, Human Rights Watch observed that "somewhere between two and three hundred thousand men and women in U.S. prisons suffer from mental disorders including such serious illnesses as schizophrenia, bipolar disorder, and major depression."[78]

Ron Honberg, Legal Director for the National Alliance for the Mentally Ill, provided the core testimony on this subject.

> My name is Ron Honberg, and I am the Legal Director for the National Alliance for the Mentally Ill, or NAMI. And I am pleased to be here today representing NAMI, which is the nation's leading organization advocating on behalf of people with severe mental illnesses. We have over 200,000 members nationwide, and more than 5,000 members and 58 local affiliates throughout New York State.
>
> I am here to make the case that the death penalty, to the extent it exists at all, should not be applied to people with severe mental illnesses. And although NAMI's primary goals are to improve treatment and services for people with these illnesses, our efforts and attention have increasingly focused on the criminal justice system in recent years. Sadly, the criminal justice system has become the de facto mental health treatment system in many communities, largely because psychiatric treatment and mental health services are frequently not available to those who most need them.
>
> Most people with severe mental illnesses in criminal justice systems have been charged with minor, non-violent misdemeanors or felonies. But, some people with these illnesses, particularly those in prisons, have been convicted of more serious, violent crimes. And, in some states, people with severe mental illnesses are significantly represented among the ranks of those on death row. The estimates are (that), nationally, about 20 percent of all death row inmates have serous psychiatric diagnoses.

Many of these death penalty cases involve individuals who sought but were denied treatment earlier in their lives. And only later, after crimes were committed, was treatment provided, usually for the purpose of achieving competence to stand trial. It's a sad irony that states frequently spend far more money on seeking executions of people with severe mental illnesses than they do on providing treatment and services to people with these illnesses who have not committed crimes.

The U.S. Supreme Court and many state legislatures have eliminated the death penalty for juveniles and people with mental retardation, juveniles at least under 16 years of age. And NAMI believes that it is time to extend these prohibitions to people with severe illnesses for the following reasons.

First, the symptoms and functional effects of severe mental illnesses, like mental retardation, diminish criminal culpability sufficiently to mitigate against the ultimate punishment of death.

Recently, the U.S. Supreme Court in a case called Atkins v. Virginia struck down the death penalty for defendants with mental retardation citing characteristics of these disorders that diminish capacity of defendants to formulate criminal intent or carry out criminal acts in cold blooded, calculated ways.

In Atkins, the court recognized that while mental retardation does not excuse criminal culpability, it does justify a lesser degree of potential punishment, thereby eliminating the death penalty as an option. Although quite different from mental retardation, severe mental illnesses similarly impact in profoundly negative ways on perception, cognition, and behavior. Thus, NAMI believes that the rationale articulated at Atkins applies equally to individuals with mental illnesses.

Severe mental illnesses are biologically based brain disorders that produce symptoms frequently beyond the control of those who experience them. For example, individuals with schizophrenia frequently experience paranoid delusions and auditory or visual hallucinations so vivid and profound that they appear real. These individuals may be unable to distinguish between delusions and reality and may sometimes act on their delusions or behave in ways that seem bizarre or incomprehensible to others. It is not uncommon for an individual experiencing paranoid delusions to perceive that he or she is under threat, when no such threat exists.

Judges and juries, faced with the monumental task of passing judgment about the culpability of individuals who commit crimes while psychotic, are essentially asked to do the impossible. It is not possible to impose logic, as the law tries to do, on biologically based brain disorders that create illogical, confused patterns of thought. Bright line tests between right and wrong do not work when it comes to evaluating the dark, unbridled confusion of psychosis, delusions, and hallucinations.

Second, there is mounting evidence that mental illness is construed as an aggravating rather than a mitigating factor in capital cases.

In virtually every state that has the death penalty, including New York, mental illness is included among a list of factors that should be considered as mitigating against the death penalty. The term used in New York State's statute is "mental or emotional disturbance at the time of the offense." Because of this, there are some who assume that the presence of a severe mental illness categorically excludes an individual from the death penalty. Unfortunately, this is not the case. In fact, there are growing concerns that evidence of severe mental illness may be viewed by juries as an aggravating, rather than mitigating, factor in capital cases.

In an article published in 2000, Professor Chris Slobogin, a leading expert on mental illness and the law, cited a number of studies showing this trend.[79] For example, a study of 175 capital cases in Pennsylvania demonstrated that all aggravating and mitigating factors listed in that state's death penalty statute correlated with the eventual sentence imposed . . . with the exception of extreme mental or emotional disturbance, which correlated positively with a death sentence.[80] In other words, if you had a serious psychiatric diagnosis, you were more likely to be sentenced to death. And other studies in states like Georgia have produced similar results.

Research suggests two possible reasons for this very disturbing trend. The first concerns the perceptions of lay people that people with mental illnesses are abnormally dangerous. Thus, jurors may view a capital defendant with schizophrenia as beyond redemption, with no amount of treatment likely to reduce that person's violent tendencies. In actual fact, the opposite is true. Psychiatric treatment has been shown to be very effective in reducing risks of violence.

A second reason may be the cynicism of jurors that mental illnesses are real – and perceptions on the part of these jurors that raising a mental illness as a mitigating factor is a subterfuge designed to enable people to escape responsibility for their own behaviors.

Third, serious concerns about fairness arise in capital cases involving defendants with mental illnesses.

The ability of a capital defendant with active symptoms of a severe mental illness to receive a fair trial or otherwise participate fully and knowingly in his or her own defense is in serious question. Let me give you a few examples. First, competency concerns. Although the U.S. Constitution requires that defendants must be capable of participating knowingly and fully in their own defense, competency standards are quite low and may be misunderstood and unevenly applied. And history abounds with defendants with mental illnesses who have been allowed to proceed to trial and even represent themselves, despite serious questions about their competency to do so.

A related concern applies to defendants with mental illnesses who forbid their attorneys from presenting evidence of mental illness. As Dr. Amador will explain, it is quite common for individuals with schizophrenia or other severe mental illnesses to deny that they are sick or require treatment. In criminal cases, this frequently translates into refusals by defendants to permit their defense attorneys to raise competency questions or to assert the insanity defense. In such cases, the New York State statute does not currently permit defense attorneys to override the defendant's wishes and present mitigating evidence of severe mental illness.

Still another problem concerns the susceptibility of defendants with mental illnesses to coercion, for example, giving confessions or waiv(ing) their right to counsel. The vulnerability of defendants with mental retardation to coercion and suggestibility was raised by the Supreme Court in the <u>Atkins</u> case, and it applies equally well to certain defendants with severe mental illnesses.

And, finally, the proliferation of so-called volunteer cases. There have been a number of these cases that have occurred in different parts of the country where capital defendants with severe mental illnesses have consistently insisted throughout the criminal process that they want to plead guilty, forego appeals, and hasten the process of execution. The desire of these individuals to proceed with their own deaths is often symptomatic of the severity of their illnesses. This is borne out by the fact that volunteers frequently change their minds after they receive psychiatric treatment.

Let me just finish up by taking just a couple of minutes to suggest a, perhaps, better approach to weighing mental illness in these kinds of cases.

As stated earlier, NAMI believes that people with severe mental illnesses should be exempted from the death penalty. And recently our Board of Directors adopted a policy that would exempt defendants with these illnesses under the following three circumstances.

First, individuals with cognitive or functional limitations equivalent to those applied to defendants with mental retardation in the <u>Atkins</u> case would be exempted, with the only difference being that the age of onset of the mental disability occurs after age 18.

Second, individuals who, at the time of their offense, suffer from mental illnesses and act on impulses or beliefs that are the product of delusions, hallucinations or other manifestations of psychosis would be exempted. Individuals whose actions are attributable solely to acute effects of alcohol or other drugs would be not included in this category.

Finally, individuals whose severe mental disabilities manifest or worsen after sentencing to the extent that they are unable to understand the nature and purpose of the death penalty or to make rational decisions about legal proceedings relevant to the death penalty would be exempted. This would avoid the types of cases we have heard about in other states . . . (in which there were) concerns about the competency of specific defendants to be executed or to waive their appeals or whether such individuals should be medicated to make them competent.

This really doesn't get out some of the very serious concerns that we have about the training of attorneys, about the training of judges and others who are called upon to make these horrendously weighty decisions, and who often times don't understand mental illnesses, defense attorneys who don't really know how to properly raise mental illness in cases. And these concerns – the very , very high probability of errors, which we've been hearing about all day in the general context of the death penalty, would suggest categorically excluding people with mental illnesses from the death penalty.

Dr. Xavier Amador.

Dr. Amador: Thank you. Thank you for letting me address the committees. My name is Dr. Xavier Amador.

I'm here to share my experiences about how the death penalty is applied in persons with serious mental illness. So a little bit of context about how I came to this issue, I think, is going to be helpful to you.

First, I'm a Professor in Clinical Psychology at Columbia University. For more than a decade, I was a Professor in the Department of Psychiatry at Columbia and also Director, for a time, of the New York State Psychiatric Institute's Psychology Department. I've been a consultant to the National Institute of Mental Health, the United States Department of Justice, which has done some research on why so many mentally ill people are flooding our jails and prisons. But even more relevant, I'm also a forensic expert. It's a kind of new part of my career. I just started seven years ago. And in the last seven years I've worked on over 25 death penalty cases in federal and state courts, (in) more than eight states, including New York State. So I'm going to talk mostly about that, not about my research or psychiatry in general, but about my experience with these death penalty cases. . . .

I'm also a victim of a homicide. My father was killed. His killer was never caught or brought to justice. I understand the feeling. I understand that emotion. One of the speakers earlier said if my wife were killed I would want to kill that person with my own bare hands. I get it. But that's not, I think, what you're all grappling with as lawmakers.

Another personal note, I have a brother with schizophrenia. So I have seen very up close and personal, this is not just book learning to me, I've seen up close and personal how that disease, that brain disorder, can change somebody. It can change their ability to understand the difference between the fact and the fiction of their dreams or illusions. But also how it can change a kind and patient person into somebody who is terrifying and menacing because his broken brain has convinced him that his life is in danger.

Well, why talk about the seriously mentally ill in this context, in the context of these hearings. I'll just say a couple of sentences about it.

President Clinton's Attorney General('s) ... report, President Bush's Freedom Committee (New Freedom Commission on Mental Health, 2003) report, and many other authoritative reports, all agree that our mental health system in this country is in shambles. We have many thousands of people flooding our jails and prisons. And, hence, that's why somebody like me can end up working on so many of these cases.

Unlike the typical forensic psychologist who makes a living at this – just a brief word about how I got into it. I was asked by the defense team in the Theodore Kaczynski case, seven years ago, the Unabomber[81] case, to help them explain to the judge why Ted Kaczynski was trying to fire them. And the reason he was trying to fire them is because the experts in the case had said to his attorneys your client has schizophrenia. The judge's expert actually later agreed with the defense experts. This man has very serious mental illness. You should use that in his defense. He'll be found guilty, very likely, but you could probably save him from death. When Ted Kaczynski heard that, because he doesn't understand he's ill, because his illness has rendered him unable to understand he's ill, (he) tried to fire his attorneys, and they asked me to bring the science into the discourse of the judge's decision about this. And there's a lot of science. About half of all people with these illnesses do not understand they're ill. And in a moment I'm going to, I think, bring that alive to you in terms of what that creates .... But my work on that case and the cases to follow really helped me to debunk some myths.

I had certain beliefs that are popular beliefs that I think a lot of people hold that are not true. And among them (is the belief that) prosecutors do not seek the death penalty for persons with very serious, well documented mental illness. That's absolutely not true. (Another myth is that) (w)e don't execute mentally ill people who are psychotic. For example, who are delusional, they're hallucinating, even defecating on themselves on the eve of execution. We do execute people like that. I've seen them. I've met them.

(Another belief is that) (s)eriously mentally ill people rambling in open court spouting irrational and paranoid accusations would never be allowed to defend themselves. In fact they are. I have many cases, if there are questions about them later, I can tell you about first hand. The other myth that really surprised me, I have to say, is that the closest relative of somebody who was murdered requests it (the death penalty) whether it's any case or a case where the person who committed the homicide is somebody with mental illness. It doesn't always change what the prosecutors do. I don't have statistics to tell you, but I've seen . . . prosecutors refuse calls from victims of cases that they were prosecuting because those victims don't want to pursue the death penalty. So I've had a lot of, I have to say, surprising moments in doing this work the last seven years. Let me talk about a couple of the cases very briefly.

Russell Weston, who the press has labeled the Capital Shooter, you may remember this case. Several years ago he raced through a metal detector at the Capital (Washington, D.C.) and shot six people, ultimately killing two police officers. The Justice Department still has the death penalty on the table in this case despite acknowledging that Weston has a 20 year history of schizophrenia. (He) . . . never before had been violent. He doesn't take medication. He wasn't taking medication. He was rushing the Capital to gain control from the great safe of the U.S. Senate, control of the ruby satellite system that he had developed when he worked for the CIA. The ruby satellite system controls our minds. Russell was terrified. I've seen my brother terrified because of the demons and delusions that he's had. Russell Weston was satisfied that the CIA was controlling his mind and other people's mind(s), and he was rushing to save his life and other people's lives. So that's just a general context of how he ended up in that situation.

In a bizarre but common twist by which delusions have become reality, the government now is pursuing his death. But even more bizarre and much more common than I ever realized, for the first time he is consistently on medication, which is a rarity in the criminal justice system, and there are a lot of statistics on that. The reason he's on medication is the prosecution has fought very hard to medicate him to make him competent to stand trial so they can prosecute the death penalty.

Weston's case highlights several common themes. First, in the cases I've seen, in the cases I've worked on, a failed mental health system is, frankly, at the root cause of many of these cases. It's certainly a theme in all of them. The other theme that his case reflects is that many of these defendants have never before been violent, outside of the context of their mental illness, have not been so-called criminals outside of the context of the onset of their mental illness. And, third, the common problem of poor insight into being ill and in the need of treatment. This problem leaves these individuals, I think, particularly vulnerable, as Ron said, to many of the miscarriages of justice you've been hearing about in these hearings.

Volunteering is a term used describing people on death row that refuse to pick up their appeals. They've decided, they've presumably made a rationale choice, to be executed.

I've worked on a number of these cases, I've said goodbye to two people who went on to be executed. In one of the cases, the man was delusional. He believed that he had written the third Bible, that God had given him the Scripture, and that he would rise from the dead. But he was found competent to be executed. In another case, well there were many cases and actually I'm going to stop there. If you're interested I can tell you more.

I can tell you that depression and psychosis lead many of the people I've evaluated to choose to volunteer for the death penalty. And because there is so little treatment available in prisons, the illnesses often times are, in fact, influencing these decisions. And these individuals are being found competent.

Let me just tell you about James Brown. This is a man with schizophrenia who had gone untreated, like many people's illnesses do, for many, many years. And the prosecutor in the case saw that he had a very longstanding history of schizophrenia, he saw that it was relevant to the crime, and the prosecutor in this instance offered him life in prison. James said no way. And the reason was because his attorney, he knew for a fact, was plotting with the prosecutor to trick him. He repeatedly was asked (to plead) by this attorney, another attorney was brought in, and again, and again, and again he said no purely on the basis of a delusion. He refused life in prison. He went to trial, was convicted, and was given the death penalty.

I was presenting some of this to the Georgia Board of Parole and Pardons and explaining how if not for his delusion this man would not be before that Board, would not be on death row, he would be serving life in prison. But that testimony and other . . . substantive testimony just about – there were witnesses that recanted and some other evidence that had to be withdrawn – didn't sway the Board and James was executed.

I've, again, many examples of judges finding mentally ill defendants competent that I and other experts have opined are not competent, whether it be to stand trial, whether it be to be executed.

There was a New York attorney who once characterized the competency standard in New York State as essentially the capacity to tell the difference between a grapefruit and a judge; if you could do that, you were competent. I laughed when I first heard that. I'm not laughing anymore because I have seen that kind of standard applied. And I ask myself as a psychologist how is this happening. And all I can tell you is that these trials are so charged, the emotion is running so high, that a tremendous amount of subjectivity goes on, and worse. . . .

Why does this happen? Frankly, the main reason I think this happens is because we're raised on the Grimm Brothers fairy tales. We learn about Hansel and Gretel. Why did that woman, I don't know if she even had a name, the old woman – she would kill children and eat them. She would kill children and eat them. We learned about what as children? Evil. And that is what I see sold by prosecutors. And even by a lot of experts, I have to say, who, in the name of science, will paint a picture of evil. We don't learn about brain disorders. We don't learn about schizophrenia or bi-polar disorder.

(T)he discourse and so-called evidence that gets presented in these cases really would never, ever, pass peer review in a journal or in any of the committees I've ever sat on in a hospital. It's really remarkable to me what does get passed as science and expert opinion.

I could go on and on. I'm just going to leave you with a couple of quick thoughts.

I believe there are three main problems. These (death penalty prosecutions) are highly emotionally charged cases that eclipse reason and make it easy to justify the seemingly unjustifiable. (J)udges, jurors, prosecutors and defense attorneys subscribe to common myths about mental illness and are largely ignorant to the nature of these disorders. The science about these disorders doesn't get presented nearly as often as I ever would have thought it did, so that basically jurors, and other triers of fact, are making decisions based on their impressions and myths about mental illness without truly understanding the nature of this defendant's broken brain. And, finally, the adversarial system is inappropriate and ill equipped when it comes to the task of uncovering the truth about a defendant's mental illness and its relevance to the case. It pits experts one against the other. When you get up and testify, it's not about the quality of your testimony, it's about your demeanor. It's about he said, she said, rather than about the objective evaluation.

Thank you for your attention.

Assemblyman Lentol: I just want to ask you one question and that is how do we fix the problem if prosecutors are going to have psychiatrists and psychologists and come in to testify that a defendant is fine when he's really a raving maniac?

Dr. Amador: I actually wrote a couple of notes in my written statement about that. I have some thoughts about that. But the fact is that I don't know if that aspect can be fixed. Let me say something about career forensic experts. These are people who make their living doing this.

As a scientist involved in brain and behavior research, you look at that context and these are people who are asked to render opinions and they end up working for one side or the other. And I just think that's always going to be the case when it's an adversarial situation.

The Andrea Yates[82] case and the reversal in that case raise some very interesting questions, and I think it's an illustration of exactly this problem. Without being too specific, I've seen experts go way out on a limb, refute 20 years of medical history. One doctor . . . says this person doesn't have schizophrenia and essentially testifies this is just a bad guy and he's making it all up. He's been faking schizophrenia. I've seen that kind of testimony fly.

I'm not sure if this aspect can be fixed. I have seen where judges will order evaluations, and those seem to be less subject to that kind of bias (and, therefore, outside evaluations might solve some of these problems).

Professor John Blume of the Cornell Death Penalty Project added:

> As for the topic of mental illness, I just wanted to briefly touch upon a few things, because a number of different studies, and even a cursory review of Appellate Court decisions, demonstrate it is not at all uncommon for persons with schizophrenia, mental retardation, fetal alcohol syndrome, autism spectrum disorders, depression, bi-polar illness to be sentenced to death.
>
> I recently completed a study of death row, what I would call volunteers, or inmates who waived their appeals nationally and essentially agree to be executed.[83] And that study demonstrated at least 70 to 75 percent of these individuals suffer from the most severe mental illnesses that we recognize currently, including schizophrenia, depression, and bi-polar illness.
>
> Now it's true there are cases where the jury hears the evidence of mental illness at trial, and decides nevertheless to impose the death penalty. And there are several ways to look at this. One would be that the jury's made the moral calculus that despite the person's mental illness, the heinousness of the offense warrants death.
>
> Even among supporters of capital punishment, reasonable people can and should debate whether that is the correct calculus. But what our studies reveal is that in a significant number of cases, defendants are sentenced to death not in spite of their mental illness, but because of it.
>
> And that is true for two reasons. The dynamics that drive capital decision making based upon our research in the Capital Jury Project, two of the most important dynamics, are jurors assessments of the defendant's dangerousness and assessments of the defendant's remorse.

And on both these issues, a person who is mentally ill is at a distinct disadvantage. Because of their mental illness, many jurors will in fact perceive the person to be unfixable and therefore more dangerous than someone else.

And also because of the mental illness, because of the powerful medications the person will be under, or just because of the illness itself, the individual will not appear to be remorseful as they sit at counsel table during the trial. So it is just inevitable that these people will be discriminated against.

So if the death penalty is to be re-enacted in New York, and it is not for me to say whether it should or should not be, there should be an exemption for persons who are severely mentally ill.

I know that Professor Blecker previously expressed some skepticism about such a proposal, arguing this would prevent the death penalty for a person who (is) what he called (a) psychopath or the worst of the worst, but that is really not the case at all.

For example, a current proposal by the ABA Task Force on mental illness and capital punishment, of which I am a member, is worded in terms which would prevent individuals with a severe mental impairment or mental illness from being executed. But it would not bar the death penalty for people who only commit a crime because of a substance abuse disorder or anti-social personality disorder.

The National Alliance for the Mentally Ill of New York submitted the following written testimony urging that defendants with severe mental illness be excluded from any new death penalty law in the state.

NAMI-New York State would like to thank Assemblyman Lentol, Chair of the Committee on Codes, Assemblywoman Weinstein, Chair of the Committee on the Judiciary and Assemblyman Aubry, Chair of the Committee on Correction for the opportunity to testify at this hearing.

NAMI-New York State is a grassroots, self-help, support, education and advocacy organization dedicated to improving the lives of all people who are affected by mental illness. We are the largest advocacy organization representing families of persons with severe psychiatric disorders, as well as consumers of mental health services, with 57 affiliates across the state.

(T)he time is appropriate to prohibit the imposition of the death penalty upon individuals who suffer from a serious and persistent mental illness, and whose disordered or psychotic thinking patterns were a factor in the commission of their crime....

Such discussion necessarily brings us to ... persons with serious and persistent mental illness who commit a capital crime, but whose behavior, at least in part, is the result of psychotic or distorted thinking patterns. Apart from the *Lavalle* case, the New York State death penalty law does permit a defendant to use a defense of "extreme emotional disturbance" as a mitigating factor in a capital case where the prosecutor is seeking the death penalty. While the statute affords a process to invoke such a defense, which if successful, provides protection against the death penalty and requires a sentence of incarceration, we believe that the time is right for New York State, and indeed the whole of the United States, to join with virtually every civilized country in the world in prohibiting the execution of people with serious mental illness.

First, we believe that much of the reasoning in the *Atkins* decision applies to persons with a serious mental illness, even though we acknowledge the substantive differences between mental retardation and serious mental illness. Do not a person's auditory or visual hallucinations, delusions, manic thinking, paranoia, or depths of depression diminish one's capacity to clearly process information, to communicate, to engage in logical reasoning, to control impulses, and to understand the reactions of others, as cited by Justice Stevens in *Atkins*. While such disordered thinking often falls short of the very high standards of an insanity plea – which is another matter altogether – there can be no question but that such distorted thinking is a primary factor and central to one's criminal behavior in virtually all cases involving persons with a serious and persistent mental illness.

We are also persuaded by the American Bar Association's Section on Individual Rights and Responsibilities policy paper, entitled "Mentally Ill Defendants: Systemic Bias in Capital Cases".[84] While there have been no executions of any defendants in this state, the story around the country is much different. And, there are numerous horror stories of persons with serious psychiatric disorders who have been executed.

The Bar Association paper cites the difficulties encountered by lay juries who unwittingly allow pejorative values and prejudices to influence their opinions and guide their decisions. The paper states that jurors, having sat through a trial and struggled in the guilt/innocence phase, are left with the impression that there is nothing about serious mental illness itself that should be considered at the penalty phase as determining that the offender should not be executed. Further, jurors without training or expertise are expected to make legal determinations and, somehow, without assistance, translate complex, conflicting medical information into the equally bewildering legal formulae given to them in instructions. The paper concludes that what results are courts and juries making psycho-legal determinations which are inherently unreliable.

We are not familiar with any such cases involving a person with a serious and persistent mental illness reaching the penalty stage in this state. However, we have certainly witnessed more than our fair share of cases which have gone to jury trials here and elsewhere in the state where we have seen juries reject psychiatric testimony and return guilty verdicts of persons with serious mental illness where we believed that a compelling case was made for an insanity plea. We have also witnessed cases in which our system of law has allowed persons who are demonstrably very ill and disordered in their thinking to be deemed competent and to represent themselves at trial where a mental health defense is never even considered. We believe it is only one small step further for juries to decide to impose the death penalty on such a person who is seriously mentally ill, unless the state death penalty statute, as constructed, is amended to bar such sentences.

According to Amnesty International, virtually every country in the world currently prohibits imposing the death penalty on persons with a serious mental illness. The United Nations Commission on Human Rights has repeatedly called for an end to the death penalty against people with mental disorders in the few countries which still employ a death penalty at all.

While NAMI-New York State has taken no official position on whether New York State should continue with some form of death penalty statute, we do believe that "standards of decency" in 2005, including our current understanding of psychiatric disorders and a recognition of the frailties of our jury system in deciding such cases, constitute a persuasive case for joining the global community in banning the execution of persons with serious mental illness. Let New York State lead the way in this country, rather than waiting for others to shape the future.

This testimony strongly suggests that these two areas of death penalty law – the impact of race on the system and the execution of the mentally ill – will receive further review in the United States Supreme Court. The outcome as to race is unclear. However, existing Eighth Amendment case law seems to support a constitutional ban on capital sentencing of the severely mentally ill.

CHAPTER SIX: INNOCENCE

For many Americans, the single greatest problem with the death penalty is innocence – the fear that we have executed, or will execute, an innocent person. The large and steadily increasing number of death row inmates who have been exonerated and released from prison, currently 139 in 26 states, drives this fear. A 2009 Gallop poll reported that 59% of Americans surveyed believed that within the past five years a person had been executed who was in fact innocent of the crime charged. By contrast, 57% of that same group continued to support capital punishment.

The innocence issue was raised directly when the Hearings Committees asked in question II. 1., "Did the 1995 statute provide appropriate safeguards to ensure that innocent persons would not be convicted and subject to the death penalty in New York? If not, what additional safeguards would be needed to meet that goal?" The New York Hearings approached these questions by examining the reliability of criminal convictions in general and capital sentences in particular. This testimony was exceptionally compelling.

The foundation for analysis of the "innocence phenomenon" was laid by noted forensic scientist and lawyer Barry Scheck. Professor Scheck is the Co-Director (with lawyer Peter Neufeld) of the Innocence Project at Benjamin N. Cardozo School of Law in New York, and is often recognized for his role in the 1995 acquittal of football star O.J. Simpson on charges stemming from the murder of Simpson's wife in California.

> Mr. Scheck: Good afternoon. My name is Barry Scheck, and I am cofounder and co-director of the Innocence Project at Cardozo Law School at Yeshiva University, where we use DNA testing to prove the innocence of people convicted of crimes. All together, there have been 153 people exonerated by post-conviction DNA testing in this country, including 14 individuals who were on death row.

Most importantly, I think, I've also served for the last 12 years as a Commissioner of Forensic Science in the State of New York. That's a regulatory body in this state that oversees all of our crime labs.

I'm here to testify against the re-imposition of the death penalty in New York because it's bad public policy. It does not deter, it is very expensive, and it will inevitably result in the execution of the innocent. It is hubris to believe otherwise.

Mandatory life without parole is a sufficiently harsh penalty for the worst of the worst offenders, and most importantly . . . vital reform legislation that protects the innocent and helps apprehend the guilty must first be passed before one can responsibly consider reinstituting the death penalty.

Reasonable people can differ as to whether it is morally appropriate to execute someone for the most heinous of crimes, but there should be no disagreement, and I don't even think Professor Blecker, who I've discussed this with many times, disagrees that we must take all appropriate measures that will prevent the execution of the innocent and help with the apprehension of the real murderers before you really consider going back on this.

A lot has changed since 1995, when New York brought back the death penalty and when many of you last considered this important vote. We now know that there are many more innocent people being convicted than anyone ever expected. Of course, DNA testing is the primary source of this knowledge. It's not just the 153 people who have been exonerated with post-conviction DNA tests, and I'm sure again, Professor Blecker would not disagree, and (you can) go to our website, InnocenceProject.org, nobody's arguing about these 153 people.

These are innocent people. But there are tens of thousands, as Mr. Morgenthau pointed out to you this morning, tens of thousands of people in this country that were indicted based on mistaken eyewitness identification, false confessions, bad forensic science, unreliable snitch testimony, or other things . . . since 1989. Tens of thousands of people and that's why all of us feel the resonance here and we know something has changed in terms of our understanding about the fallibility of the criminal justice system.

But I really would like to make a point with what Mr. (Assemblyman) Gottfried (said) before, and make it very strongly. It would be a mistake to believe that DNA testing is a panacea for what ails the criminal justice system, or (that) it can bring about a fool-proof death penalty.

Let me be the first to tell you, that's not true. It is believed by experts in this field that only 15 to 20% of cases, serious felony cases, much less homicide cases, have any biological evidence that we could subject to DNA testing to determine whether someone is guilty or innocent.

So what about the other 80% of the cases, especially the death cases? New research points to a disturbing answer. A recent survey by our colleagues at the University of Michigan looked at more than 329 post-conviction exonerations based on new evidence of innocence since 1989. Most of those involved non-DNA evidence.

Capital cases were a disturbingly high percentage of this total. Although death row inmates constitute only ½ of 1% of the American prison population, capital cases constituted 22% of the exonerations. Now, one of the reasons for this high percentage of wrongful convictions in death penalty cases is obvious and inevitable. Death cases, arising from the most heinous of crimes, stir public passion and lead to more error. We are human and our criminal justice system is extraordinarily fallible.

Just consider our state. We have learned, since 1995, through DNA testing and other forms of proof, that there were scores of murder cases from the (Mayors) Carey and Cuomo era where innocent men were convicted of murder here in New York who would have unquestionably been sentenced to death and probably executed, may very well have been executed, if there had been a death penalty. I know them. I know these people well.

I just think of these men, Jeffrey Blake, in Brooklyn, felony murder. Exonerated when it was found out this man, Dana Garner, who had been used (to testify) in this case, had lied in a whole bunch of cases. Charles Shephard, Anthony Faison, John Restivo, Hector Gonzales, Dennis Halstead, Bobby McLaughlin. These are all innocent people. They were all convicted of terrible murders. All of them could be dead.

So as Assemblywoman Cohen was saying, I mean, it works both ways. It's a terrible thing to talk to families who have had one of their own murdered. But believe me, I can tell you, it's a pretty horrible thing to talk to people who have been sentenced to death, who came within five days of execution, and (it is a horrible thing) to their families. Their families are destroyed by this. Death is different that way.

Just think, and I know them all, of the young men convicted in the Central Park jogger case. If you doubt this notion, that passion – I mean, that's one thing about Professor Blecker, he's very passionate, he has no doubts, he's coming from a moral position. I respect it. But, I have to tell you, I'm much more of a secular humanist type than a skeptic about our institutions.

I have to tell you that we can make mistakes. But think about the Central Park jogger case (in which the original defendants were all innocent) because we all remember it. Just imagine if that poor young woman had died and she almost did. Is there any question those young men could have gotten the death sentence? Is there any question that they would have been high priority executions? None of us should ever forget the passion that case generated.

One of our most prominent citizens, Donald Trump, took out full page ads talking about, let's bring the death penalty back, or this is what we need it for, expand it. And I'm not questioning it. Everybody was really, really upset about that case.

It was brought by arguably the best state prosecutor's office in this country, very skilled and responsible prosecutors tried that case. Elizabeth – Linda Fairstein oversaw it. It was overseen by Bob Morgenthau himself, who is probably one of the great district attorneys in our country's history.

They were innocent. It was false confessions. We found the real murderer. There is no question that if New York had capital punishment prior to 1995, in the Carey-Cuomo era, our situation, in terms of death row in this state, would have looked just like Illinois before Governor Ryan declared a moratorium, pardoned a number of innocents, and then gave mandatory life without parole to everybody else on death row.

We would have had scores of exonerated on death row. We would have proven them innocent based on DNA testing and other forms of proof. And if we were lucky enough to avoid executing an innocent, we would have been lucky.

Now, our situation could have been worse than Illinois because we paid court appointed lawyers during this whole period much less money to represent poor people charged with crimes than the state of Illinois. And all of you know that because you've been struggling with this problem for quite some time.

So we've learned, since 1996, a lot more about innocence. And it's a much bigger problem than anybody thought in 1995. Yet there is more we've learned about the causes of wrongful convictions and how to prevent them that should make anyone who supports the death penalty pause before bringing it back now.

There are a number of reforms, an innocence agenda, that my colleague, Tom Sullivan, can talk about because they passed most of them and went through it all in Illinois, that must be enacted, must be enacted, before you can even responsibly consider reinstituting capital punishment.

First, there is eyewitness reform. We know now how to dramatically reduce mistaken eyewitness identifications, the single greatest cause of the conviction of the innocent, without reducing in any material way correct identifications. A series of new procedures are being very successfully implemented in New Jersey, brought about by John Farmer, Republican Attorney General. The whole law enforcement (community) has been doing it for close to three years. They think it's terrific. Just adopted in Boston after a number of exonerations.

Minneapolis, Santa Clara, California, a number of jurisdictions, legislation that Tom Sullivan can tell you about that's passed in Illinois. Procedures recommended by the leading law enforcement groups in this country. When I've spoken with Ray Kelly, with others in this state, about bringing some of these reforms in, like blind use of examiners in conducting line ups, (they say) we don't have the money. We don't have the money. I don't doubt that, but this death penalty is costing us $170 million of law enforcement dollars that we can put somewhere else.

Illinois just enacted this legislation. The American Bar Association has just recommended this eyewitness reform. We have proposals that we can give to you to consider and enact before you even approach the question of capital punishment.

Similarly, measures to prevent false convictions, like the Central Park jogger case, are essential. The best way to do it is videotaping interrogations in serious felony cases at precincts. Again, Illinois, a little known state senator named Rocco Boma, carried the legislation and got it done. We have to do that in this state before we bring back the death penalty.

Crime laboratory reform is another critical area. I can tell you that. I've been working as a Commissioner of forensic science, going to New York City police departments, testing old unsolved rape cases so we can find the real perpetrators, looking at unsolved murder cases, burglary cases, we don't have enough resources there.

We're doing better than most states, but we don't have enough resources there. We have to do a lot, frankly, to bring up our crime lab and to deal with forensic issues.

I want to tell you about one (problem area) and this should be all you really need to know. Fingerprinting. We all thought fingerprinting was so reliable. But frankly, there (are) certain scientific problems with it. We're going to have to look at this very carefully in New York State. But if you're wondering about it, just think about Brandon Mayfield, the lawyer in Oregon. As you recall, this lawyer, who was married to a Muslim wife, who did divorces for people in Oregon, some of whom were alleged to have ties to Al-Qaeda, (and) it was said by the FBI that his fingerprint, a 16-point match, was found on a bomb in Madrid that blew up the trains.

They ran it through the AXIS system, they got a hit on Mayfield, 16 points of identity. The Spanish authorities are saying we're not so sure this is true, we see discrepancies. The FBI said no, we definitely believe it's true. A federal judge appointed an expert for the defense to look at it. He said, yeah, I think that's true. I think it's a 16-point match.

Then, the Spanish authorities found fortuitously, because God knows what would have happened to Mr. Mayfield, the real person's print, a known member of Al-Qaeda, and . . . (they) matched his fingerprint. Now, I came yesterday from a meeting of the American Association of Crime Lab Directors, and there is an article (about this case) that appeared about 10 days ago, I think, in the Journal of

Forensic Science, and I talked with the people at the FBI who have begun the first investigation of this.[85]

How did this mistake happen? It's quite incredible. The way it happened, they believe, at least one problem, there's some other underlying scientific problems on how fingerprints, how we have to change the standards, but the one problem deals with this whole issue of passion. They found, this is an FBI finding itself, that the principal examiner in the case who looked at the fingerprint got it wrong, (and) others were checking him and they were afraid to tell him otherwise. There was "group-think" and there was examiner bias in the way they did fingerprints. And the conclusion was, the bigger the case, the more important the case, the greater the danger of examiner bias with fingerprints. Well, that's got to be a wakeup call on this whole issue of innocence.

We're going to have to go back, incidentally, and start looking at fingerprinting in our crime labs, because the problem with fingerprinting is that when it's not being done correctly, we're missing our ability to catch guilty people too, probably more of that, as well as making some number of false matches that convict the innocent.

So, there is more. There are measures to fund defense counsel and experts, the rest of it. Let me finally address the political issue. Public support for capital punishment is diminishing. Professor Blecker is right. There's a wonderful book on this, THE CONTRADICTIONS OF AMERICAN CAPITAL PUNISHMENT, by (University of California/Boalt Hall law professor) Frank Zimring, that studies this in great detail. It is true still in Europe, that when you ask people, well, are you for or against capital punishment for the most heinous of crimes, people say yes.

And maybe 50, 60% in many European countries that are still in favor of it if you ask them that way. But they got rid of it because they can't trust the state to get it right because there is fallibility in this system.

We have enormous fallibility in this system. The public opinion polls show that people understand this. You know, (Senator and former Presidential candidate) John Kerry is a staunch opponent of capital punishment. That was never raised by President Bush, who has executed more people than any other governor in the modern era.

Why? I'll tell you why. Because it's not the third rail of American politics anymore. Because people see that the innocent are being convicted and put on death row and have been executed. And we're finding out more about this and it's a worse situation than we ever thought. So, it is not that kind of (hot political) issue anymore.

In conclusion, until we take reasonable, prudent, practical measures to prevent the execution of an innocent person in New York, we cannot even get to the question of whether restoring capital punishment is the right thing to do.[86]

As of the end of 2009, the Death Penalty Information Center estimates that 139 individuals in 26 states had been released from death row based on evidence of innocence. An exceptional historical perspective on these types of exonerations was provided by an article submitted to the Hearings by five individuals from the University of Michigan: "Exonerations in the United States" – 1989 through 2003". The authors are:

Samuel R. Gross, Thomas & Mabel Long Professor of Law, University of Michigan Law School; Kristen Jacody, University of Michigan Law School, J.D. candidate, May 2005; Daniel J. Matheson, University of Michigan Law School, J.D., May 2004; Nicholas Montgomery, University of Michigan Department of Economics and Ford School of Public Policy, Ph.D. candidate, May 2007; and Sujata Patil, University of Michigan School of Public Health, Ph.D., May 2004.

The following portions of the article,[87] which was entered in the record of the Hearings, provide extensive information on innocence and the reliability of criminal convictions in the United States as of 2003. (Numbers appearing in brackets [ ] in the text of the article are footnote numbers; these footnotes are reproduced in note 88 at the end of this book).

On August 14, 1989, the Cook County Circuit Court in Chicago, Illinois, vacated Gary Dotson's 1979 rape conviction and dismissed the charges. [1][88] Mr. Dotson – who had spent 10 years in and out of prison and on parole for this conviction – was not the first innocent prisoner to be exonerated and released in America. But his case was a breakthrough nonetheless: he was the first who was cleared by DNA identification technology. It was the beginning of a revolution in the American criminal justice system. Until then, exonerations of falsely convicted defendants were seen as aberrational. Since 1989, these once-rare events have become disturbingly commonplace.

This is a report on the study of exonerations in the United States from 1989 through 2003. We discuss all exonerations that we have been able to locate that occurred in that fifteen-year period, and that resulted from investigations into the particular cases of the exonerated individuals. Overall, we found 340 exonerations, 327 men and 13 women; [2] 144 of them were cleared by DNA evidence, 196 by other means. With a handful of exceptions, they had been in prison for years. More than half had served terms of 10 years or more; 80% had been imprisoned for at least 5 years. As a group, they had spent more than 3400 years in prison for crimes for which they should never have been convicted – an average of more than ten years each. [3]

As we use the term, "exoneration" is an official act declaring a defendant not guilty of a crime for which he or she had previously been convicted.

The exonerations we have studied occurred in four ways: (1) In 42 cases governors (or other appropriate executive officers) issued pardons based on evidence of the defendants' innocence. (2) In 263 cases, criminal charges were dismissed by courts after new evidence of innocence emerged, such as DNA. (3) In 31 cases the defendants were acquitted at a retrial on the basis of evidence that they had no role in the crimes for which they were originally convicted. [4] (4) In 4 cases, states posthumously acknowledged the innocence of defendants who had already died in prison: Frank Lee Smith, exonerated in Florida in 2000; Louis Greco and Henry Tameleo, exonerated in Massachusetts in 2002; and John Jeffers, exonerated in Indiana in 2002. [5]

This is the most comprehensive compilation of exonerations available, [6] but it is not exhaustive. The criminal justice system in the United States is notoriously fragmented – it is administered by fifty separate states (plus the federal government and the District of Columbia) and by more than 3000 separate counties, with thousands of administratively separate trial courts and prosecuting authorities. There is no national registry of exonerations, nor any simple way to tell from official records which dismissals, pardons, etc., are based on innocence. As a result, we learned about many of the cases in our database from media reports. But the media inevitably miss some cases – and we, no doubt, have missed some cases that were reported. [7]

In the great majority of these cases there was, at the end of the day, no dispute about the innocence of the exonerated defendants. This is not surprising. Our legal system places great weight on the finality of criminal convictions. Courts and prosecutors are exceedingly reluctant to reverse judgments or

reconsider closed cases; when they do – and it's rare
– it's usually because of a compelling showing of
error. Even so, some state officials continue to
express doubts about the innocence of exonerated
defendants, sometimes in the face of extraordinary
evidence. Two brief examples:

- When Charles Fain was exonerated by DNA in Idaho
  in 2001, after 18 years on death row for a
  rape/murder, the original prosecutor in the case said
  "It doesn't really change my opinion that much that
  Fain's guilty."

- On December 8, 1995, at the request of the
  prosecution, the DuPage County, Illinois, Circuit
  Court dismissed all charges against Alejandro
  Hernandez, who had spent 11½ years in prison for
  an abduction, rape and murder in which he had no
  role. By that time DNA tests and a confession had
  established that the real criminal was an imprisoned
  serial rapist and murderer by the name of Brian
  Dugan; a police officer who provided crucial evidence
  had admitted to perjury; and Hernandez's co-
  defendant, Rolando Cruz, was acquitted by a judge
  who was harshly critical of the investigation and
  prosecution of the case. Nonetheless, when
  Hernandez was released, the prosecutor said: "The
  action I have taken today is neither a vindication nor
  an acquittal of the defendant."

  Needless to say, we are in no position to reach
an independent judgment on the factual innocence of
each defendant in our data. That is not our purpose
in this report. Instead, we look at overall patterns in
the exonerations that have accumulated in the past
fifteen years and hope to learn something about the
causes of false convictions, and about the operation
of our criminal justice system in general. It is
possible that a few of the hundreds of exonerated

defendants we have studied were involved in the crimes for which they were convicted, despite our efforts to exclude such cases. On the other hand, it is certain – this is the clearest implication of our study – that many defendants who are not on this list, no doubt thousands, have been falsely convicted of serious crimes but have not been exonerated.

. . .

(The) rapid increase in reported exonerations probably reflects the combined effects of three interrelated trends. First, the growing availability and sophistication of DNA identification technology has, of course, produced an increase in DNA exonerations over time. Second, the singular importance of the DNA revolution has made exonerations increasingly newsworthy; as a result, we are probably aware of a higher proportion of the exonerations that occurred in 2003 than in 1989. And third, this increase in attention has in turn led to a substantial increase in the number of false convictions that in fact do come to light and end in exonerations, by DNA or other means. More resources are devoted to the problem – there are now, for example, 41 Innocence Projects in 31 states [11] – and judges, prosecutors, defense lawyers, and police officers have all become more aware of the danger of false convictions.

. . .

II. The Crimes for Which Exonerated Defendants
were Convicted

Ninety-six percent of the known exonerations
of individual defendants since 1989 were either for
murder – 60% (205/340) – or for rape or sexual
assault – 36% (121/340). Most of the remaining 14
cases were crimes of violence – 6 robberies, 2
attempted murders, a kidnapping and an assault –
plus a larceny, a gun possession case and two drug
cases. See Table 1.

Table 1: Exonerations by Crime and Basis			
CRIMES	NUMBER OF EXONERATIONS	BASIS	
		DNA	Other
Murder	205 (60%)	39	166
Death Sentences	*74 (22%)*	13	61
Other Murder Cases	*131 (36%)*	26	105
Rape	121 (36%)	105	16
Other Crimes of Violence	11 (3%)	0	11
Drug & Property Crimes	3 (1%)	0	3
Total	340 (101%)	144	196

. . .

2. *Why are Exonerations Heavily Concentrated
among Murder Cases, and Especially among Capital
Murders?*

What about exonerations that are not based
on DNA? In 2001, about 13% of state prisoners were
serving sentences for murder or non-negligent
manslaughter, [18] but 85% of non-DNA
exonerations (166/196) are found among this group.
For prisoners under sentence of death the contrast is

even more stark. The death-row population in America peaked in 2001, at about a quarter of 1% of the American prison population [19] – and yet 74 exonerations in the past 15 years, 22% of the total, were drawn from this tiny sliver of the prison population. What accounts for this enormous over-representation of murder defendants, and especially death-row inmates, among those who are exonerated?

There are only two possible explanations:

- One possibility is that *false convictions are not more likely to occur in murder and death penalty cases,* but only more likely *to be discovered* because of the comparatively high level of attention that is devoted to reviewing those cases after conviction. This is no doubt true, at least in part. Because of the seriousness of their consequences, murder convictions – and especially death sentences – *are* reviewed more carefully than other criminal convictions. In 1999, for example, Dennis Fritz was exonerated by DNA evidence and released from a life sentence for a rape murder he did not commit. But he was exonerated as a by-product of an intensive investigation that led to the exoneration of his co-defendant, Ron Williamson, who had been sentenced to death. If Williamson had not been sentenced to death, Fritz would probably be in prison to this day.

But could this be the entire explanation? Could it be that false convictions in capital cases really are no more common than in other cases? If that were the whole story it would mean that if we reviewed prison sentences with the same level of care that we devote to death sentences, there would have been *over 29,000 non-death row exonerations* in the past fifteen years rather than the 265 that have in fact occurred –

including more than 3,700 exonerations in non-capital murder cases alone. [21] This is a shocking prospect.

- On the other hand, if this first explanation is not the whole story, that inescapably means that *false convictions* <u>*are*</u> *more likely to occur in murder cases,* and *much more likely in death penalty cases,* than in other criminal prosecutions. There are several reasons (apart from the evidence presented here) to believe that this too is almost certainly true: the extraordinary pressure to secure convictions for heinous crimes; the difficulty of investigating many homicides because, by definition, the victims are unavailable; extreme incentives for the real killers to frame innocent fall guys when they are facing the possibility of executions. Whatever the causes, this is a terrible prospect: that we are most likely to convict the innocent defendants in those cases in which their very lives are at stake.

   Considering the huge discrepancies between the exoneration rates for death sentences, for other murder convictions, and for criminal convictions generally, the truth is probably a combination of these two appalling possibilities: We are both much more likely to convict innocent defendants of murder – and especially capital murder – than of other crimes, and a large number of false convictions in non-capital cases are never discovered because nobody ever seriously investigates the possibility of error.

. . .

SUMMARY AND CONCLUSION

The extraordinary rate of exoneration of death-sentenced defendants . . . raises deep questions about the accuracy of our system for determining guilt in capital cases. Exonerations from death row are more than 25 times more frequent than exonerations for other prisoners convicted of murder, and more 100 times more frequent than for all imprisoned felons. This huge discrepancy must mean that false convictions are more likely for death sentences than for all murder cases, and more likely than among felony convictions generally – an unavoidable and extremely disturbing conclusion.

Finally, the frequency of exonerations from death row is a chilling reminder of the consequences of these false convictions. If we managed to identify and release 75% of innocent death-row inmates before they were put to death, then we also executed 25 innocent defendants from 1989 through 2003. If, somehow, we have caught 90% of false capital convictions, than we only executed 8 innocent defendants in that fifteen-year period. Is it conceivable that a system that produces all these horrendous errors in the first place could also detect and correct 90% of those errors, after the fact? And considering the number of mistakes in capital trials, even an unlikely 90% exoneration rate would be disturbingly low.

Worse yet, the high rate of death-row exoneration is limited to defendants who have been sentenced to death. Approximately half of all defendants who are convicted at capital trials are sentenced to life imprisonment instead; and of those who are sentenced to death most are resentenced to life imprisonment at some point in the process of review; about 40% have their convictions or sentences reversed on their first appeal, and most of them are ultimately resentenced to life. [63] In other words, the bulk of defendants at capital trials are subject to the frightening risk of error that plagues capital prosecutions – they are as likely as other capital defendants to be convicted of murders they did not commit – but they get little or none of the special care that is devoted to re-examining death sentences after conviction. In all likelihood, a great majority of innocent defendants who are convicted of capital murder are neither executed nor exonerated but sentenced to prison for life, and then forgotten.

Stephen Saloom, Policy Director for the Innocence Project at Cardozo School of Law, added his views on the reasons for exonerations.

As a result of DNA testing and other advances in science, people are now extremely cognizant of how very possible it is for the criminal justice system to get it wrong, and to sentence an innocent person to death.

The Innocence Project has examined . . . 154 wrongful convictions proven by DNA evidence, and identified many of the factors that confound the criminal justice system's best intentions. These include erroneous eyewitness identifications, faulty lab work, reliance upon invalidated forensics, coerced confessions, and reliance on jailhouse informants, to name just a few.

. . .

Regardless of how sound the death penalty statute is that you might try to enact, no state can ever be so sure that it will not someday execute an innocent person. Governor (Mitt) Romney of Massachusetts has identified and recommended measures that would have made imposition of the death penalty there "as infallible as humanly possible."

But even his best effort did not convince Massachusetts prosecutors of the worthiness of such a pursuit.

Daniel Conley, the District Attorney of Suffolk County (MA), which is in Boston, said the release of four wrongly convicted inmates since he took the job in 2002 "has simply convinced me that while technology like DNA is critical in determining one's guilt or innocence, the administration of justice is a human endeavor, and we're all fallible."

Other prosecutors noted (that) the state's medical examiner's office and crime labs were already overwhelmed with work. And regarding fiscal issues, Norfolk (County, MA) District Attorney William Keating noted that employing . . . exacting standards (such as proof beyond any doubt) would cost taxpayers an estimated $5 million per death penalty case, which is nearly as much as his entire $6.8 million annual budget, which funds approximately 19,000 criminal complaints per year.

Once again, Professor Blecker provided a different point of view on the numbers and reasons for death row exonerations, although his testimony began with a rather startling, if not somewhat ambiguous, admission.

(A)bolitionists tend to point out that there can be one mistake, (that) we will inevitably execute an innocent person . . . we have probably, my guess is, executed an innocent person in the modern era. We don't know who it is, but we probably have. We have not to the best of my knowledge demonstrably executed an innocent person in the modern era.

His testimony continued:

Assemblywoman Cohen: It's the same question . . . . Given that we're fallible, human beings are fallible, how do you say after an execution, whoops, we figured out this was a mistake.

Mr. Blecker: You don't say whoops, you say sick. You feel sick. You feel sick also, say, after a car accident where you didn't spend the money to improve, to make the road abutments safer on a bridge. (What) do you say when you see mangled corpses or dying bodies in a car accident when you knew that another $100,000 in allocation would have saved them. What do you say? You don't say whoops, you feel sick. You think that you've misallocated your resources. You've made a tragic mistake. You do your best to prevent (it).

There is nobody on New York's death row in the modern era who is innocent. There is nobody on Oregon's death row who is innocent or claims to be innocent. Interesting enough, in the Illinois Commission, after their two-year study, they didn't come up with anybody of the 168 (prisoners) who they thought was innocent either.

There will be an innocent, there's likely to be an innocent person executed, it's possible. It's possible. And it's tragic and it's horrifying. Of course, there's also likely to be innocent people killed by prisoners while in prison who would have gotten the death penalty and but for (that they) would have been incapacitated, and instead (they are) turned back into the dangerous monsters that they were out here. And so in effect, by sparing their lives, you're allowing them to take other innocent lives. That's happened too. How do you feel? Sick.

But you don't balance the one against the other retributively, you just ask the question (should he or she be executed) of each individual and you do your best. Does this person deserve to die?

Assemblyman Lentol: Mr. Norman.

Assemblyman Norman: Yes, along the same line of the fallibility of the system. You indicated that there may be the possibility that an innocent person might be executed and (that) make(s) you sick. Certainly, if you are that person who is executed. But we know beyond just mere speculation that there have been people on death row who have been exonerated. Back in 2003, 12 people were freed who were on death row. In 2004, five people who were on death row were freed. In fact, since the re-imposition of the death penalty, I think there's 117 people who otherwise would have been executed who have been freed. So I find it difficult to reconcile your passion for the reinstitution of the death penalty in the context of the fallibility of the criminal justice system, where we have demonstrative, concrete, evidence that people have indeed been on death row, who were in fact innocent.

I was wondering how you might be able to reconcile what we know, factually, with what you say could be a possibility of one or two people.

Mr. Blecker: I appreciate your question. . . .

The figure of 117 or 130 generally comes from the Death Penalty Information Center, which is a leading source of information, but is not as neutral as it sounds. It is confessedly abolitionist. . . .

The probably truer figure, my best guess, best informed guess is, 30 innocent people on death row who have been released, who did not commit the crime. 30 is way too many, but remember, let's distinguish between the 30 who were eventually released, and not executed, from the . . . few, one maybe, two, maybe more, who have been executed in the modern era, who were actually innocent, but that number is very, very small. It's much smaller than those released from death row.

What concerns me is a different kind of innocence, and that's of the 3,400 people on death row today. My best guess is that if you had a true, morally refined, death penalty that was really confined to the worst of the worst, you would find that of those 3,400 the majority of them don't deserve to die, yet have been sentenced to death.

They don't deserve to die. Not because they are factually innocent, they committed murder, but they're not the worst of the worst. And because some states have too broad a death penalty, including once again, including felony murder, robbery murder, which is class biased and race biased, which is why I hope you let me come back to that, because states do have that, the number of people sent to death row is well beyond the number of people who deserve to die. That's the principle of the problem of innocence and the death penalty and that's why the Legislature must confine the death penalty to only the worst of the worst.

Assemblyman Norman: But you do concede that there is the possibility of fallibility in the criminal justice system, the mistakes can be made?

Mr. Blecker: Mr. Norman, there is a possibility that this ceiling will collapse and fall on us, full and upon us, and kill us both as we engage in this dialogue, yet you bravely risk your life to it and so do I. We are constantly risking ourselves. There is constant chance of error and danger.

Assemblyman Norman: What is your answer?

Mr. Blecker: I readily concede to you that no system is absolutely infallible, nor is life imprisonment when you keep a person in prison his whole life and he didn't do it, it's too late to make amends, even if you discovered in his lifetime, when 50 or 60 years have gone by, and the irony is, by the way, is that we pay so much more attention, as we should, to the death penalty process. . . . (I)f you eliminated the death penalty, . . . the perspective of the privileged community would be, what's the difference, they probably did something else anyway, and (the result would be less frequent and critical review of life sentences and) we would allow . . . thousands of convicted murderers, tens of whom would be a factually innocent, to spend their lives in prison, without any real concern for (that), precisely because they weren't facing the death penalty.

So the grand irony here is that the error rate, . . . a 68% error rate of the Liebman study, is not accurate in terms of the number of errors. I respect Jim Liebman very much. That's what I was just referring to.

I've even co-published with him in the Houston Chronicle, and we found common ground. But, one of the fallacies of that 68% error (rate), because I am conceding to you that there is error, but nothing like 68%, is that the study does not include the question of how many judges who reversed a death penalty sentence later affirmed another one on appeal. What we have are abolitionist judges, including some who sit on the New York Court of Appeals, who will use any pretext they can to spare (a convicted inmate from death) . . . we can't rely on the New York Court of Appeals too much longer to be our backstop, this so-called progressive New York Court of Appeals majority. . . .

That we can't rely on them. It implicitly concedes the fact that abolitionist judges will under pretext, because no trial is perfect, under constitutional pretext, prevent the death penalty from recurring. So, the error rate is overstated. It is nevertheless of great concern.

Sean Byrne of the New York Prosecutors Training Institute shared many of Professor Blecker's views on the significance of exonerations and defended the death sentences handed down under the 1995 New York capital punishment law.

Prosecutor Byrne: Your witnesses frequently attempt to bolster their argument by pointing to the hundred-plus death-row defendants who have allegedly been exonerated since 1977.

The innocent argument invites more responses. First, every defendant convicted under the 1995 New York statute was indisputably guilty. Their attorneys routinely admitted their clients' guilt in the opening statements of their comments.

Second, your witnesses have not pointed to even one innocent person who has been executed since the reauthorization of the death penalty by the Supreme Court 28 years ago. I do not deny that such a travesty could happen, but thankfully there is no proof that one has happened.

Third, different prosecutors around the United States, including the California Attorney General's Office, a former States Attorney from Illinois, and the National District Attorneys Association, have examined the purported exonerations, and have determined that the vast majority of the defendants were anything but innocent. The majority were reconvicted on the same charges. Others had key evidence proving their guilt suppressed, or their retrial was not possible for other reasons. The point is, the majority of these exonerated persons were factually guilty.

All the same, some of the exonerated defendants were, in fact, innocent. And that brings me to my fourth observation. The system is working as intended. The very point of our adversarial system with multiple capital qualified counsel, a neutral judge, a jury of ordinary citizens, and a non-waivable appellate review, and so on, is to test, certify, and recertify the accuracy of the capital charge.

. . .

As someone who has been involved in every New York death penalty case, I can assure you that every person placed on New York's death row under the 1995 statute was clearly guilty and among the worst of the worst.

. . .

Mr. Rivera: My point is that no matter what evidence you have, no matter what evidence is presented, there is still

that human element which is fallible. Would you agree that
even though we have these – all these safeguards that we
have within our law, that there's still that fallibility that
exists . . . and that innocent persons have been found guilty?

Mr. Byrne: I would agree that there is a human
element, and that when there's a human element in the
statute there's a possibility of a mistake.

Mr. O'Donnell: In your recitations about innocence
and the hundred-plus people on death row who are getting
exonerated, you said something that struck me. And that is
that you don't deny the possibility (of execution of an
innocent person), but there is no proof that it has ever
happened, and so I have a two-part question:

Are you suggesting to us that we should wait until
somebody who is innocent is executed and then address the
subject? Or are you suggesting that your position would
change were that to come to be actually shown?

Mr. Byrne: Neither, sir.

Mr. O'Donnell: Okay.

Mr. Byrne: First, I would never hope that we should
wait. That's not the point. I believe that in human
institutions and human systems there is the potential for
fallibility. When we license a hospital we know that doctors
can accidently kill patients. When we set a speed limit we
know that more people are going to die at 65 than die at 55.
Things like this happen in the institutions that involve and
are run by human beings.

So, I wouldn't want to wait for anything like that to
happen. I would like to try and prevent it from ever
happening.

. . .

Mr. Aubry: All right. Okay. Professor Blecker, and I
assume from your testimony, (you) too suggested . . . that any
human system is fallible. And ergo, even with all of the D.N.A.

and all of the protections that we have, there is an intellectual possibility that we would execute the wrong person at some point in time in our future.

For him (Professor Blecker), and I believe based on his testimony, that was sort of just what we must bear. Is that your position also, that even though he recognized the possibility that with all those protections humanly instituted, that the possibility of someone being convicted and executed who is innocent still exists for this state, but that's just the burden that we should bear?

Mr. Byrne: Sir, as I said, anytime we have a human system there's a potential for error, and you know, we should do our very best to always protect that those errors don't happen, but they could happen, yes, sir. Many, many errors happen.

Nuclear – a nuclear power plant could blow up and kill thousands of people due to human error. It happens. I understand that.

Mr. Aubry: But you would still think that a death penalty should be instituted even in light of it?

Mr. Byrne: I think that a death penalty law could be passed and appropriately implemented (in) . . . New York State even in light of that risk.

. . .

Mr. Lavine: (If such a law is passed) . . . we're always going to have these – we're always going to have these questions (legal and factual) when we have a nation that is as ambivalent as it is toward the ultimate, the ultimate penalty of death; fair enough?

Mr. Byrne: Yes, sir.

Mr. Lavine: No matter how good a job we ever try to do to pass a statute that will meet constitutional muster, because death is different, we're always going to run the substantial risk that it will, or portions will, be declared unconstitutional, and that's because – fair enough? Because we're only human too; right?

      Mr. Byrne: Yeah, well, there's always the risk that portions of it will be found unconstitutional in the future.

      Mr. Lavine: And that could apply to any law; correct?

      Mr. Byrne: Yes, sir.

      Mr. Lavine: But much more so, much more so when we're dealing with death penalty litigation.

      Mr. Byrne: Yes, sir. Our experience here is very similar to other major states who reenacted the death penalty in the '80s and after. I mean, California, I believe, it was 98 out of the first 100 cases were reversed; it was, I believe, 28 out of 28 in Ohio; something like 32 out of 32 in New Jersey. I mean, that's going to happen.

Arguments over innocence can be abstract and theoretical. The New York Hearings faced this problem by eliciting powerful testimony from convicted murderers who were exonerated while in prison, and from the lawyers who represented them. As documented by the Death Penalty Information Center, exonerations are a continuing phenomenon. For example, the DPIC reported that Nathan Fields had become the 131st person to be exonerated from death row. On April 8, 2009, Fields was acquitted of murder in the retrial of his original case. Fields served almost 20 years in prison and over 11 years on the Illinois death row. His first trial was "marred by corruption" including the payment of a $10, 000 bribe during the trial. Fields' co-defendant, Earl Hawkins, who admitted to killing 15 to 20 people, testified against Fields at the retrial but was found by Judge Vincent Gaughn to be utterly non-credible. The judge observed "if someone has such disregard for human life, what regard will he have for this oath" to tell the truth.

The following presents the voices of some of the exonerated.

      Assemblyman Lentol: Our last panel member is Madison Hobley.

Mr. Hobley: Good afternoon, ladies and gentlemen. My name is Madison Hobley and I was born and raised in Chicago and I spent 16 years on Illinois's death row for a crime that I did not commit. I've (been) out a little under two years and I give credit to being here today to Governor Ryan, the former Governor of Illinois. . . .

I'm also – presently I'm a member of the Campaign – the (anti-)death penalty (campaign) - and my mission is to have the death penalty abolished nationwide. I'd like to give you a briefing of my case. Back in January of 1987, I was accused of setting my own apartment on fire and seven people died including my wife, who was my high school sweetheart, and our 15 month old baby, baby boy, who I named after my dad, who died or was murdered prior to my graduating eighth grade.

I want to tell you exactly what happened in my case. After the police detectives learned that I survived the fire, I was taken into custody. From the moment I was taken into custody, these two white officers, they told me they did not like niggers. I was referred to as a nigger from the time I was taken into the interrogation room until the time I woke up by being suffocated with a plastic bag over my head.

To this day, I'm talking 17 years later, I still remember this one officer, Officer Dwyer, badge 44, he put a chair in front of me, said to me, it's a known fact that black and white didn't get along. As far as he was concerned, I was a nigger and I was the nigger that did it and whoever set the fire – the niggers that died in the fire, they did him a favor.

As he was telling me I couldn't relate because I'm from an interracial family and all I know is we love each other. Also, I want to let you know, these officers, what they did was, they went and got a gas can from a fire that happened a month before my building was set on fire, and they placed the can on the fire scene and said that I confessed to putting it there. Also, they concealed the results from the analysis of the fingerprint test proving that my fingerprints weren't on the can – 10 years later, we hired a fire investigation specialist and when they saw the can, they actually thought it was a joke because the can that was supposedly on the scene of the fire had a little plastic cap on it and it hadn't even been singed. But they kept that from us. We weren't allowed to talk about it.

And they also, when we found (out) through the Chicago Police Department that another can existed and we found out about it, they hurried up and destroyed it and said that the statue of limitations had passed and we had no right to it, so they destroyed it.

Again, through the courage of George Ryan and the Commission, they saw these things and George Ryan had the courage to give me a pardon with actual innocence. I've been out for two years, almost two years.

Also, what people don't understand, if you heard my story, I feel that I've been wronged twice. I was put on death row for a crime I didn't commit, and my wife and child was murdered, so I have it from both sides.

We talk about the death penalty, justice and retribution and all that. I just want to bring a point. If we really want to bring justice, and if we care about the victims, I would like these pro-death penalty people to put their money where their mouth is and instead of spending millions of dollars executing people, why not use the millions of dollars for grants for the victim's families and send their kids to college.

Instead of using the money to kill in the state, why not cover grants to the victim's families and show that you really care. That's what I'd like to say.

Assemblyman Lentol: Mr. Melendez.

Mr. Melendez: My name is Juan Roberto Melendez. I was born in Brooklyn, New York, and raised on the island of Puerto Rico.

I am the 99th death row inmate in the United States to be exonerated and released from death row since 1973. Right now, 117 death row inmates have been exonerated and released because of innocence. You will hear from three of us today but please imagine that 117 of us could be standing here before you sharing their tragic stories of terrible injustice.

As in so many of the other cases of innocence, I am a very lucky man to be alive today and able to speak with you. God only knows how many others were not so lucky and have already been executed. There was no DNA evidence in my case. In fact, DNA played a role in only 14 out of 117 cases of exoneration. It's only available in a small percentage of murder cases. I can say with certainty that I was not saved by the system. I was saved in spite of the system. I was saved by miracles. I'm a very lucky man. My case was upheld three times on appeal by the Supreme Court of Florida. First of all my first miracle was my trial attorney, and I thank God for this, he became a judge. It creates a conflict of interest and I was able to get my case out of (a) racist county and move(d) to another county. It fell into the hands of a courageous woman, a female judge by the name of the Honorable Barbara Fleischer. I can sincerely say that I owe my life to her. A woman who wanted to do the right thing.

The other thing in my case that made a big impact was, they finally took the confession of the real killer. When they took the confession of the real killer, they also found that he had confessed to more killings.

They even found physical evidence against him. But the case was on – three times. I've got to say I'm very lucky. Some people would call it luck, I call it a miracle.

I will tell you the suffering in death row. I can certainly say that I was mentally tortured, my family and I. Death row is hell. My mother and – I still get letters from, I kept the letters that my mother and my aunts wrote me. And every once in a while I read them. I saved this one in my head. She wrote me and she said, Son, I did not raise no killer. You're not a killer. I believe that you're innocent. I just built an altar. I put a statue of the Virgin of the Guadalupe in there and I cut roses. I pray five rosaries a day. You just got to have faith in God and he will get you out of there. So she was one of reasons for me to survive. She gave me hope and the will to live and I survived like that. But it was hard times. But I remember lots of times I wanted to commit suicide and I came very close many times. And believe me, a lot of my friends committed suicide. What saved me was every time I wanted to make that move and commit suicide, I just laid down and I asked our creator to send me a beautiful dream, my childhood, the happy days. And I took all those dreams as a sign of hope that one day I would be out of there.

The place is terrible, the conditions in the State of Florida. Death row is not going to get the best medication. If you're condemned to death, why waste the best medication on you. I have seen people really, they let (them) die with heart attacks .... They have to put the handcuffs and the chains and all that stuff (on) before they move you out of that cell. Security is first. Your life is nothing. Every time you move out of that cell, you got to have chains, handcuffs, and chains around your waist, shackles.

One thing that also helped me survive on death row is this. I did not know how to read and write and speak English when I went to death row. Condemned men taught me how to read, how to write, how to speak English. When I learned how to read, how to write, and how to speak, I was able to communicate better with my attorneys. I was able to understand the situation I was in. And I was able to write pen pals. And that helped me survive.

It is simple. It's real simple why it cannot be fixed. Because we're all humans. There is always going to be an overzealous prosecutor, always going to be corrupt law enforcement officers. There's always going to be somebody who is going to take that stand and swear on a stack of Bibles and still tell a lie. If you sentence a person to life in prison, and 12 years later you find out that he's innocent, you can give him his life back. But if you sentence a person to death, you cannot give him his life back if you kill him. So to avoid all this, sooner or later, if you go to the death penalty, sooner or later, this state will have an innocent man on death row and you will have killed an innocent man. I already know people that I know in my heart are innocent and they already have been executed.

I will give you full names, Jesse Tafero, Leo James and Pedro Medina. To me they all were – there is no one here who is innocent in this nation if we don't stop this death penalty madness. We're going to be guilty of murder because when the state kills, you are the one killing. So please, I plead to you, don't reinstate the death penalty in this state.

Show the rest of the nation that we don't need the death penalty, that we can deal without it and we can do a better job. The job is not killing. Killing doesn't resolve killing.

God bless you and peace and love to you all.

Mr. Lentol: Thank you very much. Please begin. Who's first? You.

Mr. Restivo

Mr. John Restivo: My name is John Restivo. I am here today as living proof that New York's criminal justice system can convict innocent people of a crime they did not commit.

In the winter of 1984 I was 26 years old. I was living in Montour, New York, just a few miles from Lynbrook, the town – the town in Long Island where I was born and raised. My father, who had just passed away, was a member of the Nassau County Police Department for more than 20 years.

I had never been convicted of any crime. I owned a small business and had just purchased a home with my fiancée, who was pregnant with our first child.

Less than six months later my world was shattered. Along with two other men who worked with me I was indicted by a grand jury for the rape and murder of a Lynbrook teenager. She had been abducted while walking home from her job at a roller rink one Saturday night.

None of us had anything whatsoever to do with that crime. In fact, we all had alibis, independent alibis, and mine was corroborated by telephone and business records. Yet somehow all three of us were convicted of rape and murder and sentenced to spend the rest of our lives in prison.

I woke up in a prison cell every day for the next 18 years. Finally in June of 2003 my codefendants and I were all set free after D.N.A. testing proved we were innocent. Our lawyers were joined by the district attorney's office in a rare joint motion to throw out these convictions, after a series of D.N.A. tests showed that another man had committed this rape and murder.

I served 6,566 days in New York's toughest prisons for a crime I did not commit. I lost my home, my family, and every penny I had to my name, but at least I am alive.

Today I can appear before you to bear living witness to the fact that our criminal justice system can and does convict innocent people of the most serious crimes. But if New York had a death penalty in the 1980s I have no doubt that I would not be here today.

This is not just because our system is run by human beings who can and do make mistakes. It's also because the kind of horrible crimes for which the death penalty is used are exactly the cases in which common sense and reason are most likely to go out the window. Believe me, I know.

It is hard to describe the fear and hysteria that ripped my community when that young girl's body was found in the woods, especially because the police had no leads on the perpetrator. To this day I still don't fully understand exactly how or why my friends and I became suspects in this case, much less were convicted.

The witnesses at my trial were a series of dubious characters, most of whom were seeking a break from their own criminal charges, (and they) falsely claimed that we had made statements somehow indicating a knowledge of the crime.

Given my alibi, and what I knew to be the truth, I couldn't imagine I would ever be convicted based on this kind of flimsy evidence. However, when I was brought into court, before any witness ever took the stand, I could feel the jury thinking if he's sitting there he must be guilty. I really thank God that the death penalty was not an option available to them at that time, because I have no doubt they would have used it.

I also want to make clear that just because D.N.A. testing has been developed since the time I was convicted, (it) is not a guarantee against a conviction or execution of an innocent person in the future. I'm here today because of the combination of determination and sheer luck. There were D.N.A. tests – there were D.N.A. test results pointing to another man in our case for more than seven years before my conviction was overturned. During that time I filed every motion and Freedom of Information request I could think of, seeking more tests to prove my innocence, but was told that additional evidence which could be tested had already been consumed.

Then three years ago, my new legal team miraculously located a test tube with an intact vaginal swab from the victim that we never knew existed. It was buried inside one of the seven boxes of police department evidence that they (the lawyers) had found and gotten permission to search by hand. The testing on that swab provided the critical piece of D.N.A. evidence that finally set me and the others free.

But that only happened because we had a dream team of lawyers and law students from the Innocence Project, Pace Law School, and a prestigious corporate law firm on our side, all of whom worked for free on the case for years and never gave up. But believe me, not everyone convicted of murder in New York is lucky enough to have Barry Scheck as their lawyer.

I also want to emphasize that while there was a lot of media attention on my case at the time I was freed from prison, the system that wrongfully convicted me has not yet been fixed.

The millions of dollars that it would take for you to bring back the death penalty in New York could instead be used to address these ongoing problems. It could provide lawyers for hundreds of people in prison who might well be innocent, but do not have the ability to prove it on their own, or videotape police interrogations of witnesses and suspects so that a full record of the process exists and can be examined by a jury, or reform grand jury procedures to identify cases of innocence earlier in the process. And there is so much that can and must be done before New York State should even consider sentencing anyone to death.

Thank you for holding these hearings and for the serious and careful consideration you're giving this issue. I only hope you will think long and hard about how I spent the last two decades before you vote to bring back the death penalty in New York.

Mr. Lentol: Thank you.

Sammie Thomas?

Mr. Sammie Thomas: Hi. I'm Sammie Thomas, and in 1975 I and my brother, older brother, were convicted of a robbery/homicide in the town of Auburn, New York. I received a sentence of 15 (years) to life. He received a sentence of 25 to life.

We spent a little over four years in prison for those charges. We weren't released until about, like I say, about a little over four years later when the Court of Appeals ordered the district attorney to turn over 18 pieces of extremely exculpatory evidence that he had.

When we got that (new) evidence it was turned over to us at a new trial. It took the jury less than five minutes to come back with a not guilty verdict. Had we had that (evidence) during the first trial, the appeals court said that outcome would have been different. . . .

This district attorney that had this evidence after we had – my attorneys had made numerous requests for this information during the trial - he said he didn't have it. And it wasn't until a new district attorney – and this district attorney (in the original case) has moved on . . . he's a superior court judge. He used our case to – as a stepping stone to become a judge. There was nothing ever done about him, what he did. But thanks to the new district attorney that came in behind him, you know, this evidence was not cast out into a trash can or something. They turned it over to us and that was a saving grace. We really – we lucked out there on that case.

Author Scott Christianson broadened the discussion of wrongful convictions with the following testimony.

Mr. Scott Christianson: Thank you for this opportunity to testify about capital punishment policy at this critical moment in New York history.

My name is Scott Christianson. I'm a former New York State criminal justice official, having served as Director of Prison Affairs for the Commission of Correction, Special Assistant at the Division of Criminal Justice Services, Executive Assistant to the State Director of Criminal Justice, Deputy Director of the Division of Probation and Correctional

Alternatives, and Deputy Director of Parole Operations in the Division of Parole.

I've also worked with several not-for-profit criminal justice organizations and I have taught courses at five universities or colleges within the state. I've worked as an investigative reporter, published hundreds of articles in scholarly and popular journals, and authored several books on criminal justice subjects. Some of my work has been cited by the United States Supreme Court.

As someone who has been deeply involved in death penalty issues over the last 30 years, I have many observations and opinions to offer, but in my brief remarks today I will try to limit myself to matters involving wrongful conviction.

Much of what I have to say is based on my work involving two recent books; one of these, CONDEMNED: INSIDE THE SING SING DEATH HOUSE, published in 2000, entailed extensive research into the internal official records of the unit at Sing Sing Prison (New York) that executed 614 persons from 1891 to 1963.

In that state's own internal official files I found many documents bearing on the issue of wrongful conviction. In my view that state's official records indicate that some actually innocent persons have been legally executed before they could prove their innocence.

My other book that is relevant here, INNOCENT: INSIDE WRONGFUL CONVICTION CASES, published in 2003, examined the current problem of wrongful conviction in New York State and some of its historical antecedents.

This study entailed looking at more than a hundred cases involving persons who were later exonerated in the courts, some of whom were paid damages by the state of New York and various localities.

For this project I also selected 12 individuals who were still in prison whom I had concluded were actually innocent and wrongfully convicted. Thus far, six have had their convictions overturned, and five of those have been released from prison, and the sixth has had his sentence drastically reduced.

Of the remaining six innocent prisoners, two are awaiting action by a federal court; one is before a judge in Suffolk County Court; and the three others are either still perfecting their appeals or preparing to go before the parole board.

I think my track record on these cases is better than the criminal justice system's.

For the purpose of this hearing I should point out that although none of the 12 cases mentioned was a capital case, 11 of these individuals were convicted of murder before the state reinstituted capital punishment in 1995. If we had the death penalty on the books at the time they were processed some of them could be dead by now.

One of these, Martin Tankleff, is still in prison for the double murder of his parents, after one of the most contentious legal battles in Long Island history. He is totally innocent and the system is guilty.[89]

Another, Fernando Bermudez, remains convicted of a 1990 murder in Manhattan based upon mistaken eyewitness testimony resulting from blundering police practices. The same practices resulted in three other almost identical wrongful arrests and convictions stemming from shootouts at other Manhattan social clubs in that period.

I have not investigated persons who were prosecuted or convicted under the 1995 capital statute, so I'm not able to comment on those cases. What I do have to say to you today is based on my historical research using official records and other sources. It's also based on what I see going on right now in police stations and prosecutors' offices and courthouses and prisons throughout the state.

Before anybody considers whether or how to quote, "fix," end quote, New York's court-invalidated death penalty law, they must address the serious and growing problem of wrongful conviction that plagues the entire criminal justice system, not only capital cases. And make no mistake about it, it's a huge problem. It's a statewide problem existing in every region, and I believe in every county. It's a problem that undermines respect for the administration of justice.

As I see it, the state's long history of erroneous convictions and a continuing trail of high profile mistakes, such as the Central Park jogger case, the state police fingerprint scandal,[90] the N.Y.P.D. Dirty Thirty scandal,[91] and the constant stream of acknowledged injustices being paraded through the press, should have long ago set off warning bells.

But criminal justice officials have resisted introducing basic accountability measures or safeguards, and you legislators have not enacted reforms. Therefore, there's no assurance that more fatal mistakes will not be made if we reestablish capital punishment here.

Several studies over the years have found New York to rank high on the nation's list of wrongful convictioners. One of these studies, by Edward M. Borchard, a professor of law at Yale Law School, was published in 1932 under the (title) . . . "Convicting the Innocent." Borchard identified 65 cases in which he claimed there had been a miscarriage of justice and New York had more of them than any other state.

Since the 1960s Professor Hugo A. Bedau of Tufts University has published numerous works documenting as many as 343 cases of wrongful conviction.

Writing with Michael Radelet, now of the University of Colorado, Professor Bedau identified three New York death sentences that were commuted based on a governor's concerns about actual innocence. These include Charles Stielow from 1915, a case which I have also examined in a film broadcast by the History Channel; Edward Larkman from 1926; and Pietro Matera from 1932. Without extraordinary intervention by a governor, all three of these men would have died.

Bedau and Radelet have also asserted that some persons have been legally executed by New York, even though they were actually innocent.

Their list includes the following, and let me read their names: Frank Cirofici, who was executed in 1913; Thomas Bambrick, executed in 1916; Max Rybarczyk in 1930; Steven Grzechowiak in 1930; Everett Applegate in 1936; George Chew Wing in 1937; and Charles Sberna in 1939.

Since this study was published I've come across information in the Sing Sing death house archives about one of these cases, Sberna, and it further supports Bedau and Radelet's conclusion.

Based on my review of the archival records and other sources, I've concluded that the list for New York that was provided by Professors Bedau and Radelet only scratches the surface. There are indications of many other mistaken executions here, and certainly there have been dozens, dozens of wrongful capital convictions that have thankfully been stopped before they resulted in wrongful execution.

. . .

Today, . . . with the advent of D.N.A. and possibly other definitive technologies, actual innocence in some cases threatens to become positively established even after an offender has been convicted or even legally executed. In my view such a happening could have a devastating effect on public confidence about the quality of justice being meted out in the state.

It's bad enough that 50 years after her execution at Sing Sing, Ethel Rosenberg's accuser has revealed that his key testimony against her was a lie. Just imagine if D.N.A. later popped up to exonerate her or some other high-profile executed person.

The state should convene a blue-ribbon panel to hold public hearings and report its findings on wrongful convictions. Police should be required to videotape in full all interrogations, and to make a copy of the tape available to suspects. Although this can help to protect the police from unfounded allegations of coercion, some police, including the New York Police Department, have resisted it.

Police should utilize sequential photo lineups such as New Jersey has done; the state must overhaul its inadequate public defense system to ensure that indigent defendants will receive effective legal representation; prosecutors should not enjoy total immunity from civil liability; the law should make it easier for an inmate to get a new trial based on newly discovered evidence; whenever a wrongful conviction has been shown, the police department, prosecutor, defense attorney, and judge involved, should file a damage report explaining what went wrong and suggesting what can be done to prevent a reoccurrence.

(W)ithout extraordinary safeguards any execution would amount to legalized lynching. The state's legalized killing of one innocent person would make murderers of us all. The inevitability of error is just one reason why the death penalty is a bad idea, but it's one that fair-minded citizens, even punitive ones, can understand.

(W)e also have to recognize that wrongful convictions can probably never be totally eliminated, until and unless we have ensured a perfect system of justice. Absent that perfection we should not impose the irrevocable punishment of death.

That concludes my prepared remarks and I'd be happy to respond to any questions.

Testimony on innocence continued with Myron Beldock, Lawyer for Yusef Salaam, and exonerated defendants Yusef Salaam, Karey Wise, and Robert McLaughlin.

Mr. Beldock: Yes, I'll proceed. I thank the members of the Assembly for this opportunity to speak on this most important subject. I submit this statement in opposition to reinstatement of the death penalty. My name is Myron

Beldock. Over my 44 years as a lawyer I've had some experience which I hope will provide relevant information and insight as to why the death penalty should not be reinstated.

My general theme is innocence and I start with the Central Park Jogger case and then I want to talk about some other cases I've been involved in. The Central Park Jogger case was not a death penalty case of course but the victim was so near death, so near to death, and it involved the kind of facts which cause those in favor of the death penalty to cry out for vengeance, for punishment by death of the persons who could have committed such a horrible, sexually perverted and brutal attack.

The young woman's injuries were calamitous and her survival miraculous. Had she died, particularly in this kind of case, the public clamor and pressure for death to the attackers would have been tremendous. Yet, as we all know, the convicted defendants turned out to be innocent.

After my remarks you'll hear from my client Yusef Salaam, one of the exonerated defendants in that case . . . and there is an added person here, Karey Wise, one of the other defendants in the jogger case who wants to make a statement, who wasn't scheduled. I trust in speaking . . . Yusef will positively influence your thinking.

Yusef had just turned 15 when he and 4 other Manhattan youths, three 14 year olds and one 16 year old, were charged in 1989 with that horrible sexual assault and beating of the jogger. Their 1990 convictions were reversed in December 2002. After (they) all had suffered many years in prison and had years on parole and this happened when Matias Reyes, (the) sole perpetrator, came forward to accept responsibility, and his DNA and related evidence proved that he was the only assailant. And this happened only after the New York County DA's office thoroughly reinvestigated the initial 1989 investigation to determine that the charges and trials were fatally flawed and the convictions should be set aside.

In that case my client's so called confession barely qualified as such .... (I)t was a statement allegedly rewritten by a detective in his notebook days later which Yusef neither signed nor read. But there were extensive written statements and video statements taken from his four co-defendants, all of which turned out to be false as well. Those confessions, which were previously embraced as the only possible truth, particularly because of their tell-tale details, are now exposed as being totally unreliable and unworthy of belief.

Let me give you one other example of innocence in the face of the death penalty. In late 1974 ... I became counsel for (the well-known boxer) Rubin Hurricane Carter, seeking and ultimately obtaining a new trial in the 1966 Patterson New Jersey triple murder case. I think most of you know about Hurricane's case because of the long saga, the publicity and public attention, the three books and the movie.

Anyhow, before my involvement in Hurricane's case, after the first trial and conviction, there was actually a death penalty hearing. Fortunately for Rubin and his co-defendant, John Artis, a jury that convicted did not vote for death. Still, it took 13 years on our watch once we came in the case for our volunteer team of lawyers to win freedom for Rubin and John through a Federal habeas corpus proceeding. It went all the way up to the US Supreme Court.

The ... Carter and Salaam cases are striking examples of wrongful convictions of innocent persons. If the death penalty is reinstated, then we will once again have (the) state killing innocent persons. You can bet on it. This is an intolerable circumstance which we should avoid at all costs....

I urge you not to reinstate the death penalty because it is morally wrong for the State to take life and in the process, the State will inevitably take the lives of innocent persons who have been wrongfully convicted. It should never be reinstated. Thank you.

The testimony of exonerated defendant Yusef Salaam was presented in detail in Chapter Three's discussion of retribution as a justification for the death penalty. Some of that testimony is reproduced here on the issue of innocence.

> Speaker Lentol: Yusef?
>
> Mr. Salaam: To the distinguished panel and members of the Assembly of the State of New York, I am Yusef Salaam. I was one of the five innocent youths convicted of brutally attacking and raping the Central Park Jogger, Ms. Patricia Meili. . . .
>
> It is only by sheer happenstance that I appear before you today, in flesh and spirit and a free man rather than as one more statistic, unjustly mob or state murdered or incarcerated, and (a) therefore lost human being . . . .
>
> Members of the panel, I respectfully submit to you that you collectively and individually can and indeed have an obligation to stop this cycle of death and sanctioned murder. It's only by happenstance that I appear before you today. I was 15 years old, just a boy, when these events changed my life forever.
>
> Because I was the tallest and presumably the darkest skin of my co-defendants, people pointed at me saying things like what we need to do is hang him; for what they did they don't deserve a trial; he needs to be made an example of; he needs to be under the jail; death threats and much more of the like.
>
> We were labeled as scourge of the earth, wolf pack, wilding. So vicious was the media-inspired atmosphere that even few people of color sought justice for us. Not even the judge in the case sought justice. Until exoneration by the courts, I had spent and lost nearly 14 years of my life under the weighty, spiked wheels of the Criminal Justice System.

That period represents my life between the ages of 15 through 28.

In normal life, what would have happened to me by the time I turned 16? In a normal life, what would have happened for me by the time I would have turned 18? In a normal life, what would have happened for me by the time I turned 21? And likewise, what would have happened in a normal life by the time I turned 25?

In a state with the death penalty, what would have happened had Ms. Patricia Meili unfortunately died as a result of the attack? In all likelihood, instead of being here with you now I would have either been executed or instead of being here with you now, I'd be waiting execution. Honorable members of the panel, again, it's only by happenstance that I sit before here, sit before you today.

In 2002, thirteen years after our false confessions, convictions rather, the real rapist of the Central Park Jogger, Matias Reyes, voluntarily came forward and confessed to the crime and he confessed that he was the only one involved. Our convictions were reversed but fourteen years of our lives had been erased. At the time of his confession, Reyes was already in prison for the rape and murder of other women. Ironically, by the time of his confession, the statute of limitations had run out on the crimes that he committed in the Central Park Jogger case. Some still say however, that justice was served because we served his time. Had this been a capital crime, we also would have served his death penalty.

Honorable members of the panel, the wrongful convictions of the Central Park Jogger case speak volumes concerning serious and disastrous flaws in . . . (the) implementation of the death penalty. This is so regarding the likelihood of innocents being executed by the state and it also speaks volumes concerning the processes involved in a state making the choice to sanction the death penalty. With the foregoing notwithstanding this case speaks volumes concerning the desperate number of people of color in prison and languishing on death row.

Some politicians and other advocates for the death penalty have been known to glibly remark that justice can't be perfect. In effect . . . admitting that some innocent people have to die for what Patrick Buchanan calls help to public order. What a despicable and backward and inhuman position for a person to take. What a despicable and backward and inhuman position for the state to take. Members of the panel, I respectfully submit that you (must) end the State sanctioned death machine. This from a man who appears to you today only happenstance.

Mr. Salaam was followed by another Central Park Jogger defendant.

Speaker Lentol: Karey Wise, though not previously scheduled to speak, we understand you wanted to briefly address the Committees?

Mr. Wise: Good afternoon Committee. It's a pleasure to be here. My name is Karey Wise, from the Central Park Jogger file, case, who just came home . . . (I) served a good 14, 14 and a half, years for a crime I did not commit. I never had a record, a criminal record. I'm glad it doesn't exist no more. Many suns later. But my experience of incarceration, it was a death sentence. It was. And I don't know how I made it out of there, but it was the will of God, but it was a death sentence.

I then died every year for ten years. And I thank God to have my mother still around because she did a great deal of that with me. I don't know exactly what she's going to experience since we're home, but as far as me being behind the wall for 15 years of my life since the age of 16, it was a death sentence for me.

I carry the world on my back so that was a death sentence for me. I'm glad that I came, I'm glad that Matias Reyes made it his business to come before me, and to do what he did. Do I hate him? No. I understand that the man is sick. But for him to come forward to do this here instead of us, instead of me and my co-defendants having to dig up some sort of evidence to bring it back to the courts, is better late than, his news is better late than never.

It took a great deal of years out of my life. It's very hard for me to pick that back up. But I'm here, still strong, still holding on, and the death penalty . . . I'd advise you not to . . . bring that out because there's a lot of people out on death row that really got to beat that (death sentence because) they are innocent. Thank you, thank you. . . .

Robert McLaughlin, an exonerated convicted murderer, testified about the circumstances of wrongful convictions.

Mr. (Robert) McLaughlin: Hello. Thanks for having me here today and listening. My name is Robert McLaughlin and I'm out of Brooklyn, New York. I grew up here. And I was wrongly convicted, when I was 20 years old, of a murder I didn't commit.

It was basically based on an eyewitness, (and) that's where a lot of the mistakes are made today. And eyewitness (testimony) is so hard to reverse . . . .

There were many mistakes made in my case. There was a coerced witness, (and) another suspect with the same name as my name, but they went to get me instead of the other guy. There (were) a lot of little mistakes that happened in my case that weren't made (known) to the jury, and the jury didn't have this information.

They didn't know there (were) two Bob McLaughlins. I'll just give you a brief summary. One witness picked out a perpetrator. His name was William Farrell. Well, on the back of his . . . ID (was a note about) . . . a previous robbery that he had (committed). . . (and the note contained) the name Bob McLaughlin.

So they went and got me instead of the other Bob McLaughlin and put me in the line-up. Well, the detective told the ... 15-year-old witness that (since) they did a previous robbery (Farrell and McLaughlin), that they probably committed this one together.

So with all this combined, the witness eventually picked me out and I was convicted of murder. But this didn't come out – the line-up was actually thrown out of court before the trial because it was so tainted. But the witness was still allowed to testify (at trial) which was based on everything that was tainted. So it was ridiculous.

To cut the story short, I ended up going to trial and getting sentenced to fifteen to life and sent upstate to some of the worst prisons in New York State.

And when I was in prison, I don't think there's a lot of people here that could testify what it's like in prison, okay? It's a living hell. When somebody is sentenced to life in prison, and I heard people saying, oh, they watch TV and this and that. I feared every day for my life in there. People do not have fun in there. It's miserable ....

And some people say the system worked because I got out. The system didn't work because I got out. My foster father – I'm just going to tell you how I got out. I exhausted all my appeals to get out, which means the next step, if the death penalty was in effect, I would have been killed.

So at that point, after six years, my foster father went to bat for me. And believe me, my foster father believed in justice. He believed the system worked. And that's what a lot of people believe when they read the paper. Oh, they must have got that guy. He's guilty. Let's kill him.

Well they don't know what happens behind the scenes. You know, they don't know how they got to this – how they got this guy, how it all happened. And a lot of times mistakes are made.

But my dad believed in the justice system, and when this went wrong and he knew I was innocent, he went to bat for me, and he dragged up every bit of phone numbers, people I knew, to see if I was connected to this other guy . . . and nothing added up, and he believed in my innocence.

Actually, he didn't believe in my innocence in the beginning. He says, Bob, how do I know you didn't do this? And I was like, Dad, believe me, I didn't do this. You know, but because he was such a law-and-order-type person, I actually had to take a lie detector test to prove it to my dad, in the beginning. So that was something that shocked me.

But then we went to trial and got convicted. And like I said, after many years, five or six years, he went to bat for me. And the only thing he could do, I exhausted all my remedies to get out, he had to write letters to get somebody to listen. And he wrote letters to the local church right up to the President.

Well, he got people to listen. A Civil Liberties Union (lawyer) listened, Barry Scheck got involved with my case. There was a number of people. Back then there wasn't an Innocence Project of New York, so he just gathered up whoever he could. (The television show) 20/20 came up and did a story on me.

And that's what sparked – (the) media had to spark somebody to listen and put pressure on them. And what happened was, they reopened the case for an investigation. And back then Mario Cuomo was the governor who was opposed to the death penalty.

But I was – actually, the investigation happened and they reopened the case after about six years, eight months, and Elizabeth (Holtzman) was in office at the time, and she opened it up for investigation.

The one 15-year-old witness against me finally came forward and said, I was never really sure. The detectives kind of coerced me into saying what happened. And I was released. Like I said, people think that the justice system was fixed because I got out. That wasn't it.

And it ruined my life after I got out also. You know, I was involved with drugs and alcohol. I didn't know what to do, you know, and I just went in the wrong direction. I tried to make up for lost time.

Well that's why I came here today, to oppose the death penalty. We're going to kill innocent people. It's inevitable. If we have the death penalty, it's going to happen. And it's just wrong. It's wrong.

Like I said, I was in there, I know what it's like. It's worse to keep them (prisoners) alive. It is. They're having a miserable time in there. It's miserable for them in there, period. It's worst to keep them alive.

When you kill (them), okay, you just let them out of jail mentally, because they're out of jail and they don't think about it no more. They're dead, they're gone, it's done. So in my own opinion it's worse to keep them in there. They're suffering more.

And if that's not enough, you can put a little stipulation, you put them in segregation. If it's such a hideous crime where it's so bad, stipulate that they do not associate with general population. Believe me, that would drive them absolutely nuts.

Thanks for listening to me.[92]

(Applause)

Professor William Hellerstein of Brooklyn Law School provided further commentary on the problem of wrongful convictions.

Mr. Hellerstein: My name is William E. Hellerstein. I am a Professor of Law at Brooklyn Law School. I teach Constitutional Law, Criminal Procedure, and Civil Rights Law. I am also the Director of the Brooklyn Law School's Second Look Clinic, which is an innocence project, a non-DNA innocence project. I also currently serve as the co-chair of the New York State Commission on the Future of Indigent

Defense Services, having been appointed by Chief Judge Kay last January.

Prior to my joining the Brooklyn Law School faculty in 1985, I spent 21 years with the Criminal Appeals Bureau of the Legal Aid Society, of which I was Chief for 17 years.

I have been practicing criminal law now for 40 years, at least, during which time I have secured personally the freedom of a number of defendants who were totally innocent of the crimes for which they were convicted, and my colleagues at Legal Aid did the same. I am also representing at the present time two individuals who I believe to be innocent and hope to be able to establish that in our courts of law.

I am familiar with the numerous studies and data which document the hundreds of other exonerations nationally, including those within the State of New York. It is my firmest belief, probably firmer than anything else I believe in life, that the death penalty should not be reinstated in New York. It is a belief that is founded on a single harsh reality: that the capacity for error in our criminal justice system is so great that the possibility of the execution of an innocent man or woman is the . . . unbending reality of our system. It's (a) fact of life whose prevalence cannot be ignored and one which repudiates, in my mind, intrinsically, any countervailing argument in favor of the retention of the death penalty. The evidence is there and it cannot be minimized. I will first give you a very brief synopsis of the national picture, as I have come to understand it, as to wrongful convictions, and let me give you some case histories from our own State of people who were sentenced to death (and) who were (later) established innocent and saved from the death penalty.

You heard this morning, I think, one statement that no one in New York has ever been executed who was innocent. I don't think anyone can make that statement, especially when you look at how close these individuals that I will tell you about came. And finally I would like to tell you about some of my own cases in which I was able to establish that my client was innocent and one in which I failed to do so, but someone else was successful. All three of those cases were cases which would have drawn the death penalty had we had one in effect at that time. They were homicides and more.

Let me tell you just very briefly about the comprehensive national picture that emerged from a study entitled, Exonerations in the United States, 1989 through 2003, which was just published this past April by Professor Samuel Gross of the University of Michigan Law School and his colleagues. And here, just a few of the findings.

From 1989 through 2003, there were 328 exonerations, 316 men and 12 women; 145 of them were cleared by DNA, 183 by other sorts of evidence. They had served an average of over ten years in prison for crimes for which they should never have been convicted. Four defendants were exonerated posthumously, after they had died in prison.

The database did not include at least 135 additional defendants who were framed by rogue police officers and cleared in two mass exonerations: in 1999-2000, in Los Angeles, in the aftermath of the discovery of the Rampart area police scandal; and in 2003 in Tulia, Texas, where a single dishonest undercover officer was shown to have framed 39 innocent drug defendants. He was just convicted last month of perjury and he got probation.

Almost all of our exonerations, 97 percent, grew out of convictions for the two most serious crimes of violence – 199 cases, 61 percent of all exonerations (involved murder), including 73 innocent defendants who were sentenced to death, 22 percent; and 120 . . . cases (involved rape), 37 percent.

Defendants convicted of murder constitute about 13 percent of American prisoners, but 61 percent of all exonerations, and 87 percent of the non-DNA exonerations. Death row inmates number about one-quarter of one percent of the prison population, but 22 percent of the exonerated.

The four leading states for exonerations of falsely convicted defendants were Illinois, 54; New York, 35; Texas, 28; and California, 22. All four of which . . . (were) states with capital punishment.

The leading cause of false convictions in the murder exonerations was perjury, including perjury by the real killers, and by supposed participants or eyewitnesses to the crime; perjury by jailhouse snitches and other police informants; and perjury by police officers and state forensic scientists.

New York's own history with the death penalty until 1963, the year of the last execution, also contains numerous instances where the death penalty was imposed on an innocent man. I will just make reference to several which are documented in studies by Hugo Adam Bedau in his book THE DEATH PENALTY IN AMERICA.[93]

For example, in 1915, Charles Stielow was sentenced to death for murder. Forty minutes before his scheduled execution, Stielow received a stay. After three years, he was exonerated and released when the real perpetrator confessed; Stielow's conviction had been obtained by a coerced confession.

In 1925, Edward Larkman was convicted of murder and sentenced to death. In 1927, the sentence was commuted to life, and in 1929 another convict confessed to the crime. Governor Lehman unconditionally pardoned Larkman in 1933.

In 1940, Louis Hoffner was convicted of murder and sentenced to death. The sentence was commuted to life imprisonment by Governor Dewey. In 1955, Hoffner was released and indemnified for false imprisonment.

Now, I would like to turn to three of my own cases that would have, I think, qualified for the death penalty.

Nathaniel Carter. On June 5, 1982, Mr. Carter was convicted by a jury in the Supreme Court, Queens County (N.Y.), of murder in the second degree. He was found guilty of the murder of his former mother-in-law, Clarice Herndon, who had been stabbed in her home 38 times. Nathaniel was sentenced to 25 years to life imprisonment. At his sentencing, Justice John Leahy said that for such a brutal crime, he would have been happy to impose the death penalty. I undertook the investigation and was able to prove that Nathaniel was framed by his ex-wife, Delissa, who also committed the murder. In January 1984, my motion to vacate Nathaniel's confession was granted and he was freed.

There is a cruel, or call it whatever you wish, irony to Nathaniel's case that I want to tell you about in the context of this Committee and its work.

Nathaniel grew up in Peekskill, New York, and he was the star of the Peekskill High School basketball team in his senior year. One of his teammates was George Pataki, our Governor. Governor Pataki is also a neighbor of mine in Garrison, New York, in Putnam County. In 1984, shortly after Nathaniel's conviction had been thrown out, Mr. Pataki, whom I knew and still know, walked over to my driveway and expressed his gratitude for the work I had done on behalf of his former teammate Nathaniel. I thanked Mr. Pataki and said, "you know, George, it's a good thing we don't have the death penalty in New York. Time might have run out on my attempts to exonerate Nathaniel." And here, why was Nathaniel convicted? We couldn't figure it out. He wasn't even in New York at the time.

I spoke to several of the jurors in part of my investigation and asked them how did you convict – and he testified in his own behalf. I read the record. The prosecution didn't lay a finger on him in terms of cross-examination. Three jurors said when he testified he was phlegmatic. He was calm. He wasn't angry. I said did you hear any inconsistencies? No, but he wasn't angry. And anyone charged with such a crime should be angry. Well, I went and told Nathaniel that. He said, Mr. Hellerstein, I knew that I was innocent so I wasn't angry. In fact, his personality is such that he's not angry.

I spoke to his coach. His coach said when he wanted to play it was 35 points a night, but when he didn't want to play they had to bench him, pull him out after the first ten minutes of the game. It was just that kind of personality. He was a religious person.

Let me tell you about the case that was the most difficult case of my life which I just was successful with this past month. It certainly would have qualified for the death penalty.

On August 24, 1987, David Wong, a Chinese immigrant, serving a sentence in Dannemora, was convicted in County Court, Clinton County (N.Y.), for the murder of Tyrone Julius on March 12, 1985, in the yard of Dannemora Prison. It was like the (movie) Shawshank Redemption scenario if you can think of it. He was sentenced to 25 years to life imprisonment on top of the sentence he was serving for robbery. More than two years ago with my students in the Second Look Clinic, I entered the case. Our investigation established that another inmate, not David, had killed Mr. Julius in pay back, in revenge, for this other inmates having his leg broken by Julius when they were both at Rikers Island together.

We had an evidentiary hearing in April and May of 2003 in Clinton County. And despite presenting ten witnesses, including the widow of the deceased who was a witness for us on certain evidentiary items, the county judge rejected all of those witnesses' testimony and I had to take an appeal to the Appellate Division, Third Department. But on October 21, of this year, the Appellate Division, Third Department, reversed, disagreeing on credibility grounds that our witnesses were believable and what the trial judge concluded was not acceptable.

The Appellate Division then remanded it. A new judge was assigned. And on December 20, Judge Richard Giardino from Johnstown acting up in Clinton County dismissed the indictment and said in this opinion, "on this record the situation facing this Court appears to be both rare and compelling. The defense clearly contends and, while not stating so specifically, the prosecution essentially admits that a trial at this juncture would likely result in acquittal." And of course it would.

But here was a case of a homicide committed in prison by a person serving a term in prison. Had Mr. Wong faced the death penalty in that situation (he could have been executed), remember it took me three years and this was a 17 year old conviction. I don't want to tell you the details of how difficult it was even after the Appellate Division reversed.

My last case is the case of Eric Jackson, and, certainly, this would have qualified for the death penalty.

Eric Jackson was convicted on March 2, 1981, in Supreme Court, Kings County. Six counts of felony murder for causing the death of six New York City firefighters in what was then known as the Waldbaum's Supermarket fire on Ocean Avenue in Brooklyn. He was sentenced to six concurrent 25 years to life terms of imprisonment. I represented Mr. Jackson on his appeals to the Appellate Division and the New York Court of Appeals but I was unable to persuade the courts that he was innocent. It was my belief based on the evidence in the record that the testimony of the prosecution's own forensic expert contradicted the other prosecution witness (who stated) that there had not been arson. So I argued that in the Appellate Courts but, of course, you know that's an issue for the trial court. And the (trial) attorney representing Mr. Jackson would not have won the Clarence Darrow Award for competency at that time.

After I left Legal Aid and joined the faculty at Brooklyn Law School, Robert Sullivan, a lawyer representing the widows of firefighters called me and said he believed Jackson was innocent based on material that he had discovered in pre-trial discovery in the civil cases and could I be of assistance. Well, Bob Sullivan fought that case, took it, handled it, and it was established that Jackson was not the person who committed the crime because there was no crime. There was no arson. It was an accidental fire. And he was free.

So the issue that I address today before you is should the death penalty be reinstated in New York. I'm not going to tell you about other cases in which I have been successful in freeing innocent people because they weren't capital cases. But these same elements of wrongful conviction are present in all. Poor representation, mistaken identifications, particularly cross-racial identifications, snitches, the works. But those cases, for me, are germane to the singular ground upon which I have based my argument to you; that given the possibility of error in our system of justice that is so substantial, that to risk an innocent man or woman to be executed is a risk that no civilized society should wish to assume, or as a matter of human decency should want to assume. There is no blinking (to) the fact that, unlike any other criminal sanction, death is final and cannot be undone. However, as long as a person remains alive, an erroneous conviction can be undone. And no society, I submit to you, can legitimately ask any innocent individual to pay with his or her life in order to retain a death penalty that some in that society value, whether that value is founded on assumptions about deterrence, retribution, or closure to the families of homicide victims.

Thank you for affording me the opportunity to present these views.

Much of the present thinking on innocence and exoneration comes from the work of the so-called Ryan Commission in Illinois. In that state, the sheer numbers of wrongful convictions led the then Governor, George Ryan, to commute all death sentences to life in prison without parole. Attorney Thomas P. Sullivan was a member of that Commission.

Assemblyman Lentol: Mr. Sullivan.

Mr. Sullivan: Ladies and gentlemen, my name is Thomas Sullivan and I am a lawyer from Chicago. I'd like to just take a minute to establish my credentials since I'm not from New York. I have been practicing law in Chicago for 50 years and been a member of the Bar for 52. I was United States Attorney of the Northern District of Illinois during the Carter administration, but almost all of my practice has been on civil and criminal work, and in the criminal work, mostly for the defense.

I did prosecute for four years, but in the federal system . . . the death penalty was not really an issue in Chicago. During my time, I have done a great deal of work for indigent clients in the state courts of Illinois, including murder cases, death penalty cases. I helped Mr. Albert Jenner, my mentor and senior partner, when he argued the Witherspoon[94] case in the Supreme Court of the United States which (was a) landmark opinion in this area. I was a member of Governor Ryan's Commission on capital punishment. Frank McGower, a former Chief Judge of the District Court, was the Chair, and former (U.S.) Senator Paul Simon and I were the co-chairs.

I do not come to capital punishment with a moral sense of outrage and I certainly don't come to it with the certainty of views that Professor Blecker has. Indeed, having been raised in Catholic schools all my life, it was my impression that the Pope was the only one that claimed infallibility, but that seems to, he's going to have to move over for Mr. Blecker. Just kidding. In any event. When we studied – we had 13 exonerated defendants in Illinois that led Governor Ryan to put a moratorium on the death penalty and then to appoint the Commission of 14 people that studied what needed to be done to make the system more accurate, fair and just. We did not deal with the question of abolition. 13 was about a 10% error rate.

Now, since then there's been four more (exonerated), so we're up to 17. So think in terms of a doctor who gets it wrong, kills 10% of the patients by mistake, and (then) ask yourself if you would . . . want to have . . . an operation (from that doctor) . . . .

But here's one of the things that I found interesting when I listened to Professor Blecker, he's talking about this (Scott) Peterson (California) case and how the jury expressed the community's outrage. I can tell you that in 17 cases in Illinois, the jury expressed the community's outrage and imposed the death penalty on those people. And when we studied these cases, and this is in our report, we wondered not only why the 13 we were dealing with got the death penalty but why they were prosecuted at all. The evidence was thin. It's the same inverse thing that Barry Scheck was talking about. The worse the crime, it seems, the less evidence you need of guilt in order to get a conviction. Now, the former prosecutors here might know that. I didn't prosecute street crime. But I think that there's that phenomenon. In Illinois, if it hadn't been for a young woman named Cathy Sullivan, no relationship, who was in the journalism school at Northwestern, who checked on what we called the Ford case, and found a witness who had identified the real killers and rapists within a week of the crime, two of those men would be dead today and the other two would still be sitting in prison. As it turned out, they sat there for 17 years.

So I am opposed to the death penalty because I think it's a terribly dumb idea. It's really a dumb idea. It doesn't work right. You members of the Legislature have a responsibility to put into operation things that are going to work and get rid of those that don't work.

Another member of the Ryan Commission, attorney and well-known author Scott Turow, made similar comments on the innocence question and other matters central to this book. His written testimony follows.[95]

December 14, 2004
Dear Chairs Aubry, Lentol and Weinstein:

Thank you very much for the opportunity to express my point of view on the very important questions you are considering in your public hearings on the future of capital punishment in New York State. I am an attorney and a writer, probably best-known as the author of novels including *Presumed Innocent.* I am a former Assistant United States Attorney in Chicago, who, since leaving that office in 1986, has been a partner at Sonnenschein Nath & Rosenthal in Chicago. My practice has concentrated on criminal defense. In that connection, I have served as counsel in post-conviction proceedings in a number of capital prosecutions. Because of those experiences, I was appointed by former Illinois Governor George Ryan as one of the fourteen members of the Illinois Commission on Capital Punishment that published its recommendations in April, 2002.

My reflections on the questions you have posed about capital punishment are best expressed in a short book I wrote on the subject, *Ultimate Punishment: A Lawyer's Reflections on Dealing With the Death Penalty,* which expands on an essay I originally published in *The New Yorker.* A copy of *Ultimate Punishment* is enclosed for anyone who cares to browse it.

I came to my service on the Illinois Commission as a so-called 'death penalty agnostic.' I did not regard the moral issues as clear-cut either way. I knew there were certain horrible crimes, like those of the serial killer John Wayne Gacy, which seemed to scream out for the severest punishment. But I was unsettled by the mistakes I'd seen the capital system make in cases I had handled, including the conviction and death sentence of my innocent client, Alex

Hernandez. Alex was freed after nearly 12 years in prison when DNA tests, and revelations of false police testimony, lent near-indisputability to the confession of another man to the crime for which Alex and his co-defendant, Rolando Cruz, had once been sentenced to die.

At the end of my time in the Illinois Commission, I realized that I had been asking myself the wrong question about capital punishment. The proper inquiry, I believe, is not whether there are occasional cases, like Gacy's, for which death seems the just punishment. The right question, I think, is whether a capital system can ever be devised that reaches only those right cases, without also sweeping in the wrong cases, the cases of the innocent, or of those who are undeserving by light of any sense of proportionate punishment. My inalterable conclusion is that the answer to that question is no.

Capital punishment, no matter how well-intended or comprehensive the legislative reforms, is doomed by two major fallacies: an inherent propensity to convict the innocent; and an inescapable arbitrariness about who will be selected to die. Capital punishment, properly applied, presents an extraordinary paradox. If the sentence is confined, as the U.S. Supreme Court has required, to only the gravest offenses, to the so-called 'worst of the worst,' that very proper restraint ends up exaggerating the potential of convicting the innocent. That is because the worst of the worst are the cases that most seriously challenge our ability to reason; they are the cases that fill us with loathing, anxiety and outrage, emotions that often lead police, prosecutors, judges, juries (and even, sometimes, defense lawyers) to embrace false leads to make up for the lapse that let a savage killer loose in our midsts, to rush to judgment in order to calm a fearful public, and to reverse the burden of proof against defendants, who, far too often, are convicted by juries that don't want to take the risk of letting suspected monsters go. Simply put, it is easier to arrest, prosecute and convict an

innocent person of a horrible murder than of shoplifting.
Unless we recognize this propensity in the justice system and
abandon capital punishment, we are bound now and then to
condemn and execute the innocent, which is certainly the
most profound abnegation of the law imaginable.

Second, the same desire to punish the worst of the
worst leads to the inherent arbitrariness with which capital
punishment is imposed. Nationally, only one in fifty first-
degree murderers ends up sentenced to death. I challenge
anyone to find reason in the pattern of who gets selected.

Legislators can all agree that Gacy-type cases belong
in the most extreme category, but are frequently baffled,
given public sentiments, about where to draw the line at the
other end of death-eligibility. Is the murder of a child the
worst of the worst? A contract murder? The killing of a
firefighter? Or a witness? Because each victim family's loss
is fundamentally the same, they apply an in-built pressure to
expand the categories for death eligibility. To them, whether
their loved one died by the hand of Gacy or a repeat drunk-
driver, the loss is largely the same and surely the worst of the
worst that could happen to them. For these reasons, there is
a constant expansion of eligibility categories nationwide, and
certainly in Illinois, where the legislature added another
eligibility factor even after Governor Ryan had declared his
moratorium on execution. The wider the path for eligibility,
the greater the variation in who gets selected for death.

Other structural factors exacerbate this tendency to
arbitrariness. The quality of defense counsel, how able the
prosecuting county is to bear the financial burden of a capital
prosecution, the willingness of a defendant to plead guilty,
the gender of the offender, the ambitions and temperament
of the prosecutor, and whether the crime is committed in a
rural area, where violent offenses tend to receive harsher
sentences than crime-beset cities, all make the decision to
impose death nothing less than (a) dart-shoot on a statewide basis.

Race is also a contributing factor, and in a deeply troubling way. According to David Baldus, the pre-eminent death penalty researcher at the University of Iowa, fifty-five percent of homicides nationally are committed by African-Americans. This is a horrifying statistic that calls for remedies far more profound than the criminal justice system can provide. But it also means from the start that capital punishment, if applied, will have a disproportionate impact in the African-American community. Our efforts to be conscious of race effects, and to put African-Americans in decision-making positions in police and prosecutors' offices, have reduced, in some states, the state of affairs that existed thirty years ago when a black defendant, without more, was more likely to be sentenced to death than a white defendant. Now in Illinois, and some other states, a white defendant is somewhat more likely to be death-sentenced. But the reasons for that are hardly race-neutral. We live in a segregated society and whites deal more often with whites; and killing a white person turns out to be the important variable. In Illinois, we found that killers of white persons were three and a half times more likely to be sentenced to death than the killers of African-Americans. The factors contributing to the result are complex. Some have to do with gang crime. But much also has to do with the imbalance of wealth, status and power in this society that makes it so often the case that a lost white life seems more important to a jury. In this way, the capital system, despite our determined efforts, continues to replicate the inherent inequities in America.

Let me very briefly touch on two other subsidiary issues. First, when I started on the Illinois Commission, I was persuaded that if the death penalty was a general deterrent to murder – that if killing killers kept others from becoming murderers – the death penalty needed no further justification. I studied the question in the most disciplined way I could. I am convinced that there is no compelling evidence that the death penalty is a general deterrent. This can be explained many ways, but let me offer a simple observation sharpened by more than a quarter of a century of criminal practice. Criminals commit crimes because they believe they aren't going to get caught, or because they are not thinking about the prospect. Since they are in that belief state, the degree of punishment is irrelevant to whether crimes are committed.

Second, despite my profound sympathy for victim families, who have endured a unique loss, our discussions of victim rights are fundamentally dishonest. We focus on the wishes of victims in that one case in fifty where death is imposed, without mentioning the forty-nine cases in fifty where death is not the punishment. In many, many of those remaining cases, the victim families would prefer death, but their wishes are ignored by police and prosecutors because, for one reason or another, capital punishment does not seem to be merited. In other words, we most often listen and then override the victims' wishes. It is a canard to pretend the victims' desires should be determinative in the one case in fifty, where, in fact, we are using them as a fig-leaf for our own retributive impulses.

Again, I thank you for the opportunity to present my views. Please let me know if I can provide any further information.

Very truly yours,
Scott Turow

Some simple historical perspective from a legendary figure in the New York debate over capital punishment, Richard J. Bartlett, revealed a link of past to present in the debate over capital punishment in New York.

Chairman Lentol: Distinguished Assemblyman, who I believe served in the Assembly with my father.

Mr. Bartlett: Ms. Weinstein and gentlemen, I'm happy to have the opportunity to speak to you today on this most important subject.

I come before you today as a former member of this House, having served from 1959 through 1966, as a former member of the Temporary Commission on Revision of the Penal Law and Criminal Code, which I had the honor to chair from its inception in 1961 until our work was completed in 1969, as a former Supreme Court Justice and Chief Administrative Judge, as a former Dean of Albany Law School, and as a lawyer who was practiced in the state and federal courts of New York for 56 years. That's a lot of formers, I know.

It was my service on the Penal Law Commission and the Report we issued nearly 40 years ago on Capital Punishment, which was followed by the virtual abolition of the death penalty in New York, which the Legislature and Governor Rockefeller accomplished in 1965, which has motivated my participation in this proceeding.

When the Commission started its work, frankly, I had no personal position on the issue of capital punishment. I suspect I had some vague notion that the reasons advanced for its need must have been compelling for our criminal justice system to have retained the death penalty throughout our recorded history.

But in the process of our studies our public hearings, and the earnest discussions among us on this most important issue, I concluded, with a majority of the Commission, that the death penalty could not be rationally supported, that its retention would be bad public policy. Forty years later, I am of the same mind.

The final word on innocence comes from retired Chief Justice of the Florida Supreme Court, Gerald Kogan.

Chairman Lentol: Good morning, Judge. Mr. Kogan, would you like to begin?

Mr. Kogan: Yes, Mr. Chairman. Thank you, very much. First of all, let me introduce myself to you and give you the benefit of my background and experience dealing with capital cases.

(I) am a native of the state of New York, having been born and raised in New York City, and migrated to Florida 57 years ago. In the state of Florida, I have had the following experience in dealing with capital cases.

Early on in my career I was the chief prosecutor of the Miami, Florida, State Attorney's Office, for homicides and capital crimes. I myself tried individuals who were charged with murder in the first degree, asked juries to return the death penalty in some of those cases, and had prosecutors who worked for me in my division also ask juries to return the death penalty.

Upon leaving the State Attorney's Office, I went into private practice, and at that time was the recipient of numerous cases from judges who appointed me to represent persons who were charged with first degree murder capital cases.

From there, I went on the trial bench and tried numerous cases involving the possibility of the death penalty. I then served twelve years on the Florida Supreme Court, my last two years of which I was Chief Justice.

On that Court, death penalty litigation took up approximately half of the amount of time of the Court, although it comprised only 3 percent of our entire case load. We spent half of our time considering 3 percent of (our) cases.

While I was on the Florida Supreme Court, 28 persons were actually put to death on a death penalty approved by the Court on which I sat. On most of those cases, I voted to uphold the jury's verdict and the judge's sentence of death.

Where does that put me now after almost a lifetime of dealing with these types of cases? It comes and develops over a period of time. The first thing you begin to realize, as your career goes along, is that nothing is either black or white. It's usually a shade of gray.

You begin to learn that not only do guilty people get convicted in a court of law, but there are innocent people who are also convicted.

Prior to about five years ago, the argument concerning capital punishment was either you were morally opposed to it or you were morally in favor of it. And those two sides could never really mesh. Neither one could agree with the other, their beliefs were so strong.

And then all of a sudden something came along called DNA. And what did we discover? That low and behold there were a number of cases of people sitting on death row who, because of the DNA analysis of their cases, were in fact, factually innocent of the crimes for which they had been convicted and sentenced to death.

Now I want to point out to you that DNA testimony is only available in a very small minority of cases. You have to have some type of bodily fluid left in order to be able to make a DNA comparison. Most cases involving capital offenses do not have DNA testimony.

But what they do have is faulty, unreliable eyewitness identification, situations where confessions have been in some instances coerced from defendants, and these defendants find themselves on death row.

Now just limiting ourselves to the question of DNA. What happened to these people who had DNA, but it was not available to be tested, and they in fact were not guilty of the crime for which they were convicted? Well it doesn't take a rocket scientist to tell you that in years gone by, those people, innocent as they may be, were in fact executed.

Now I know there are going to be those who tell me, well that may have occurred, but nowadays we're going to be much more careful the way we do these things.

Well in the state of Florida, when I was on the Court, we averaged 375 people at any one time sitting on death row. Some of them had been there for 20 or 25 years. And now the matter has increased and increased, and I don't really know how many are on death row right now, but I would assume it's probably in excess of 400.

These people who did not have DNA available to them, who were in fact innocent, obviously had been executed. There are people who say, well how about those people where the guilt is no question at all? It's not beyond a reasonable doubt, but it's beyond and to the exclusion of every possible doubt.

Now the question that you have to face is, if you're going to keep the death penalty, are you willing to change the standard of proof that has been in existence in this country since its founding. And that is, that you (would) have to prove people (guilty) far beyond a reasonable doubt (standard). You must prove their guilt to an absolute certainty. And I submit to you that that is a very difficult thing to do.

This is a system that is imperfect at best, and it is a system that is operated by human beings. And God knows that we are not perfect individuals. So here we have imperfect human beings operating a system at best which is not perfect, attempting to come up with a perfect solution.

Do we change the law? Does New York become the only state in the United States who now says that guilt in a capital case has to be beyond and to the exclusion of every doubt whatsoever? I'm sure that law enforcement personnel would scream blue and bloody murder because that is almost an impossible task.

So I say to you at this particular point that based upon what I've seen after more than 40 years of dealing with these cases . . . capital punishment has no place in the judicial system of any state. And the reason it has no purpose and it has no position in your system, is because it is fraught with error, it is fraught with mistake.

Now I can go ahead and tell you that in Florida alone we have had more than 25 people released from death row, not only for DNA, but for faulty eyewitness identification, for forced confessions. What would have happened years ago? Probably most of those people would have been executed.

How many more people remain on death row in the state of Florida who are factually innocent? That is something that we may never know. Even though Florida does have all these people sitting on death row, Florida last year only executed two people. In my twelve years on the Court, that was about the average. Two people per year were executed.

Even Texas, a state which has long been known for executing people by the barrel full, has cut down dramatically on the number of people that are being executed. Why? Simply because not only prosecutors and defense attorneys, but judges as well, who sit over these particular cases and preside over them, have realized that because the system is fraught with the danger of error, that you cannot take the chance of convicting and executing an innocent person.

If you, in fact, convict an innocent person, and they're locked away in a prison, and you find out that in fact they are innocent, you can always go there, open up the door and say I'm sorry we convicted you, it was a mistake. But Members of the Assembly, if you make a mistake and execute somebody, it is irrevocable. You don't dig up a coffin in a grave yard and open it up and say I'm sorry, we made a mistake. Our justice system demands more than just that.

CHAPTER SEVEN: THE INTERNATIONAL PERSPECTIVE

The New York Death Penalty Hearings included consideration of
international law and the death penalty practices of foreign nations.
Hearings question I. 6. asked, in part, "What do the trends and experiences of
other . . . nations which have considered or implemented the death penalty . .
. teach us about whether capital punishment should be reinstated in New
York?". Several witnesses noted that the majority of countries in the world
have abolished the death penalty. Hearings testimony suggested that the
continued commitment of the United States to capital punishment isolates
America from the rest of the world and aligns our nation with several highly
repressive political regimes.

International law generally condemns the death penalty. A most
forceful rejection of capital punishment is found in the International
Covenant on Civil and Political Rights (ICCPR) and its Second Optional
Protocol. Enacted by the United Nations, they provide:

> ICCPR (1976) Part III Article 6 (1). Every human
> being has the inherent right to life. This right shall be
> protected by law. No one shall be arbitrarily deprived of his
> life. (2) In countries that have not abolished the death
> penalty, sentence of death may be imposed only for the most
> serious crimes in accordance with the law in force at the time
> of the commission of the crime . . . . (5) Sentence of death
> shall not be imposed for crimes committed by persons below
> eighteen years of age and shall not be carried out on
> pregnant women . . . . Article 10 (1) All persons deprived of
> their liberty shall be treated with humanity and with respect
> for the inherent dignity of the human person.[96]

> SECOND OPTIONAL PROTOCOL TO ICCPR (1991).
> Article 1 (1) No one within the jurisdiction of a State party to
> the present Optional Protocol shall be executed. (2) Each

State party shall take all necessary measures to abolish the
death penalty within its jurisdiction.[97]

Similar restrictions can be found in the U.N. Convention on the
Rights of the Child,[98] The American Convention on Human Rights,[99] and the
African Charter on the Rights and Welfare of the Child.[100] Especially
important are Protocols 6 and 13 to the European Convention for the
Protection of Human Rights and Fundamental Freedoms (1985).

No. 6. Considering that the evolution that has
occurred in several member States of the Council of Europe
expresses a general tendency in favour of abolition of the
death penalty. Article 1. The death penalty shall be
abolished. No one shall be condemned to such penalty or
executed. Article 2. A State may make provision in its law
for the death penalty in respect of acts committed in time of
war or of imminent threat of war . . . .

No. 13. Convinced that everyone's right to life is a
basic value in a democratic society and that the abolition of
the death penalty is essential for the protection of this right
and for the full recognition of the inherent dignity of all
human beings;

Wishing to strengthen the protection of the right to
life guaranteed by the Convention for the Protection of
Human Rights and Fundamental Freedoms signed at Rome
on 4 November 1950 (hereinafter referred to as "the
Convention");

Noting that Protocol No. 6 to the Convention,
concerning the Abolition of the Death Penalty, signed at
Strasbourg on 28 April 1983, does not exclude the death
penalty in respect of acts committed in time of war or of
imminent threat of war;

Being resolved to take the final step in order to
abolish the death penalty in all circumstances,

Have agreed as follows:

Article 1 – Abolition of the death penalty
The death penalty shall be abolished. No one shall be
condemned to such penalty or executed. [101]

Pursuant to these various provisions, much of the world has freed itself from the burdens and costs, moral and material, of capital punishment. Based on data from the Death Penalty Information Center, at the end of 2009, an estimated 139 countries were abolitionist on the death penalty, either in law or practice. By comparison, 58 countries still retained capital punishment.[102] Because membership in the European Union[103] is conditioned on banning the death penalty, and based on the fact that all 46 nations of the Council of Europe have stopped executions (40 member countries ratified Protocol No. 6), Europe (with the exception of Belarus) is now a no-execution zone covering 800 million people.[104] International bodies established by the United Nations to hear cases involving genocide, war crimes, crimes against humanity, and other extremely serious criminal charges have been denied the authority to impose the death penalty. Examples include the International Criminal Tribunal for the Former Yugoslavia, the similar Tribunal for Rwanda, and the International Criminal Court.

At the present time, a very rough estimate is that there are at least 20,000 prisoners on death row worldwide.[105] For the past few years, the top executing countries were China, Iran, Pakistan, Saudi Arabia, Iraq and the United States.[106] Other active practitioners of capital punishment included Sudan, Yemen, Vietnam, Mongolia, Jordan and Singapore.[107] In 2006, there were 1591 executions, down 25% from 2005.[108] For 2007, executions decreased an additional 22% to 1252.[109] During the same year, a minimum of 3347 death sentences were imposed as compared to 3861 for 2006.[110] Yet, in 2008, executions increased to 2390 in 25 countries and death sentences skyrocketed to an estimated 8838[111] These increases were directly attributable to China's reporting of more accurate information about that country's execution practices.

International developments in recent years show movement away from capital punishment. In 2007, Rwanda voted to abolish the death penalty;[112] France amended its constitution to ban capital punishment; the Third World Congress Against the Death Penalty was held in Paris; and the EU and Council of Europe observed the "European Day Against the Death Penalty." Of critical importance, in an unprecedented act of unity on the issue, the United Nations General Assembly passed a resolution calling for a global moratorium on executions. The vote was 104 in favor, 52 opposed, and 29 abstaining.[113] The United States voted "no." The resolution commits signatory countries to: (1) progressively restrict the use of the death penalty and reduce the number of offences for which it may be imposed; (2) establish a moratorium on executions in each country with a view to abolishing the death penalty worldwide; and (3) not reintroduce capital punishment once it is abolished.[114]

In June of 2008, the Council of the European Union reaffirmed its 1998 Human Rights Guideline on the Death Penalty and committed itself to working towards universal abolition of capital punishment.

The year 2009 saw the United Nations High Commissioner for Human Rights, Navi Pillay, mark the twentieth anniversary of the optional Protocol to the ICCPR by calling for global abolition of capital punishment. Ms. Pillay urged countries to adopt a moratorium on executions pending such abolition and noted such problems with the death penalty as "the fundamental nature of the right to life; the unacceptable role of executing innocent people by mistake; the absence of proof that the death penalty serves as a deterrent; and . . . the inappropriately vengeful character of the sentence." The President of Kenya, Mwai Kibaki, commuted the death sentences of more than 4000 death row inmates to life imprisonment. A repeal of the death penalty in that country may be forthcoming. Burundi and Togo abolished the death penalty. U.N. Special investigator Philip Alston submitted a report to the U.N. Human Rights Council criticizing the use of the death penalty in the U.S. and calling for a study of all state and federal death penalty cases.[115]

The action of the United States in voting not to join much of the civilized world in eliminating capital punishment is representative of its approach to numerous human rights issues. On the death penalty alone, the

United States steadfastly refused to join the ban on executing juveniles imposed by the Convention on the Rights of the Child.[116] It took a reservation to the ICCPR protecting its right to continue executions[117] and declined to sign the Second Optional Protocol.[118] America has refused to accept the jurisdiction of the International Criminal Court[119] and withdrawn from the jurisdiction of one of the most important human rights tribunals in the world, the International Court of Justice, on matters involving the Vienna Convention on Consular Relations.[120]

Representatives of Amnesty International and Human Rights Watch, two of the most active anti-death penalty organizations in the world, presented much of this global picture at the Hearings.

William Schultz of Amnesty International was first.

Mr. Schultz: Ladies and gentlemen, I am William Schultz, the Executive Director of Amnesty International here in the United States, speaking on behalf of 1.7 million Amnesty members, tens of thousands of them here in New York State. Thank you for letting me appear before you.

Amnesty, of course, opposes the death penalty under all circumstances. I am going to, however, today limit my remarks in light of the time to one point and one point only. And as a person trained as a clergyman, I'll assure you that's a difficult thing to do. But I am going to do it. And I'm going to speak solely to the issue of the international trends in regard to this subject.

We meet here today just a few days after our celebration of Dr. Martin Luther King, Jr.'s birthday. Dr. King said that the arc of the universe bends toward justice. Twenty-five to 50 years from now the practice of the death penalty will be regarded as barbaric as we today regard the practice of slavery. The fact is that the United States today stands alone among industrialized, democratic societies, with the sole exception of Japan, in retention of the death penalty. We stand with only Iran in the execution of juvenile

offenders (now eliminated by U.S. Supreme Court decision),
but we stand alone with the exception of Japan with regard
to the practice of the death penalty itself among advanced
democratic societies. The global trend is quite clearly toward
abolition. Over half the countries of the world have
abolished the death penalty in law or in practice, including
such diverse nations as Argentina, Australia, France and
Mozambique. Indeed, over the past decade, more than three
countries a year have abolished the death penalty in law or,
having abolished it for ordinary crimes, have gone on to
abolish it for all crimes.

In 1999 alone, for example, Albania, hardly regarded
as a model of democratic practice, Bermuda, Cypress, East
Timor, Latvia, Nepal, Turkmenistan, one of the most
repressive countries in the world, and Ukraine all effectively
abolished the death penalty. In 2003, Protocol 13 to the
European Convention on Human Rights went into effect –
this is the first legally binding international treaty to abolish
the death penalty in all circumstances with no exceptions.
We have also witnessed significant progress in Africa, where
last month Senegal abolished the practice, and where Sierra
Leone's Truth and Reconciliation Commission has
recommended doing away with the death penalty in its
entirety.

It's not just a coincidence that so many countries
have abolished the death penalty as part of the transition to a
more democratic form of government. In countries as
diverse as Haiti, Paraguay, and Romania, the death penalty
was abolished once dictatorships came to an end. And in
South Africa back in 1990, the apartheid government
declared a moratorium on the death penalty when it released
Nelson Mandela and opened negotiations with the African
National Congress. This process reached fruition in 1995
when capital punishment was abolished altogether in the
new South African constitution. In each of these countries,
the death penalty was understood to be part of repressive

machinery of a dictatorial state. And once a more democratic
society had been established there was a fundamental
determination to do away with the most terrible prerogative
that any government can exercise.

It's an unsettling fact that in stark contrast to this
global shift away from capital punishment, the United States,
which has always regarded itself as the premier model and
leader of human rights throughout the world, the United
States consistently ranks among the top executing countries
in the world. In 2003, the United States, China, Iran and
Vietnam accounted for 84 percent of all recorded judicial
executions. While 118 countries have now abolished the
death penalty in law or practice, since 1977 the United States
has shot, gassed, electrocuted, hanged, or poisoned to death
950 men and women. There are currently over 3,400
prisoners under the sentence of death in this country. The
United States' refusal to abandon this anachronistic
punishment diminishes its self-proclaimed status as an
international human rights defender.

The question I ask is this. I don't claim that this
argument is by itself definitive. I know it won't be definitive
for you, but it is part of a larger historic process of that arc of
the universe bending toward justice. And I hope you'll ask
yourselves, why should a great progressive state like New
York count itself in the ranks of those who mimic the
practices of such countries as China, Saudi Arabia, and Cuba
instead of those nations whose political traditions we claim
to share – the United Kingdom, Canada, France, Ireland,
Israel, and Italy, among many others – all of whom have long
since abolished the death penalty.

We talked about Professor Blecker. Professor
Blecker is a personal friend of mine, despite our
disagreement on this issue, but in one respect he's absolutely
wrong. He testified that the people of Europe, for example, in
contrast to their governing elites, the people of Europe
actually favor the death penalty, he said, and were they given

an opportunity to vote on the question, they would restore its use readily. Well, not only does such an argument rest on the condescending assumption that voters of democratic Europe are somehow incapable of electing leaders who truly reflect their values but it is an argument that is belied by straightforward fact. For in June 2001 there was exactly such a referendum on the ballot in Ireland that called for permanently removing the death penalty, even in times of war or civil unrest, and we know how that country has been plagued by that. Even in those times, this referendum called for the removal of the death penalty from the Republic's constitution. Ireland's last execution was in 1954, but crime rates and public fear had been rising. Turnout for this vote was massive and the result was clear; death penalty abolition was approved by more than 60 percent of the Irish voters.

In conclusion, I urge you to go with the flow of the arc of history and not try and retard it. Remember what will be said of you and of New York State 25 to 50 years from now. And I urge you to place this state . . . (as part) of the worldwide trend . . . (towards) abolition of the death penalty. In doing so, you'll not only be promoting human rights in the State of New York, but you will also be setting a fine example for other states and, indeed, for countries around the world like China and Saudi Arabia and Cuba, countries in whose company, I trust you agree, we don't want New York to be counted.

The contrary views of New York Law School's Professor Robert Blecker were as follows.

Mr. Blecker: Gallup polls, while distorting and under-counting true support for the death penalty, have consistently shown that most of the support is based upon retributive feelings. The reason that the people of the United States embrace the death penalty, and may I add, the reasons we've heard Europe discussed, the reason that Europe embraces the death penalty, because make no mistake about it, while the death penalty has been abolished by western Europe, . . . the overwhelming majority of the people supported it. And this doesn't come from me, this comes from Roger Hood, death penalty law (international expert) – a leading abolitionist.

This comes from Carol . . . (Streiker), a law Professor at Harvard.

So the support still remains in Europe. The majority of Europeans, those whose values most resemble ours, still supports the death penalty, as the majority in Canada still supports the death penalty. What the polls have shown consistently is that that majority is principally made up of people whose primary issue is the (just) desert that is that the past counts. The past counts independently of the future benefits.

Concluding remarks on this subject were presented by Dorit Radzin, Advocacy Associate, Human Rights Watch.

Assemblyman Lentol: Thank you for staying all day.

Ms. Radzin: It's been a pleasure hearing everybody, and hearing all the different perspectives, and hearing all of your insightful comments and questions.

I represent Human Rights Watch, an international human rights organization based in the United States that has been documenting and exposing human rights abuses for over 25 years. We monitor human rights in over 70 countries around the world, including the United States, as we believe international standards of human rights apply to all people equally. Despite the freedoms that Americans enjoy and the historical strength of the United States democracy, the human rights of people in this country are not always respected. We often research and report on abuses that occur within the criminal justice system and are particularly concerned about laws, policies, and practices that fly in the face of human rights standards.

The system of capital punishment in the United States is deeply flawed. Across the country, numerous state and national studies have identified serious problems that undermine the fairness and integrity of capital punishment. In Illinois, a 2000 bipartisan commission released a report based on an exhaustive two-year study of the administration of the death penalty in that state. The report identifies numerous ways that error, arbitrariness, and prejudice can influence capital punishment decisions. In Texas, several organizations have recently documented the prevalence of prosecutorial misconduct . . . and inadequate representation in the death penalty system. In Maryland, in 2003, a study by the University of Maryland, commissioned by the governor, found substantial racial and geographic disparities in the administration of the death penalty. Nationwide, these flaws have contributed to death sentences being imposed on innocent people. Since 1973, 117 innocent persons have been released from death row in 25 states, some within hours of their scheduled execution.

The continued use of capital punishment in the United States ignores a worldwide trend against it. Since 1990, more than 35 counties and territories have abolished the death penalty for all crimes. An additional 117 countries, or 118 as William Schulz said, I have to check my number on that, have either abolished the death penalty or have allowed it to fall out of practice by not carrying out an execution in the last ten years. But in 2003, as you also heard, the United States, along with Iran, China, and Vietnam, carried out 84 percent of the known executions worldwide. The United States is even more isolated in the world in carrying out executions of juvenile offenders (now eliminated). In the last three years, the United States has executed four of the six juvenile defenders put to death worldwide. By being one of the dwindling number of countries that continue to carry out state-sponsored executions and defend the practice, the United States undermines its ability to champion democracy and human rights around the world and harms its moral leadership.

International human rights law, as codified in the International Covenant on Civil and Political Rights, favors the abolition of capital punishment, even though it does not prohibit it categorically. The United Nations Commission on Human Rights, however, has passed numerous resolutions affirming its opposition to the death penalty. In one recent session, a resolution passed stating, "the abolition of the death penalty contributes to the enhancement of human dignity and to the progressive development of human rights."

Human Rights Watch opposes the death penalty in all circumstances. The intrinsic fallibility of all criminal justice systems assures that even when full due process of the law is respected, innocent persons are sometimes executed. The death penalty is inherently cruel and executions are inevitably carried out in an arbitrary manner, inflicted primarily on the most vulnerable – the poor, the mentally ill, and persons of color.

We urge the Assembly in the strongest terms not to reinstate the death penalty in the State of New York. Thank you.

CONCLUSION

In the Spring on 2005, the Codes Committee of the New York Assembly voted 11-7 to reject legislation that would have restored capital punishment as a criminal penalty in New York. This decision reflected the majority view of witnesses testifying at the New York Death Penalty Hearings that the death penalty should be abandoned as a criminal sentence in the state.

Since that vote there have been occasional attempts to reenact the death penalty. In 2006 the New York Senate passed a bill to reinstate capital punishment by correcting the jury instruction provisions invalidated by the New York Court of Appeals in <u>People v. LaValle</u>. The Assembly rejected this legislation. When four New York police officers were shot during a two week period in the Spring of 2007, the temporary Senate President and Republican Majority Leader, Joseph L. Bruno, called on then Governor Spitzer to push for new death penalty laws. Mr. Bruno criticized the April 27, 2007, vote of 97 Assembly Democrats against an amendment to impose the death penalty on police killers. His statements emphasized the continued willingness of the New York Senate to re-introduce capital punishment in the state.[121] This political stalemate continues, and makes New York, for now, a non-death penalty jurisdiction.

On the national level, the debate over capital punishment continues. The issues raised by the New York Death Penalty Hearings and presented through witness testimony in this book frame this debate. At its center is the fact that Americans are still deeply divided over capital punishment. An October 2009 Gallup Poll indicated that 65% of Americans support the death penalty while 31% oppose it. Yet, when asked by Gallup in May of 2006 to decide between death or life in prison without parole, 48% of those surveyed favored life without parole to 47% for capital punishment. These figures have been relatively stable for almost a decade.

Intense disagreements and debates continue over such questions as, is retribution a justification for the death penalty; is the death penalty an effective deterrent; how significant is the issue of cost; is capital punishment racially discriminatory; and what should be done about the persistent possibility of executing an innocent person. As Japan moves away from the death penalty with the appointment of Keiko Chiba, an active abolitionist, as Justice Minister, the United States is further isolated from the international community by its status as the only industrialized democracy in the world still actively imposing the death penalty.

The goal of this book is to bring understanding to the debate over capital punishment. Neither the law, nor the facts, nor the passion of the advocates on both sides of the controversy, have changed significantly since the end of the New York Death Penalty Hearings in 2005. It is hoped, then, that readers of VOICES will enter this debate with new insights and a commitment to reaching the best possible public policy on these critical matters of life and death.

Appendix A: Index to Witness Statements

*Title/Affiliation at the time of the Hearings.

Appendix B: Assembly Committee Chairs and Appearances

Committee on Codes, Chair, Assemblyman Joseph R. Lentol

Committee on Correction, Chair, Assemblyman Jeffrion L. Aubry

Committee on Judiciary, Chair, Assemblywoman Helen E. Weinstein

Appearances*

Assemblyman Michael Benjamin

Assemblyman Jonathan L. Bing

Assemblyman James Brennan

Assemblywoman Adele Cohen

Assemblywoman Vivian Cook

Assemblyman Michael Gianaris

Assemblyman Richard Gottfried

Assemblyman Ryan S. Karben

Assemblyman Thomas J. Kirwan

Assemblyman Charles D. Lavine

Assemblyman Clarence Norman, Jr.

Assemblyman Daniel J. O'Donnell

Assemblyman Thomas F. O'Mara

Assemblyman Chris Ortloff

Assemblyman Felix Ortiz

Assemblywoman Crystal D. Peoples

Assemblyman Peter M. Rivera

Assemblyman Scott M. Stringer

Assemblyman Fred W. Thiele, Jr.

Assemblyman Mark S. Weprin

Assemblyman Keith L. Wright

*Based on Appearances noted in the official transcripts of Hearings testimony. Other members of the Assembly were not listed but participated in the Hearings at various stages.

NOTES

---

[1] 817 N.E. 2d 341 (N.Y. 2004).

[2] Appendix B lists the names of the Chairs of these Committees.

[3] Final report on the Hearings, New York State Assembly, The Death Penalty in New York (April 3, 2005), *available at* http://www.assembly.state.ny.us/comm/Codes/20050403/ (Final Report on Hearings).

[4] *See* People v. Cahill, 809 N.E. 2d 561 (N.Y. 2003); *see* Russell G. Murphy, *People v. Cahill, Domestic Violence and the Death Penalty Debate in New York*, 68 ALB. L. REV. 1029 (2005).

[5] The moratorium was in effect during the pendency of a case, Baze v. Rees, 128 S. Ct. 1520 (2008), that challenged the prevailing method for executions (lethal injection) in the United States. The moratorium was lifted after the Court upheld the constitutionality of that method.

[6] Federal Death Penalty Act of 1994, Pub. L. No. 103-322, tit. VI, 108 Stat. 1796, 1959 (codified as amended in scattered sections of 8, 18, and 49 U.S. C. (1994)).

[7] G. Pierce and M. Radelet, *The Impact of Legally Inappropriate Factors on Death Sentencing for California Homicides, 1990-1999*, 46 SANTA CLARA L. REV. 1 (2005).

[8] Twice during 2009 the U.S. Supreme Court refused to grant appellate review to cases challenging these lengthy delays as unconstitutional under the Eighth Amendment. *See* Johnson v. Bredesen, 130 S. Ct. 541 (2009). Bresden was confined for 29 years in a solitary cell in a Tennessee prison. *See* Thompson v. McNeil, 129 S. Ct. 1299 (2009). Thompson had been on death row in Florida for 32 years at the time the Court denied review.

[9] Death Penalty Information Center, Report of the California Commission on the Fair Administration of Justice (2008), *available at* http://www.deathpenaltyinfo.org/costs-death-penalty.

[10] John Roman, Aaron Chalfin, Aaron Sundquist, Carly Knight & Askar Darmenov, The Cost of the Death Penalty in Maryland, Urban Institute Justice Policy Center (2008), *available at:* http://www.deathpenaltyinfo.org/CostsDPMaryland.pdf.

[11] Update on Cost, Quality, and Availability of Defense Representation in Federal Death Penalty Cases, Office of Defender Services of the Administrative Office of the U.S. Courts (2008), *available at* *http://www.uscourts.gov/defenderservices/FDPC_Contents.cfm.*

[12] Tennessee Comptroller of the Treasury Office, Tennessee's Death Penalty: Costs and Consequences, (2008), *available at* http://www.deathpenaltyinfo.org/costs-death-penalty.

[13] Legislative Division of Post Audit, State of Kansas, Performance Audit Report: Costs Incurred for Death Penalty Cases: A-K-GOAL Audit of the Department of Corrections (2003), *available at* http://www.kslegislature.org/postaudit/audits_perform/04pa03a.pdf.

[14] Katherine Baicker, The Budgetary Repercussions of Capital Convictions, Working Paper No. w8382 (National Bureau Economic Research July 2001) *available at* http://www.deathpenaltyinfo.org/costs-death-penalty.

[15] 428 U.S. 153 (1976).

[16] U.S. Const. art. III, § 2. The President shall be the Commander in Chief.

[17] U.S. Const. art. II, § 8. The Congress shall have the power ... to declare war.

[18] U.S. Const. art. VI. This Constitution, and the Laws of the United States which shall be made in pursuance thereof, ... shall be the supreme Law of the Land; ... any Thing in the Constitution or Laws of an State to the contrary notwithstanding.

[19] U.S. Const. amend. X. The powers not delegated to the United States by the Constitution, nor prohibited by it to the states, are reserved to States respectively, or to the people.

[20] *See* LaValle, 817 N.E. 2d 341.

[21] U.S. Const. amend. VIII. Excessive bail shall not be required, nor excessive fines imposed, nor cruel and unusual punishments inflicted.

[22] 408 U.S. 238 (1972).

[23] 428 U.S. 153 (1976).

[24] 428 U.S. 242 (1976).

[25] 242 U.S. 153 (1976).

[26] Roper v. Simmons, 543 U.S. 551 (2005).

[27] Atkins v. Virginia, 536 U.S. 304 (2002).

[28] Tison v. Arizona, 481 U.S. 137 (1987).

[29] Coker v. Georgia, 433 U.S. 584 (1977); *See also* Kennedy v. Louisiana, 128 S. Ct. 2641 (2008).

[30] Rees, 128 S. Ct. 1520.

[31] This controversial method involves a mixture of sodium thiopental, pancuronium bromide, and potassium chloride, injected directly into a vein. Problems have developed with the mixing of the drugs and their administration. The state of Ohio tried for 2 hours to execute Romell Broom before giving up on trying to find a workable vein. Some states are moving towards a single drug, thiopental sodium, that is often used in euthanizing animals.

[32] 481 U.S. 279 (1987).

[33] U.S. Const. amend. XIV, § 1. No State shall ... deprive any person of life, liberty, or property, without due process of law; nor deny to any person within its jurisdiction the equal protection of the laws.

[34] *See, e.g.*, Antiterrorism & Effective Death Penalty Act of 1996 (AEDPA), Pub. L. No. 104-132, 110 Stat. 1214 (1996) (codified as amended in scattered sections of 8, 18, 22, 28, and 42 U.S.C); Terrorist Death Penalty Enhancement Act of 2005, Pub. L. No. 109-177, 120 Stat. 230 (2006) (codified as amended in 18 U.S.C. 3599).

[35] Select Questions to Which Witnesses May Direct their Testimony:

I. Should the Death Penalty be Reinstated in New York?

1. Is it possible to design a death penalty law which is fairly administered and consistently applied, free from impermissible racial, ethnic, or geographic bias and prevents the conviction of the innocent?

2. Is the death penalty an appropriate societal exercise of retribution against persons who commit intentional murder?

3. What evidence is there that New York's death penalty or the death penalty in general deters intentional murder more effectively than other sentencing options?

4. Are the results which New York has achieved over the past nine years in administering the death penalty worth the significant public resources which have been expended? Could those resources have been used more effectively for other crime control or public purposes?

5. Is the currently available sentence of life imprisonment without the possibility of parole an effective alternative to the death penalty in New York? Or is it imperative that this current sentencing option be supplemented with the death penalty?

6. What do the trends and experiences of other states and nations which have considered or implemented the death penalty or life imprisonment without parole teach us about whether capital punishment should be reinstated in New York?

II. If the Death Penalty in New York Were Reinstated, What Should It Provide for?

1. Did the 1995 statute provide appropriate safeguards to ensure that innocent persons would not be convicted and subject to the death penalty in New York? If not, what additional safeguards would be needed to meet that goal?

2. Have the close family members and loved ones of the deceased murder victims been given appropriate input and involvement in decisions about seeking the death penalty and in the death penalty process under the 1995 law? How could the role of these family members and loved ones be improved?

3. Did the 1995 statutes provide appropriate protections against convictions and the imposition of the death penalty by virtue of bias applicable to the race or ethnicity of death penalty defendants or murder victims? If not, what additional steps would be necessary to achieve that goal?

4. As noted above, New York's death penalty law, as amended, provided the death penalty option for thirteen kinds of intentional murder. Should those categories be expanded, contracted or otherwise modified if the death penalty is reinstated?

5. New York's law provided a system of capital defense through a Capital Defender Office and contracts with other institutional defenders and private attorneys. Has this system worked effectively? How might it be improved?

6. Under New York's death penalty law, prosecutors were given unfettered discretion to seek or not seek the death penalty in any first degree murder case. Is such unlimited discretion appropriate? Did this system of prosecutional discretion work effectively and fairly?

7. Three death sentences imposed under the 1995 law came from Suffolk County with one each coming from Kings, Queens, Onondaga, and Monroe counties. The chances that a defendant would be subject to a death penalty prosecution in New York over the past nine years varied widely, depending upon the county in which a defendant's crime occurred. Is this a permissible result in a death penalty system? Should the imposition of the death penalty vary depending upon the county in which a defendant is prosecuted?

8. Has the state provided sufficient financial resources to law enforcement, victims' services, defense providers and the judicial system to administer the death penalty over the past nine years? What change in state funding for administering the death penalty could be considered?

9. What do the experiences of other states with death penalty laws and the federal government teach us about how any death penalty statues should be structured in this state?

10. What changes in evidentiary rules or the appellate process might be considered if the 1995 law were reinstated?

11. On August 11th [2004], the Senate passed Governor's program legislation which seeks to remedy the unconstitutional jury deadlock instruction identified by the Court of Appeals in the *LaValle* decision (S. 7720). The bill would seek not only to reinstate the death penalty for future cases, but would also purport to retroactively apply the new statute, both to crimes which occurred prior to the *LaValle* decision and crimes which occurred subsequent to *LaValle* but prior to the law's enactment, during a time period when no valid death penalty law was in effect in New York. The bill's retroactive provisions have been criticized as being violative of the *Ex Post Facto* clause of the United States Constitution and therefore invalid, particularly with respect to cases occurring subsequent to *LaValle*.

(a) Should the prospective provisions of S-7720, which seek to reinstate the death penalty be adopted without any further modifications to the statute?

(b) Are the retroactive provisions of S-7720 which seek to reinstate the death penalty with respect to prior crimes constitutionally valid? Should these provisions be adopted?

12. The 1995 statue generally barred the execution of mentally retarded persons but contained an exception for the first degree murder of a corrections officer committed by a prison or jail inmate. The United State Supreme Court, in its 2002 decision in *Atkins v. Virginia,* barred the execution of mentally retarded persons. How does the *Atkins* holding impact the 1995 law's limited provisions authorizing the execution of mentally retarded persons?

13. The 1995 statute contained extensive provisions related to a jury's consideration of a defendant's possible mental impairment when determining whether the death penalty should be imposed. How well did these provisions operate? Would these provisions need to be revised if the death penalty in New York were reinstated?

14. The 1995 law set eighteen as the minimum age for the imposition of the death penalty. Should that minimum age be modified if the death penalty is reinstated?

15. The 1995 law contained provisions for disqualifying jurors from death penalty guilt and penalty phase proceedings who harbored opinions for or against the death penalty which would preclude them from rendering an impartial verdict or exercising their discretion to determine an appropriate sentence. Has the provision, as it has been interpreted by New York's courts, been applied fairly and appropriately? Should this provision be modified in the event the death penalty is reinstated?

16. The 1995 statute established procedures for housing death-sentenced inmates and carrying out death sentences. The State Department of Correctional

Services has also implemented a number of policies in administering the 1995 law. Should any of these laws or policies be changed, in the event death penalty is reinstated?

[36] Universal Declaration of Human Rights, G.A. Res. 217A, at art. 3, U.N. GAOR, 3d Sess., 1st plen. mtg., U.N. Doc. A/810 (Dec. 12, 1948). Everyone has the right to life, liberty and security of person.

[37] Author Scott Christianson noted in his Hearings testimony: "It's bad enough that 50 years after her execution at Sing Sing Ethel Rosenberg's accuser has revealed that his key testimony against her was a lie. Just imagine if D.N.A. later popped up to exonerate her . . . . "

[38] *See, e.g.*, Michael L. Radelet and Traci L. Lacock, *Do Executions Lower Homicide Rates?: The Views of Leading Criminologists*, 99 JOURNAL OF CRIM. L. & CRIMINOLOGY 489 (2009); *Cf.* Cass R. Sunstein and Adrian Vermeulle, *Is Capital Punishment Morally Required? Acts, Omissions and Life-Life Tradeoffs*, 50 STAN. L. REV. 703 (2005) with Carol S. Streiker, *No, Capital Punishment is Not Morally Required: Deterrence, Deontology, and the Death Penalty*, 58 STAN. L. REV. 751 (2006). For an excellent summary of current research on deterrence see Roger Hood and Carolyn Hoyle, THE DEATH PENALTY: A WORLD WIDE PERSPECTIVE, CHAPTER 9 (Oxford University Press, 4th ed. 2008).

[39] Richard Berk, *New Claims About Executions and General Deterrence: Déjà vu All Over Again*, 2 JOURNAL OF EMPIRICAL STUDIES 303 (2005).

[40] Ted Bundy, American serial killer of at least 3 women, was executed in Florida in 1989; John Wayne Gacy killed and raped at least 33 young men and boys, and was executed in Illinois in 1994; Donald "Pee Wee" Gaskins tortured, mutilated, and murdered at least 80 young children throughout the South until he was executed by electrocution in South Carolina in 1991; Aileen Wornos killed seven men whom she alleged had raped or attempted to rape her. Her execution by lethal injection in Florida, in 2002, led to the 2003 movie "Monster". Actor Charlize Theron played Wornos in the film and won an Academy Award for Best Actress.

[41] Violent Crime Control and Law Enforcement Act of 1994, Pub. L. No. 103-322, 108 Stat. 1796 (1994).

[42] James S. Liebman, et al., *A Broken System: Error Rates in Capital Cases*, 1973 - 1995 (2000), http://www2.law.columbia.edu/instructionalservices/liebman/.

[43] William C. Bailey, *Deterrence, Brutalization, and the Death Penalty*, CRIMINOLOGY (1998); See also William C. Bailey, *Deterrence, Brutalization, and the Death Penalty: Another Examination of Oklahoma's Return to Capital Punishment*, 36 CRIMINOLOGY 711 (2006).

[44] Printed with the permission of Mr. Byrne. (Phone conversation and email, February 18, 2010).

[45] B. Chevigny and H. Prejean, DOING TIME: 25 YEARS OF PRISON WRITING (PEN American Center, 1999).

[46] For a more recent analysis of the issue of costs, see the Fall 2009 report from the Death Penalty Information Center, Smart on Crime: Reconsidering the Death Penalty in a Time of Crisis, *available at* http://www.deathpenaltyinfo.org/documents/CostsRptFinal.pdf. "(A)ll of the studies conclude that the death penalty system is far more expensive than an alternative system in which the maximum sentence is life in prison."

[47] It appears that Mr. Deiter was referring to Wiggins v. Smith, 539 U.S. 510 (2003), in which the Court found ineffective assistance of counsel in the failure of a defense lawyer to investigate and present mitigating evidence at a death penalty sentencing proceeding.

[48] 91 N.Y. 2d 214 (1997).

[49] Ex parte Burdine, 901 S.W. 2d 456 (Tex. Ct. Crim. App. 1995). In March of 2010, the U.S. Supreme Court heard argument in the case of Holland v. Florida (Docket #09-53278). Holland was convicted of murder and sentenced to death in 1996. Holland's lawyer on appeal failed to file a timely habeas corpus petition that would have challenged the validity of his conviction. Despite repeated efforts by Holland to get the lawyer to act, the deadline for filing the petition passed. The lawyer's conduct was at least "grossly negligent" and, according to legal ethics specialists who filed a brief supporting Holland, was "intolerable, thoroughly unacceptable behavior." The decision by the Court in Holland will define, once again, the extent to which innocence arguments can be silenced by poor lawyering.

[50] 173 App. Div. 2 512, 513, *rev. denied,* 78 N.Y. 2d 1015 (1991).

[51] 531 U.S. 98 (2000).

[52] William J. Bowers and Wanda D. Foglia, *Still Singularly Agonizing: Law's Failure to Purge Arbitrariness from Capital Sentencings,* 39 CRIM. L. BULLETIN 51 (2003).

[53] Morgan v. Illinois, 504 U.S. 719 (1992).

[54] Atkins, 536 U.S. 304; Roper, 543 U.S. 551; and Kennedy, 128 S.Ct.2641.

[55] David Baldus & George Woodworth, *Race Discrimination in America's Capital Punishment System Since Furman v. Georgia (1972): The Evidence of Race Disparities and the Record of Our Courts and Legislatures in Addressing This Issue* (1997) (report prepared for the American Bar Association), cited in Richard C. Dieter, The Death Penalty in Black and White: Who Lives, Who Dies, Who Decides (Death Penalty Information Center, Washington D.C., 1998).

[56] David Baldus, Charles Pulaski & George Woodworth, *Comparative Review of Death Sentences: An Empirical Study of the Georgia Experience,* 74 J. CRIM. L. & CRIMINOLOGY 661 (1983).

[57] Kemp, 481 U.S. 279.

[58] Professor Baldus asserted: "The reason for this gap is that a substantial majority of New York black defendant cases involve a black victim which draws down the death-sentencing rate for black defendants as a group."

[59] DEATH PENALTY SENTENCING: RESEARCH INDICATES PATTERN OF RACIAL DISPARITIES (U.S. General Accounting Office Report to the Senate and House Committees on the Judiciary, February 1990), available at http://archive.gao.gov/t2pbat.11/140845.pdf.

[60] Miller-El v. Cockrell, 537 U.S. 322 (2003).

[61] Williams v. Woodford, 270 F. 3d 915 (9th Cir. 2001) *rev'd en banc,* 245 F. 3d 1075.

[62] Kemp, 481 U.S.279 (statistical studies showing racially discriminatory effects of death penalty system in Georgia held insufficient to overturn defendant's capital conviction absent showing of purposeful racial discrimination in his case).

[63] Excellent background information on the effects of race on the death penalty system can be found in an analysis prepared by Richard C. Deiter, Executive Director of the Death Penalty Information Center in "The Death Penalty in Black and White: Who Lives, Who Dies, Who Decides" (June 1998) *available at*

http://www.deathpenaltyinfo.org/death-penalty-black-and-white-who-lives-who-dies-who-decides. As an example of racial prejudice in prosecutors' use of peremptory challenges to potential jurors and the resulting discrimination in the system, Executive Director Deiter cited a situation in Philadelphia, PA, in which "one district attorney prepared a training tape for new prosecutors in which he offered advice on how to develop race-neutral reasons as a pretext for rising peremptory challenges to black jurors." For more recent studies, interested readers should refer to S. Phillips, *Racial Disparities in the Capital of Capital Punishment*, 45 HOUSTON LAW REVIEW 807 (2008), and B. Butler, *Death Qualification and Prejudice: The Effect of Implicit Racism, Sexism and Homophobia on Capital Defendant's Right to Due Process*, 25 BEHAVIORAL SCIENCES AND THE LAW 857 (2007).

[64] 476 U.S. 79 (1986). In <u>Batson</u>, the Supreme Court dispensed with the notion that a consistent, long-term, pattern of racial discrimination during jury selection is necessary to trigger a violation of the Equal Protection Clause. In holding that a defendant may make a prima facie showing of purposeful racial discrimination based on the facts of his or her particular case, the Court established a set of criteria to determine whether a violation has transpired. The burden is on the defendant to first show that he or she is a member of a cognizable racial group and that the State exercised peremptory challenges to remove from the list of potential jurors members of the defendant's race. The defendant is entitled to rely upon the fact that peremptory challenges are a practice that allows "those to discriminate who are of a mind to discriminate." The defendant must finally show that these facts and any other relevant circumstances raise the inference that the State used its peremptory challenges to exclude the members of the defendant's race from the jury. The Court requires the trial judge to consider all relevant circumstances when deciding whether the defendant has made the required showing. Once the defendant makes a prima facie showing, the burden shifts to the State to proffer a neutral explanation for its challenges. This explanation need not rise to the level of justification for cause. The State may not, however, rebut the defendant's prima facie case by simply stating that the jurors were challenged on the assumption they would be partial to the defendant because of their shared race. The neutral explanation must be related to the particular case being tried. <u>Batson</u>, 476 U.S. at 95-99.

[65] 10 A.D. 3d 531 (1st Dept. 2004).

[66] 510 U.S. 1141 (1994)

[67] Justice Blackmun went to say "It is virtually self-evident to me now that no combination of procedural rules or substantive regulations ever can save the death penalty from its inherent constitutional deficiencies. The basic question – does the system accurately and consistently determine which defendants "deserve" to die? – cannot be answered in the affirmative. It is not simply that this Court has allowed vague aggravating circumstances to be employed, *see, e.g.,* <u>Arave v. Creech</u>, 507 U.S. 463 (1993) (relevant mitigating evidence to be disregarded); *see, e.g.,* <u>Johnson v. Texas</u>, 509 U.S. 350 (1993), (vital judicial review to be blocked); *see, e.g.,* <u>Coleman v. Thompson</u>, 501 U.S. 722, (1992). The problem is that the inevitability of factual, legal, and moral error gives us a system that we know must wrongly kill some defendants, a system that fails to deliver the fair, consistent, and reliable sentences of death required by the Constitution." Id.

[68] The Federal Death Penalty System: Supplementary Data, Analysis and Revised Protocols for Capital Case Review, U.S. Dept. of Justice (June 6, 2001) *available at* http://www.justice.gov/dag/pubdoc/deathpenaltystudy.htm. [old web link was slightly off]

[69] *See* David S. Baime, Special Master, Report to the New Jersey Supreme Court: Systemic Proportionality Review 2004-2004 Term (December 15, 2005) *available at* http://www.judiciary.state.nj.us/pressrel/Baime2005Report12-16-05.pdf. New Jersey legislatively abolished the death penalty on December 17, 2007. Capital punishment was replaced by the sentence of life in prison without parole. This N.J. law was the first statutory ban on the death penalty since it was constitutionally reinstated in the U.S. in 1976. The state held hearings similar to the N.Y. Hearings prior to taking this action. *See* Report of the New Jersey Death Penalty Study Commission issued January 2, 2007.

[70] *See* Richard L. Weiner, *Death Penalty Research in Nebraska: How Do Judges and Juries Reach Penalty Decisions*, 81 NEB. L. REV. 757 (2002).

[71] A felony murder is generally an unintentional death caused during the commission of a separate dangerous felony crime. The robbery and burglary aggravators involve intentional murders that take place while those crimes are being committed.

[72] 476 U.S. 28 (1986).

[73] *See, e.g.*, Theodore Eisenberg, Stephen Garvey and Martin Wells, *Victim Characteristics and Victim Impact Evidence in South Carolina Capital Cases*, 88 CORNELL L. REV. 306 (2003); John H. Blume, Theodore Eisenberg, and Sheri Lynn Johnson, *Post-McCleskey Racial Discrimination Claims in Capital Cases*, 83 CORNELL L. REV. 1771 (1998).

[74] A more recent, targeted, study of racial differences is presented in Scott Phillips, *Racial Disparities in the Capital of Capital Punishment*, 45 HOUSTON L. REV. 807 (2008).

[75] The American Psychiatric Association, in its draft fifth edition of the Diagnostic and Statistical Manual of Mental Disorders, (DMS-5, 2010), proposes substituting the term "intellectual disability" for "mental retardation."

[76] Atkins, 536 U.S.304.

[77] N.Y. Mental Hyg. Law § 1.03 (20).

[78] Ill-Equipped: U.S. Prisons and Offenders with Mental Illness, Human Rights Watch (2003), *available at* http://www.hrw.org/en/node/12252/section/1. *See* USA: The Execution of Mentally Ill Offenders, Amnesty International (2006), *available at* http://www.amnesty.org/en/library/asset/AMR51/003/2006/en/75c16634-d46f-11dd-8743-d305bea2b2c7/amr510032006en.html.

[79] Christopher Slobogin, *Mental Illness and the Death Penalty*, 1 CAL. CRIM. L. REV. 3 (2000), *available at* http://www.boalt.org/CCLR.

[80] *See* David Baldus et al., *Racial Discrimination and the Death Penalty in the Post – Furman Era: An Empirical and Legal Overview, with Recent Findings from Philadelphia*, 83 CORNELL L. REV. 1638, 1688-89 (1998).

[81] Theodore "Ted" Kaczynski was named the "University and Airline Bomber", or, Unabomber. From 1978 to 1995, Kaczynski sent 16 mail bombs that killed three people and injured 23. He ultimately entered a plea agreement under which he

avoided the death penalty in exchange for a sentence of life in federal prison without possibility of parole.

[82] Andrea Yates drowned her five young children in the bath tub of her home in Houston, Texas. She had suffered severe postpartum depression and psychosis for years. After two trials for capital murder, she was eventually found by a Texas jury to be not guilty by reason of insanity. She was committed to mental health facilities in Texas.

[83] *See* John H. Blume, *Killing the Willing: 'Volunteers,' Suicide and Competency*, 103 MICH. L. REV. 361 (2005).

[84] ABA Section of Individual Rights and Responsibilities, Dorean Marguerite Koenig, "Mentally Ill Defendants: Systemic Bias in Capital Cases" (2001). available at http://www.abanet.org/irr/hr/summer01/koenig.html.

[85] *See*, e.g., Katherine Schwinghammer, *Fingerprint Identification: How "The Gold Standard of Evidence" Could Be Worth Its Weight*, 32 AM. J. CRIM. L. 265 (2004 - 2005).

[86] *See* Robbie Brown, *Judges Free Inmate on Recommendation of Special Innocence Panel*, N.Y TIMES, February 17, 2010, *available at* http://www.nytimes.com/2010/02/18/us/18innocent.html. One such practical measure could be innocence panels. In 2006, North Carolina established a first-of-its-kind body, the North Carolina Innocence Commission, with jurisdiction to hear claims of innocence from prisoners or any other person with relevant information. If the eight-member Commission finds merit to a claim it refers the case to a three judge panel. On February 18, 2010, such a panel issued its first exoneration ruling. Gregory F. Taylor was found innocent of murder a prostitute in 1991. He served 6,149 days in prison.

[87] Reprinted by special permission of Northwestern University School of Law, The Journal of Criminal Law and Criminology.

[88] Footnotes corresponding to these numbers in the text of the reproduced article are as follows.

[1.] Rob Warden, The Rape That Wasn't: The First DNA Exoneration in Illinois, Center on Wrongful Convictions, *available at* http://www.law.northwestern.edu/wrongfulconvictions/exonerations/ilDotsonSummary.html.

[2.] Because men make up over 96% of the total, we generally refer to exonerated defendants using male pronouns.

[3.] This is a conservative estimate of the direct consequences of these wrongful convictions. We have not counted time spent in custody before conviction. Nor have we included time spent on probation or parole, or time on bail or other forms of supervised release pending trial, retrial, or dismissal, even though all of these statuses involve restrictions on liberty, some mild, some onerous.

[4.] We have excluded any case in which a dismissal or an acquittal appears to have been based on a decision that while the defendant was not guilty of the charges in the original conviction, he did play a role in the crime and may be guilty of some lesser crime that is based on the same conduct. For our purposes, a defendant who is acquitted of murder on retrial, but convicted of involuntary manslaughter, has not been exonerated. We have also excluded any case in which a dismissal was entered in the absence of strong evidence of factual innocence, or in which – despite such evidence – there was unexplained physical evidence of the defendant's guilt.

[5.] *See* Sydney P. Freedberg, *He Didn't Do It*, St. Petersburg Times, January 7, 2001, at 1A (Frank Lee Smith); J.M. Lawrence, *Ex-prosecutor apologizes to Salvati, Limone*, The Boston Herald, May 12, 2002, at 6; Ralph Ranalli, *Congressional Probe; FBI Used Hit Man as Informant, Transcripts Reveal Bureau Recruited Killer Despite Past*, The Boston Globe, Dec. 4, 2002, at A30 (Louis Greco and Henry Tameleo); Jon Yates and Kevin Lynch, *Confession Leads to 2 Arrests in '75 Killing; Man Convicted in Indiana Case Died in Prison*, Chicago Tribune, August 29, 2002 at 1 (John Jeffers).

[6.] Most of the exonerations we include in this database are listed on one or more the web cites that are maintained by three organizations: The Death Penalty Information Center, *available at* http://www.deathpenaltyinfo.org; the Innocence Project at Cardozo Law School, *available at* http://www.innocenceproject.org; and the Center on Wrongful Convictions at Northwestern University Law School, http://www.law.northwestern.edu/depts/clinic/wrongful. We have gathered additional information on most of the cases from these three lists, reviewed them carefully, and excluded some cases that do not meet our own criteria for an exoneration.

[7.] An earlier version of this paper was released in April of 2004, listing a total of 328 exonerations. *See* http://www.law.umich.edu/newsandinfo/exonerations-in-us.pdf. After that report was released we learned about 15 additional exonerations between 1989 and 2003, mostly by way of e-mails individuals who contacted us about cases we had missed. We have also excluded three cases we listed in that initial report because additional information revealed that the defendants had not been "exonerated" as we define the term: Edward Ryder in Pennsylvania in 1996, and Dennis Halstead and John Restivo in New York in 2003. Halstead and Restivo were removed from the list because it remains theoretically possible that charges will be retried. *See* Chan Lam, *1984 Teen Homicide; Hair May Play a Role in Case*, Newsday, December 5, 2004 at A53. More likely they will be added to the list of exonerees in 2005 or 2006 rather than 2003 . . . .

. . .

[11.] Calculated from list *available at* http://www.innocenceproject.org/

. . .

[18.] Calculated from Bureau of Justice Statistics, Prisoners in 2002, Table 15.

[19.] There were 3,577 prisoners on American death rows at the end of 2001 (Bureau of Justice Statistics, Capital Punishment, 2002, Table 4), and approximately 1,404,032 prisoners in federal and state adult correctional facilities. Bureau of Justice Statistics, Prisoners in 2002, Table 3.

[21.] There were 3,577 prisoners on American death rows at the end of 2001 (see above, note 19); if exonerations from that population had occurred at the same rate as on death row, there would have been 29,046 non-death row exonerations since 1989. (If we restrict our focus to prisoners who were convicted of murder, the expected number of exonerations would be 13% of that total or about 3,776.) This is a conservative estimate, since death-sentenced defendants spend more time in prison than the average inmate, and therefore are an even smaller proportion of the total population of defendants who are convicted of felonies and pass through prisons in any given time period.

[63.] Andrew Gelman, James S. Liebman, Valerie West, and Alexander Kiss, *A Broken System: The Persistent Patterns of Reversals of Death Sentences in the United States*, 1 JOURNAL OF EMPIRICAL LEGAL STUDIES (2004).

[89] In December 2007, Mr. Tankleff was released from prison after serving 17 years. In January, 2008, Suffolk County, N.Y., District Attorney Thomas Spofa dismissed all charges against him.

[90] In 1992 and 1993 it was discovered that several New York State Police officers had been fabricating evidence against criminal defendants. Craig D. Harvey, a 16-year veteran of the force, pleaded guilty in 1993 to fabricating evidence in three cases. After a four-year investigation, a special prosecutor called the cases that worst scandal in State Police history.

[91] The Dirty Thirty scandal got its name from multiple crimes committed by NYPD officers in the 30th Precinct covering Harlem, N.Y. City.

[92] Ultimately, Mr. McLaughlin was awarded $1.93 million as compensation for his wrongful conviction. McLaughlin v. State, N.Y.L.J. Oct. 27, 1989, col. 4. *See also* N.Y. TIMES, Oct. 19, 1989, at B28, col. 1.

[93] HUGO ADAM BEDAU, THE DEATH PENALTY IN AMERICA: AN ANTHOLOGY (Aldine Publishing, Chicago, 1964). *See also* HUGO ADAM BEDGAU, DEBATING THE DEATH PENALTY (Oxford University Press, 2005).

[94] Witherspoon v. Illinois, 391 U.S. 510 (1968). A statute that granted the state unlimited challenges to jurors who had "conscientious scruples" against capital punishment violated the constitutional right to an impartial jury. A jury seated pursuant to this statute would inevitably be biased in favor of the death penalty.

[95] Reprinted with permission of the author and subject to Mr. Turow's notice of copyright. (Email dated February 11, 2010).

[96] International Covenant on Civil and Political Rights, G.A. Res. 2200A (XXI), at 52, U.N. GAOR, Supp. No. 16, U.N. Doc. A/6316 (Mar. 23, 1976) [hereinafter ICCPR].

[97] Second Optional Protocol to the International Covenant on Civil and Political Rights, Aiming at Abolition of the Death Penalty, G.A. Res. 44/128, at 207, 44 U.N. GAOR Supp. No. 49, U.N. Doc. A/44/49 (Jul. 11, 1991) [hereinafter Second Optional Protocol to ICCPR].

[98] Convention on the Rights of the Child, U.N. GAOR, 44th Sess., 61st plen. mtg. art. 37, U.N. Doc. A/44/49.

[99] American Convention on Human Rights, art. 4, §§ 2-6, Nov. 22, 1969, O.A.S.T.S. No. 36, 1144 U.N.T.S. 123.

[100] African Charter on the Rights and Welfare of the Child, OAU Doc./ CAB/LEG/24.9/49 (1990), entered into force Nov. 29, 1999. Article 5 (3).

[101] Protocol No. 6 to the [European] Convention for the Protection of Human Rights and Fundamental Freedoms, E.T.S./114, entered into force March 1, 1985. Protocol 13 to the European Convention on Human Rights and Fundamental Freedoms, adopted by the Council of Europe's Committee of Ministers on February 21, 2002. This treaty was the first legally binding international treaty to ban capital punishment in all circumstances and without exceptions; currently ratified by 42 countries.

[102] *See* DPIC, The Death Penalty: An International Perspective, Abolitionist and Retentionist Countries, http://www.deathpenaltyinfo.org/abolitionist-and-retentionist-countries (last visited March 30, 2010). *See also*, Amnesty

International, Abolitionist and Retentionist Countries,
http://www.amnesty.org/en/death-penalty/abolitionist-and-retentionist-countries
(last visited March 30,2010).

[103] On June 16, 2008, the Council of the European Union issued a statement
reaffirming its goal of "working towards universal abolition of the death penalty"
and identified that goal as an "integral part of the EU's human rights policy." Press
Release, General Affairs and External Relations, Council of the European Union,
Dimitrij Rupel, President (June 16, 2008). The statement lauded the vote of the UN
General Assembly that called for a moratorium on executions world-wide and noted
that abolition "contributes to the enhancement of human dignity and the
progressive development of human rights."

[104] W. CLARKE AND LAURELYN WHITT, THE BITTER FRUIT OF AMERICAN JUSTICE:
INTERNATIONAL AND DOMESTIC RESISTANCE TO THE DEATH PENALTY, 7 (Northeastern
University Press 2007).

[105] Amnesty International, Death Penalty: Death Sentences and Executions in 2009,
http://www.amnesty.org/en/death-penalty/death-sentences-and-executions-in-
2009 (last visited March 30, 2010).

[106] DPIC, The Death Penalty: An International Perspective, Executions Around the
World, http://www.deathpenaltyinfo.org/death-penalty-international-perspective
(last visited January 15, 2010).

[107] Id.

[108] DPIC, International News and Developments: 2007,
http://www.deathpenaltyinfo.org/node/2256 (last visited January 15, 2010).

[109] DPIC, International: Amnesty International Reports Worldwide Drop in
Executions, http://www.deathpenaltyinfo.org/node/2354 (last visited January 15,
2010).

[110] Death Penalty: Death Sentences and Executions in 2007, *supra* note 97; Amnesty
International, Death Penalty: Death Sentences and Executions in 2006,
http://www.amnesty.org/en/death-penalty/death-sentences-and-executions-in-
2006 (last visited January 15, 2010).

[111] Death Penalty An International Perspective, Executions Around the World, *supra*
note 98; Amnesty International, Death Penalty, Death Sentences and Executions in
2008, http//www.amnesty.org/en/death-penalty/death-sentences-and-executions-
in-2008 (last visited January 15, 2010).

[112] DPIC, International News and Developments: 2007,
http://www.deathpenaltyinfo.org/node/2256 (last visited January 15, 2010).

[113] Italian Premier Romano Prodi called for a worldwide moratorium on the death
penalty: "we shall perform a great political act through the adoption of this
resolution. It will demonstrate that humankind isn't capable of making progress
only in science but also in the field of ethics."

[114] *See* Press Release, General Assembly, General Assembly Adopts Landmark Text
Calling for Moratorium on Death Penalty, U.N. Doc. GA/10678 (Dec. 18, 2007),
available at http://www.un.org/News/Press/docs//2007/ga10678.doc.htm
(discussing resolution placing moratorium on death penalty).

[115] International News and Developments: 2008-2009, *supra* note 63.

[116] Convention on the Rights of the Child, *supra* note 90. The United States has never ratified the United Nations Convention on the Rights of the Child and refused to recognize its ban on the death penalty for juveniles. Id.

[117] ICCPR, *supra* note 88 at 175 (prohibiting capital punishment for anyone under 18 at the time of offense and signed and ratified by the United States subject to a reservation regarding Article 6(5)).

[118] Second Optional Protocol to ICCPR, *supra* note 89

[119] *See* The International Criminal Court and Landmines: What are the Consequences of Leaving the U.S. Behind, 11 EUR. J. OF INT'L L. 77 (2000) (evaluating U.S. rejection of International Criminal Court).

[120] *See* Letter of March 7, 2005, from U.S. Secretary of State Condoleezza Rice to the United Nations Secretary General stating that "the United States of America . . . hereby withdraws from . . ." the Optional Protocol Concerning the Compulsory Settlement of Disputes arising under the Vienna Convention and that, as a result, "the United States will no longer recognize the jurisdiction of the International Court of Justice reflected in that Protocol." *See* Charles Lane, *U.S. Quits Pact Used in Capital Cases*, WASHINGTON POST, March 10, 2005, at A01.

[121] Mr. Bruno retired from the New York legislature in July of 2008. In January of 2009 he was indicted by the United States Attorney for the Northern District of New York and charged with 8 counts of using his legislative position to give contracts and grants to businesses that paid him $3.2 million in consulting fees or other compensation from 1993 through 2006. In December, 2009, Mr. Bruno was convicted on two fraud counts of the indictment, acquitted on five other counts, and had a hung jury on one other count. Sentencing was scheduled for March 31, 2009. Mr. Bruno's lawyers pledged a vigorous appeal.

Breinigsville, PA USA
29 June 2010
240802BV00005B/1/P